The Great Railway

ILLUSTRATED

The Great Railway

ILLUSTRATED

WRITTEN AND EDITED BY

PIERRE BERTON

DESIGNED BY FRANK NEWFELD

MCCLELLAND AND STEWART
LIMITED
TORONTO

0-7710-1329-9

The Canadian
Publishers
McClelland
and
Stewart
Limited
Illustrated
Book
Division
25 Hollinger Road,
Toronto 374

PRINTED AND
BOUND
IN CANADA

iv

As these opening
photographs show,
Canada was made
vertebrate by the
building of the CPR.

HALF TITLE
*A new station and
a new town, somewhere
on the prairies*

TITLE PAGE
*A work train on
the "Loop" of the
Illecillewaet
below Glacier House*

THIS PAGE
*In the canyon of
the Kicking Horse,
workmen struggle
to lay a roadbed.*

NEXT PAGE
*The first passenger
train arrives at
Vancouver, B.C.*

CONTENTS

First Train in Vancouv[er]

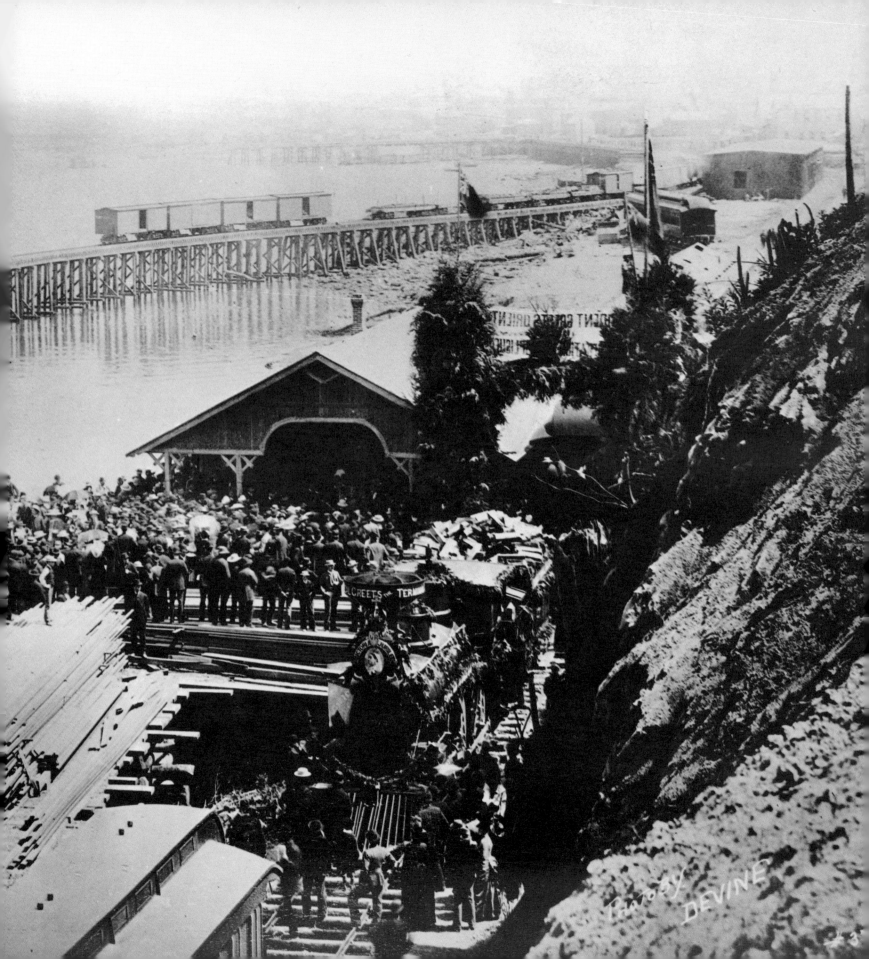

From Sea to Sea

It is New Year's Day, 1871, the year in which Canada will become a transcontinental nation, and in most of British North America it is bitterly cold. In Ottawa, where it is 18 below, the snow, gritty as sand, squeaks eerily beneath the felted feet of morning church-goers. A cutting wind, blowing off Lake Ontario, is heaping great drifts against the square logs of the Upper Canadian barns, smothering the snake fences and frustrating the Grand Trunk's Montreal-Toronto passenger schedule. On the St. Lawrence, in front of Quebec City, that annual phenomenon, the ice bridge, is taking form. In the harbour of Saint John, the rime hangs thickly upon the rigging, turning schooners and barquentines into ghost ships.

Only at the colonial extremities is New Year's Day a green one. In the English gardens of Victoria, British Columbia, the occasional yellow wallflower still blooms shyly, and in the verdant colony of Prince Edward Island the fields are free of frost. The editorial comments are as salubrious as the climate. The potato farmers of Souris and Summerside read their Saturday Islander with approval: "In our cosy little Island we have scarcely experienced anything but the blessings of Providence," it says. "It is probable that never at any previous period of our existence were we as rich a community as we are at the moment." There is cause for rejoicing: the colony is eagerly awaiting new proposals from Canada calculated to entice it into Confederation; the rumours say that these will be far more liberal

than the ones that have been rejected. And why not? After all, British Columbia has been promised a railway!

Three thousand miles to the west, the steam presses of the British Colonist are pumping out a New Year's salutation for the morrow. For British Columbia, the editor writes, the outlook has never been brighter: "Clad in bridal attire, she is about to unite her destinies with a country which is prepared to do much for her." The paper carries a reprint from a Tory journal back east, praising the Government for the nuptial present it is about to bestow.

The world is in its customary turmoil – the Germans at the gates of Paris, the insurrectionists bedevilling Cuba – but in Canada there is nothing but good humour. Even George Brown, the caustic editor of the Globe, is in a mellow mood. One can almost surmise a half-smile lighting up those long, Scottish features as he scribbles an unusually benign editorial in his Toronto office. "Peace and plenty prevail," he writes, "and there is nothing for us but hope and encouragement as we welcome the advent of another year."

It is the Lord's Day and all across settled Canada the curtains are drawn and the church bells are sounding. Only an eccentric would resist their summons. Because of the Sabbath, all the elegant and sometimes lusty New Year's rituals of the Canadian social classes have been postponed for a day. The brass and rosewood, the sterling and cut glass have all been polished to a high gloss by an army of servants, making ready for Monday's "calling." Then will the gentlemen of the towns, frock-coated and convivial, trudge unsteadily from threshold to threshold, to be greeted by well-bustled matrons with puckered lips and full decanters. The temperance movement is crying out against such debauchery. In Montreal, it is reported, some of the ladies have been persuaded to serve coffee. That city, a correspondent notes, has already given the New Year "a sober and orderly welcome."

Far off beyond the sombre desert of the Canadian Shield, at Fort Garry in the new province of Manitoba, the welcome is not so orderly. Fiddles screech, pipes skirl, and the settlers caper like souls possessed to an endless succession of Red River reels, while nearby tables groan with smoking joints of venison and buffalo. The great Scottish feast of Hogmanay – New Year's Eve – is far more important than Christmas.

For one Scotsman, there is a special reason to celebrate. Donald A. Smith, late of Labrador, has just won a federal seat in his adopted province's first election. It is a significant victory. The events set in motion by the decisions of 1871 will change the current of Smith's life and enshrine his likeness in the history books of a later century, linking him forever with a symbolic railway spike in a distant mountain pass.

That pass is one thousand miles to the west of the Red River and for all that thousand miles scarcely a light flickers or a soul moves. Awesome in its vastness and its isolation, the newly acquired North West – the heart of the new Canada – sleeps beneath its blanket of snow. Walled off from the Pacific by the vertebrae of the Cordilleras and from the settled East by a granite Precambrian wasteland, the great central plain is like an unconquered island.

The North West! The name is beginning to take on overtones of romance. In the winter, when the blizzard strikes and the heavens are blotted out, it can be a white hell; in the summer, by all accounts, it is an enchanted realm. One can travel for days, they say, along the ruts of the Carlton Trail between Fort Garry and Fort Edmonton without encountering human kind – only ridge after ridge of untrammelled park land rolling on towards the high arch of the sky. Out there, they say, the eye can feast upon acres and acres of tiger lilies and bluebells, stretching to the horizon "as if a vast Oriental carpet had been thrown across the plains." The prairie chickens, they say, are so numerous that they mask the sun, while the passenger pigeons roost so thickly on the oaks that the very branches snap beneath their weight. And there are exquisite lakes, speckled with geese and swans, broad meadows where the whooping cranes stalk about in pairs, and everywhere the ultimate spectacle of the buffalo, moving in dark rivers through a tawny ocean of waist-high grass. Only a privileged few have gazed upon these marvels; the events of 1871 will ensure that they will soon be just a memory.

How many white men inhabit this empty realm? Perhaps twenty-five hundred. Nobody knows for certain because there has never been an accurate census. The North West is a scattered archipelago of human islets, each isolated from the others by vast distances and contrasting life-styles – Scottish farmers, Métis buffalo hunters, Yankee whiskey traders, French missionaries, British and Canadian fur merchants. In the lonely prairie between these human enclaves the nomadic and warlike Indian bands roam freely.

For all of the decade, this wild, misunderstood domain will be the subject of endless speculation, curiosity, political manoeuvre and debate. There are few Canadians yet who care greatly about it; most provincial politicians, indeed, are "either indifferent or hostile to its acquisition." Yet by the fact of its acquisition, the young dominion has set itself upon a new course. The Conservative prime minister, Sir John A. Macdonald, has just promised British Columbia a great railway across the North West to Pacific tidewater. Once that decision is confirmed, as it must be in this pivotal year of 1871, nothing can ever again be the same.

*A Cree camp on the unfenced prairie at the elbow of the
Saskatchewan, September, 1871. A dozen years would
pass before the long-awaited railway would come this way.*

1

When the Railway Was Only a Dream

The prairies before the railway

An ocean of buffalo bones bleaches the tall grass
in the vicinity of the modern city of Lloydminster,
Alberta. This was the last great corral of the Cree
chieftain, Poundmaker. The photo was made in 1874.

Burrard Inlet before the railway

Out of the green jungle of cedar and Douglas fir,
a single cabin rises on the site of present-day
Vancouver. This photograph was taken in 1868,
three years before British Columbia joined Canada.

Victoria before the railway

The only settlement of any size west of Toronto in the 1860's was the English colonial community on Vancouver Island. To Victoria, Canada was a foreign country and Canadians were known as "white Chinamen."

Winnipeg before the railway

Between Toronto and Victoria there existed one pin-point of civilization. Main Street, shown here in 1872, grew out of an old trail, made wide because, to avoid ruts, the Red River carts were staggered.

The vision of the North West

WHEN JOHN A. MACDONALD promised British Columbia a Pacific railroad in just ten years, his opponents pretended to believe the Prime Minister had gone mad. "Insane" was the word the Liberal leader, Alexander Mackenzie, used to describe the pledge. It was, he said in the spring of 1871, "an act of insane recklessness," and there were a good many Canadians who thought he was right.

Here was a country of only three and a half million people, not yet four years old, pledged to construct the greatest of all railways. It would be longer than any line yet built – almost one thousand miles longer than the first American road to the Pacific, which the United States, with a population of almost forty million, had only just managed to complete.

The Americans had more money, shorter mileage, and fewer obstacles; for one thing, they knew where they were going – there were established cities on their Pacific coastline. But the only settlement of account on the Canadian Pacific coast was on an island; the indentations in the mainland were uncharted, the valleys were unexplored, and the passes were unsurveyed.

For another thing, the United States was not faced with any barrier as implacable as that of the Precambrian Shield. If the railway followed an all-Canadian route, its builders would have to blast their way across seven hundred miles of this granite wasteland. There were ridges there that would consume three tons of dynamite a day for months on end; and, where the ridges ended, there was another three hundred miles of muskegs, which could (and would) swallow a locomotive at a single gulp. This was land incapable of cultivation. There were many who held with Alexander Mackenzie that to build a railway across it was "one of the most foolish things that could be imagined."

John A. Macdonald during his first term as Prime Minister. The photograph was taken at the time when his life savings had been wiped out and just before an attack of gallstones that brought him to the brink of death.

Alexander Mackenzie was the antithesis of Macdonald. He did not, in his own words, possess his opponent's "happy frame of mind." Unlike John A., he was never able to relax or put aside the daily burden of political cares.

After the Shield was breached, the road was to lead across the North West – a tenantless empire of waving grass (which many thought to be unproductive desert) bordered by the thinly forested valley of the North Saskatchewan River. Every sliver of timber – railroad ties, bridge supports, construction materials – would have to be hauled, league after league, across this desolate land where it seemed the wind never ceased.

At the far limit of the plains the way was blocked by a notched wall of naked rock, eight thousand feet high. Beyond that wall lay a second wall and beyond that wall a third. At the end of the sea of mountains lay the unknown coastline, tattered like a coat beyond repair. George Etienne Cartier, acting for his ailing leader, had promised British Columbia that the railway would reach that coastline, ready to operate, within ten years. To Edward Blake, the intellectual giant of the opposing Liberal (or Reform) Party, it was "a preposterous proposition." Many of Macdonald's own followers agreed with him.

The Government had promised the railway to British Columbia in order to lure that colony into the new confederation of Ontario, Quebec, New Brunswick, Nova Scotia, and Manitoba. Macdonald's vision of Canada did not stop at the Great Lakes; his dream was of a transcontinental British nation in North America – a workable alternative to the United States. To achieve this dream and stitch the scattered provinces and empty territories of the West together, the Prime Minister insisted, the railway was a necessity. But there were also more pragmatic reasons. Macdonald needed the diversion of the railway to maintain himself in office. If he succeeded in fulfilling his pledge, the Conservative Party could probably look forward to a generation of power.

If the sceptics had considerable logic on their side, Macdonald had emotion. Could a country of three and a half million people afford an expenditure of one hundred million dollars at a time when a labourer's wage was a dollar a day? Perhaps not;

17

but Macdonald meant to persuade the country that it could not do without a railway if it wanted to be a nation in the true sense of the word. Besides, the Government insisted, the railway would not bring any rise in taxes: it could be paid for with land from the North West.

Why the fixed date of ten years? As Macdonald's opponent, Mackenzie, said, most of the railway would run through an uninhabitable wilderness: "It wouldn't be necessary to construct the greater portion of the line for another thirty years." That was also perfectly true; but Macdonald's attitude was that there might be no nation in thirty years without a railway. If the land remained empty, the Americans would move in to fill the vacuum. Besides, he had the assurance of the chief British Columbia delegate, Joseph Trutch, that the ten-year clause was not a "cast iron contract"; the province would not hold the Canadian government to the letter of the wording.

It was the apparent insistence on an all-Canadian line that brought the harshest criticism. Few Canadians really believed that any railway builder would be foolhardy enough to hurdle the desert of rock between Lake Nipissing and the Red River. Macdonald's opponents were all for diverting the line south through United States territory, and then into Manitoba from Duluth. If North America had been one nation that would have been the sensible way to go. But Macdonald did not believe that Canada could call herself a nation if she did not have geographical control of her own rail line. What if Canada were at war? Could soldiers be moved over foreign soil? In the half-breed uprising of 1869, the troops sent to the Red River had taken ninety-six days to negotiate the forty-seven portages across the Canadian Shield. A railway could rush several regiments to the North West in less than a week.

Macdonald's opponents might feel that the price of holding the newly acquired North West was too high, but he believed that the United States government "are resolved to do all they can, short of war, to get possession of the western territory."

18

FROM HALIFAX TO VANCOUVER.

MISS CANADA—"THIS IS WHAT WE WANT, COUSIN JONATHAN. IT WILL GIVE US REAL INDEPENDENCE, AND STOP THE FOOLISH TALK ABOUT ANNEXATION."
JONATHAN—"WAL, MISS, I GUESS YOU'RE ABOUT RIGHT THAR; BUT I'LL BELIEVE IT WHEN I SEE IT!"

A TEMPTING OFFER.

The Pacific railway was originally seen as a bulwark against American expansionism. Before 1870 there was, as the cartoon at left put it, a good deal of "foolish talk about annexation." But anti-Yankee feeling also ran high as the work of five different artists demonstrates here. The Uncle Sam figure, then known as Brother or Cousin Jonathan, is seen in the role of suitor, seducer, lecher, and outright devil, vainly seeking the hand of an innocent Miss Canada. All these cartoons were published in Diogenes in 1869 except for the one at lower right, which appeared in 1876 when Canada won several prizes at the Philadelphia Centennial Exposition.

CHANDLER ON THE RAMPAGE.
A NEW WAY OF MAKING LOVE.

A PERTINENT QUESTION.

Mrs. BRITTANIA: "Is it possible, my dear, that you have ever given your Cousin Jonathan any Encouragement?"

Miss CANADA: "Encouragement? Certainly not, Mamma; I have told him we can NEVER be United.

COMING HOME FROM THE FAIR.

Bro. Jonathan:—Adieu, fair Canada. I have long adored you, but never so much as now. May I not hope some day to claim you as my own?
Canada (kindly but firmly):—Never. I hope always to respect you as my friend and well-wisher, but can never accept you as my lord and master. Farewell.

That being so, he wrote in January, 1870, "we must take immediate and vigorous steps to counteract them. One of the first things to be done is to show unmistakeably our resolve to build the Pacific Railway." In the Canada of 1871, "nationalism" was a strange new word. The six scattered provinces had yet to unite in a great national endeavour or to glimpse anything remotely resembling a Canadian dream; but both were taking shape. The endeavour would be the building of the Pacific railway; the dream would be the filling up of the empty spaces and the dawn of a new nation.

Out beyond the sprawl of billion-year-old rock lay an immense frontier, of which Canadians were dimly becoming aware. It was now their land, wrested in 1869 from the great fur-trading monopoly of the Hudson's Bay Company after two centuries of isolation; but they did not have the means of exploiting it. A railway could give them access to that empty empire. Canada in 1871 was a country whose population was trapped in the prison of the St. Lawrence lowlands and the Atlantic littoral. A railway would be the means by which the captive finally broke out of its cage.

The North West was, at that time, an almost totally unknown realm. Until the sixties, it had been generally considered worthless to anyone but fur traders – a Canadian Gobi, barren, ice-locked, forbidding, and unfit for settlement. In 1855 the Montreal *Transcript* wrote that it would not even produce potatoes, let alone grain. This attitude was fostered and encouraged by the Hudson's Bay Company, whose private preserve it had been for almost two centuries. The last thing the great fur-trading empire wanted was settlers pouring in.

James Young, the Galt politician, in his reminiscences of those days recalled that "even the most eminent Canadians were deceived by these representations": in 1867 Cartier was strongly opposed to the acquisition of the North West and Macdonald had no idea of its value.

Macdonald's indifference terminated abruptly in 1869 when the Red River uprising under Louis

Riel inflamed the nation. By 1871, with the events from the Red River country still fresh in their minds, Canadians began to look upon their new North West with a mixture of wonder, guilt, and apprehension. *It must be wonderful to see it! Oh, if only one* COULD *see it, but it was so remote, so hard to reach! Something ought to be done about developing it; they said parts of it were very rich. But would you want to* LIVE *there – so far away from everything, in that dreadful climate? One day, of course, millions would live there – that was certain. One day . . .*

If the attitudes to the North West were vague, confused, and uncertain, part of the reason lay in

John Palliser (left) with James Hector. A typical Victorian adventurer, he was fluent in five languages and had already trekked across the American plains.

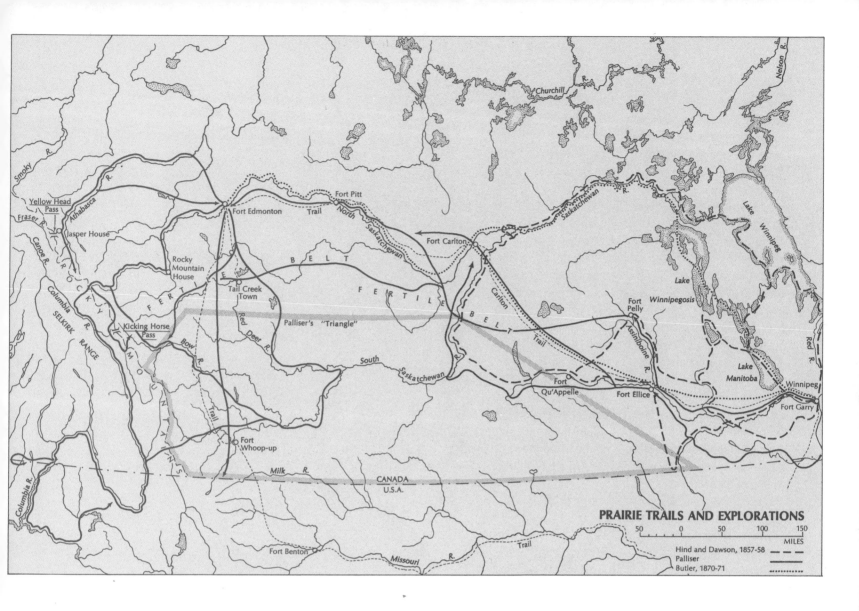

PRAIRIE TRAILS AND EXPLORATIONS

50   0   50   100   150
MILES

Hind and Dawson, 1857-58 — — —
Palliser ————
Butler, 1870-71 ················

Hector, kicked insensible by a horse and almost buried alive, discovered the pass the CPR eventually chose to cross the Rockies.

the conflicting reports about it. Some said it was little more than a desert; others saw it as a verdant paradise. Even the two official government explorations of the territory launched in 1857 – one by the British, one by the Canadians – differed in their assessments.

The best-remembered of these expeditions was that of the British, mounted by a dashing Irish bachelor named John Palliser, who left his name on a triangle of supposed desert in what is now southern Alberta and Saskatchewan.

The expedition, backed by the Royal Geographical Society and the Imperial government, was asked to explore an empire from Lake Superior to the Rockies and to report on *everything* – agriculture, minerals, settlement possibilities, and, of course, possible transportation routes.

Palliser and his companions were two years in the field and their accomplishments were monumental. They explored, by a variety of routes, all of the country between Lake Superior and the Pacific coast. One of Palliser's associates, James Hector, discovered the Kicking Horse Pass through which the CPR would eventually travel. But the idea of a railway in the shadows of those rumpled peaks was far from Palliser's mind. His knowledge of the

21

country, he reported, would never lead him to advocate a railway "exclusively through British territory." Across the prairies, certainly; but that armoured barrier north of Lake Superior "is *the* obstacle of the country and one, I fear, almost beyond the remedies of art."

However, the government of the united Canadas had mounted similar expeditions, and the Canadian explorers were far more optimistic about an all-Canadian railway than their British colleagues. One, George Gladman, did not feel the difficulties to be "insuperable to Canadian energy and enterprise." Another, Henry Youle Hind, thought Palliser too sweeping in his condemnation of the route across the Shield. Hind, a geology professor from Toronto, agreed that the Great American Desert had its apex in the Far West, but along the wooded valley of the North Saskatchewan and some of its tributaries there was "a broad strip of fertile country," which could be "settled and cultivated from a few miles west of the Lake of the Woods to the passes of the Rocky Mountains." In Hind's view this was the route that any railway must take.

Hind's enthusiasm for the Fertile Belt, as it was called, was to have a profound effect on the railway planners; from that point on few gave serious consideration to taking the CPR farther to the south. Hind also helped promote the North West as a land of promise. "A great future lies before the valley of the Saskatchewan," he declared. "It will become the granary of British Columbia, the vast pasture field by which the mining industry of the Rocky Mountains will be fed."

In 1871, a decade after Hind wrote those words, his vision still belonged to the future. To cross the North West, in the days before the railway, was a considerable feat attempted by only a hardy few. The chief form of transportation was by Red River cart. These generally travelled in brigades, some of them as long as railway trains, and they left deep ruts in the soft prairie turf, furrowing the plains like the creases on a human palm. The most famous trail was the Carlton, winding for 1,160

Henry Youle Hind, a self-assured young professor of geology from the University of Toronto, thought Palliser too sweeping in his condemnation of the route across the Canadian Shield, which was "of vast importance to Canada." But, like Palliser, he felt that the "Arid Belt" of the southern prairies was unfit for human habitation. The railway surveys followed his advice.

Sandford Fleming as he looked in 1862 when he placed before the government the first carefully worked out plan for building a railroad to the Pacific. He recommended that the job be done in gradual stages: a road first, then a telegraph line, and finally a line of steel. It would take, he estimated, twenty-five years and it would cost a hundred million dollars.

William Francis Butler, photographed on the prairie in 1873 a year after his book was published. Though too poor to purchase a commission, as was the practice of the day, he rose through sheer ability to become a lieutenant-general.

miles from Fort Garry to the Yellow Head Pass in the Rockies. For half a century this was the broad highway used by every explorer, settler, trader, or adventurer who set his sights for the West. When the railway was planned, almost everybody expected it to follow the general course of the Carlton Trail. This was not to be, but a later railway did just that: it forms part of the Canadian National system today.

One man who followed the Carlton Trail and excited the imagination of the nation was an impulsive young subaltern named William Francis Butler. His subsequent book, *The Great Lone Land*, with its haunting descriptions of "that great, boundless, solitary waste of verdure" caught the imagination of the Canadian public. The title, in fact, went into the language of the day. For the next fifteen years no description, no reference, no journalistic report about the North West seemed complete without some mention of Butler's poetic phrase.

The Great Lone Land was published in 1872. The following year another popular work on the North West made its appearance and its title, *Ocean to Ocean*, also became part of the phraseology of the period. It was the saga of two bearded Scots who, in one continuous passage by almost every conveyance available, travelled entirely through British territory to the Pacific coast – a feat which again captured the public's imagination.

The author of *Ocean to Ocean* was a remarkable Presbyterian minister from Halifax named George Monro Grant, who was to become one of the most distinguished educators and literary figures of his time. He was the choice of Sandford Fleming, newly appointed engineer-in-chief of the Pacific Railway, for the post of secretary to the expedition that Fleming organized in 1872 to follow the proposed route of the new railway.

Fleming was an impressive man, physically as well as intellectually, with a vast beard, a rugged physique, and a questing mind. He was forty-five years old at the time, and he still had half of his life ahead of him in which to complete the Intercolonial and plan the Canadian Pacific, devise a workable system of standard time, plan and promote the Pacific cable, act as an ambassador to Hawaii, publish a book of "short daily prayers for busy households," become Chancellor of Queen's University, and girdle the globe.

In Grant he had a trail-mate who was leather-tough and untroubled by adversity, a good man in the best sense, from whose bald brow there always seemed to shine the light of Christian good humour, in spite of an invalid wife and one retarded son. He himself had come through the fire, having been thrice at death's door in the very first decade of life: scal-ded half to death, almost drowned and given up for dead, and mangled by a haycutter, which cost him his right hand.

The expedition set out across the Great Lakes by steamer into the stony wasteland of the Shield where Fleming's surveyors were already inching their way. Not long after embarkation, Fleming's attention was attracted by the enthusiasms of an agile man who invariably leaped from the steamer the instant it touched the shoreline and began scrambling over rocks and diving into thickets, stuffing all manner of mosses, ferns, lichens, sedges, grasses, and flowers into a covered case which he carried.

Members of Fleming's party, photographed at the outset of their adventure. Left to right: Fleming's son, Sandford Fleming, George Grant, Dr. Arthur Moren. It was this trip that convinced Fleming that the Yellow Head Pass route was the most practicable for the railway to follow.

This was John Macoun, a self-taught professor of natural history, enjoying a busman's holiday in the wilds. Fleming asked him casually if he would care to come along to the Pacific, and Macoun, just as casually, accepted. The accidental meeting was immensely significant. Macoun became enamoured of the North West and ultimately helped change the course of the railway and thus, for better or for worse, the very shape of Canada.

It was, by any standard, an impressive journey that Fleming and his companions made. In 103 days they travelled 5,300 miles by railway, steamer, coach, wagon, canoe, rowboat, dugout, pack and saddle horse, and their own sturdy legs. They made sixty-two camps on prairie, river bank, rock, brush, swamp, and mountainside; and they were convinced that the future railway would follow their route across the Shield, up along the Fertile Belt and through the Yellow Head Pass, which was Fleming's choice from the moment he first saw it. This physical accomplishment was magnificent but its subtle concomitant was far more significant: in the most graphic and dramatic fashion, the clergyman, the botanist, and the surveyor gave to the Canadian public a vision of a nation stretching from sea to sea.

In the days before the railway, the only method of reaching Winnipeg by an all-Canadian route was by the so-called Dawson Road, which led out of Thunder Bay across the Shield to the Red River country. This drawing from the Canadian Illustrated News *gives an idea of the difficulties encountered on the Dawson portages by troops attempting to reach Fort Garry to quell the Riel uprising.*

25

For all of the 1870's, while scandal and political argument kept Ottawa occupied, the North West remained as isolated as the moon – the preserve of the Indians and Métis and the newly arrived North West Mounted Police. Here at Fort Walsh in the Cypress Hills, the Mounties built a military stockade complete with palisades and whitewashed buildings to replace the whiskey forts they were sent west to stamp out. In these sere hills, a genuine Canadian myth was in the making.

Sir Hugh Allan makes
his move

THE DEBATE on the terms of admission of British Columbia was not yet over when the first of the railway entrepreneurs arrived in Ottawa. These were Alfred Waddington of Victoria, seventy-five years old and a fanatic on the subject of a Pacific railway, and his partner, a promoter of unbuilt railroads named William Kersteman. There was no possibility of either of them successfully promoting a line of steel to the Pacific. Historically, they were merely the means by which the sinister figure of George W. McMullen was introduced to the Pacific railway scheme.

McMullen, a Chicago newspaper proprietor at twenty-seven, came originally from Picton, Ontario. Interested in railways, canals, and anything else that might make him a dollar, he had an agile, inquisitive mind which, for all of his long life, intrigued him into the most curious ventures – the growing of aphrodisiacs, for example, and the development of a long-distance cannon. He had come to Ottawa in the spring of 1871 as part of a Chicago delegation seeking the enlargement of the Chicago and Huron Shipping Canal. Waddington and Kersteman were both ardent Yankeephiles. Armed with surveys, maps, pamphlets, and copies of speeches, the two enthusiasts approached McMullen, who was sufficiently allured to seek further support in the United States.

By July, McMullen had brought a covey of American businessmen into the scheme: Charles Mather Smith, a Chicago banker; W. B. Ogden, an original incorporator of the Northern Pacific; General George W. Cass, heir apparent to the presidency of the Northern Pacific; and, more important, Jay Cooke, the Philadelphia banker who controlled the railroad's purse strings and who had his clear, boyish eyes focused on the Canadian

North West, which he hoped would become a tributary of his railroad.

Cooke's first hope was for out-and-out annexation, which would give the Northern Pacific a total monopoly west of the lakes. Failing that, Cooke and his agents intended to work for a Canadian line which would be dependent on the U.S. road for an outlet. In his dreams, Cooke visualized an international railway, running from Montreal through American territory south of Lake Superior and then cutting back into Canada by way of the Red River to proceed westward across the prairies. The railroad, and eventually the territory itself, would be totally under American control.

The American representatives arrived in Ottawa in mid-July about a week before the contract was signed with British Columbia. The Prime Minister agreed to see them but made it quite clear that any railway scheme, at that stage, was premature. To Macdonald, the only value this patently Yankee delegation had was as a kind of lever to force Canadian capitalists to take the matter of the railway seriously. And *the* Canadian capitalist was Sir Hugh Allan, the most powerful financier in the country, whose annual income was estimated at more than half a million dollars in an era when a dollar was worth four or five times its value a century later.

Allan's interests encompassed telegraphs and railways, coal and iron, tobacco and cotton, cattle, paper, rolling mills, and elevators. He himself was an imperious and uncommunicative martinet who had a hearty disdain for public, press, and politicians. The first, he believed, could be ignored; the last two could be purchased. His only politics, as one commentator remarked, were the politics of steamboats and railways.

It was to Sir Hugh Allan that Sir Francis Hincks, Macdonald's minister of finance, dropped the news, early that August, that some Americans were interested in building the Pacific railway. It was too bad, Hincks added casually, that a work of such importance should be entrusted to foreigners.

Alfred Waddington: the first promoter

Jay Cooke: he wanted to seize the North West

28

Allan was immediately interested: as the country's leading shipowner he could benefit, perhaps more than anyone else, from a steel link to the Pacific. He lost little time in getting in touch with the Americans whose names Hincks had obligingly supplied and in September proceeded to form a company which, though ostensibly Canadian, would be almost entirely controlled and financed by the Northern Pacific; it was planned, in fact, that it would be part of the Northern Pacific complex. Allan's reward was to be a large block of stock and a secret fund of fifty thousand dollars to distribute, in McMullen's phrase, "among persons whose accession would be desirable." One such person was Sir George Etienne Cartier, Macdonald's dynamic but ailing Quebec lieutenant, who was unalterably opposed to any U.S. participation.

The Americans signed a formal but secret agreement with Allan on December 23, 1871. A pretense would be made that an all-Canadian route was being built north of Lake Superior. Its actual construction, however, was to be delayed for years while a Montreal-Duluth link through the United States was put into operation, financed by Canadian Pacific bonds sold in London to investors who believed they were promoting an Imperial project.

Jay Cooke was then at the peak of his meteoric career – dreaming dreams of a railway empire that would devour half of Canada for America's manifest destiny, and secure in the belief that "the country belongs to us naturally and should be brought over without violence or bloodshed." The instrument used to achieve this scheme would be the new Canadian Pacific railway in which he and his associates were to have a fifty-five per cent interest.

Allan, meanwhile, was engaged in a lavish shopping spree, using the Americans' money in an attempt to buy up politicians, newspapermen, and business opponents, such as Senator David Macpherson, who was putting together a rival company to compete for the contract. Macpherson's Interoceanic company had a directorate of prominent Toronto and Ontario capitalists. His stated object

*Senator
id L. Macpherson
of Toronto*

*Sir Hugh Allan, the shaggy laird of Ravenscrag,
put business ahead of nationalism. His secret deal with
Jay Cooke would have made the Canadian Pacific
a mere branch line of an American-controlled railroad.*

29

was to defeat Allan's scheme, which the Liberal press was denouncing almost daily as a front for the Northern Pacific.

Allan did his best to buy Macpherson off – or so he told his American backers. Macpherson's subsequent account differed. Allan, he said, had called upon him to join in forming the Canadian Pacific Railway Company with the understanding that he, Allan, would head it. There would be eleven directors – six Canadians, including Allan and Macpherson, and five Americans, all of them directors of the Northern Pacific. Macpherson objected strenuously to the Americans' involvement; all they needed to control the company was one vote – Allan's – and if they controlled the purse strings they certainly controlled that. The naïve idea that the Americans would own the railway and yet allow the Canadians to run it was too much for Macpherson. He washed his hands of Allan and set about getting a charter for his all-Canadian company.

The downfall of Cartier

GEORGE ETIENNE CARTIER was one of the leading architects of Canadian Confederation and, next to Macdonald, the most important politician in Canada. Before Allan could succeed he must have Cartier with him. To achieve that end he was prepared to use brutal methods.

Cartier controlled the parliamentary action of forty-five Quebec members who voted in a phalanx. The Government needed this Quebec vote since its majority was considerably less than forty-five. The defection of half could, on a tightly fought issue, put it out of office. If Allan could win over a slice of Cartier's following he would then control the means to manipulate their leader. The lever, he shrewdly decided, would be the Quebeckers' hunger for a railroad along the north shore of the St. Lawrence from Quebec City through Montreal to

Ottawa. He himself headed the Northern Colonization Railway which planned to build the Mont-
real-Ottawa link of the coveted line. Cartier, who
had connections with the rival Grand Trunk Railway, could be presumed to oppose it. Allan began
at once to spend the money provided by his American backers to stir up the French Canadians along
the proposed route against Cartier. He paid several
French-Canadian lawyers to write up the matter in
the press. He bought controlling stock in newspapers and subsidized others. He stumped the country through which his proposed railway would go.
In the end, he won over twenty-seven of Cartier's
forty-five followers and felt he could control the
Government. With an election announced for the
late summer of 1872, Cartier's surrender was total.

Meanwhile, Senator Macpherson and his rival
Interoceanic company were proving an embarrassment to Macdonald. Macpherson remained utterly
convinced that Allan was prepared to deliver the
railway into the hands of Yankee freebooters. The
Prime Minister was faced with an impossible choice:
he could choose the Toronto group and alienate
French Canada, or he could choose the Allan group
and alienate Ontario. Clearly an amalgamation was
indicated. Macdonald genuinely believed that Allan
was the only possible choice to head the venture,
but Macpherson continued to insist stubbornly that
Allan was a tool of the American railway; he would
welcome amalgamation, but not with Allan as president.

As it turned out, Macpherson was right. It ought
to have been clear to Allan by this time that the
government had no intention of allowing American
control of the railway; and yet, while pretending
publicly that his was an all-Canadian company, the
imperious shipbuilder retained his secret ties with
New York and Chicago.

In vain Macdonald tried to effect a *rapproche-
ment* between Macpherson and Allan. The Tory
party desperately wanted to place the *fait accompli*
of a strong railway company before the electors;
but the principals remained deadlocked.

By this time Allan was hard at work trying to
restore the political fortunes of the badly battered
Cartier who had been transformed from enemy into ally by his machinations of the previous spring.
Though he did not know it then, Cartier had less
than a year to live: the telltale symptoms of Bright's
disease – the swollen feet, the impaired judge-
ment – had already appeared.

If Allan threw himself heart, soul, and pocket-
book into the election, it was because he believed
he had a pledge from the Government to give him
the charter for the railway. The events of July 29
and 30, when promises were made by Cartier and
Macdonald, and election funds were pledged by Allan, can only be understood against the background
of the political morality and practice of the time.

Elections were fought with money, and often
enough it was the candidate who spent the most
who cornered the votes. Dollars spoke louder than
ideas and out-and-out bribery was not uncommon.
There was still no secret ballot in the 1872 election; it did not make its appearance until 1874. This
meant that bribery was extraordinarily effective
since the party agents could check on the loyalty of
their paid supporters.

The election was particularly hard fought, especially in Ontario. Macdonald himself was badly
pressed for funds. Cartier was equally desperate,
since he faced an uphill battle in his own constituency. For him the moment of truth came
at the close of July. Allan had conferred with him
on several occasions, urging him to procure the
amalgamation of the two companies "upon such
terms as I considered would be just to myself" –
in short, the presidency for Allan. On the thirtieth,
he and his lawyer, J. J. C. Abbott, M.P., visited
Cartier once again for a meeting that was to become
memorable. Cartier had received, on July 26, a telegram scribbled by Macdonald in Kingston. The
Prime Minister had been unable to change Macpherson's mind. "Under these circumstances," he
wired, "I authorize you to assure Allan that the
influence of the Government will be exercised to

secure him the position of President. The other terms to be as agreed on between Macpherson and Abbott. The whole matter to be kept quiet until after the elections. . . ."

Four days later Cartier showed the wire to Allan. It was not quite enough for the shipping magnate. What if Macpherson continued to be stubborn? Cartier was forced to concede that, if a new amalgamated company could not be formed, then Allan's Canada Pacific company would be given the charter. But Allan wanted that promise nailed down in writing.

Cartier suggested that Abbott draw up the necessary document and return with it that afternoon. As Allan and Abbott rose to leave, Cartier asked in his abrupt way: "Are you not going to help us in our elections?" When Allan asked how much Cartier wanted, Cartier replied that it might come to one hundred thousand dollars. Allan, the model businessman, suggested he put that in writing, too.

That afternoon he and Abbott were back again with two letters. One, to be signed by Cartier, promised Allan the charter; the other, also to be signed by Cartier, asked for financial help in the elections. Cartier was not satisfied with either of the letters and both were rewritten. One was to become notorious:

"The friends of the Government will expect to be assisted with funds in the pending elections, and any amount which you or your Company shall advance for that purpose shall be recouped by you. A memorandum of immediate requirements is below.

NOW WANTED

Sir John A. Macdonald	$25,000
Hon. Mr. Langevin	15,000
Sir G.E.C.	20,000
Sir J.A. (add.)	10,000
Hon. Mr. Langevin	10,000
Sir G.E.C.	30,000."

In spite of promises to recoup, Allan did not really expect to see his money again.

Meanwhile, in Kingston, Macdonald was impatiently awaiting a reply to his telegram of July 26. When it finally arrived he was appalled. He could not afford to take time off from last minute electioneering, but he wired Cartier, repudiating the letter: his original telegram of July 26 must be "the basis of the agreement." *Agreement!* The ambiguity of that word would return to haunt Macdonald.

Cartier broke the news to Allan, who gracefully withdrew the letter; but he did not withdraw his financial support. He increased it. Altogether he distributed more than $350,000 among Conservative candidates.

And for what? The Conservative government barely squeaked into power. In Ontario it was badly battered and in Quebec, where most of the

Allan's shrewd lawyer, John J. C. Abbott, survived the Pacific Scandal and went on to become legal adviser to the CPR, mayor of Montreal, and, briefly, Prime Minister of Canada. Macdonald did not care for him. When his secretary, Joseph Pope, remarked that Abbott's smile was sweet, John A. slew him with a single phrase. "Yes," he said, "a sweet smile. All from the teeth outward."

32

Allan funds had been spent, it managed to capture only a bare majority. Without the West and the Maritimes, Macdonald would have been ruined politically. As for Cartier, he suffered a stunning personal defeat, which had its own ironies. By some mysterious process, a large slice of Allan's money had been appropriated by the other side. On the day of the election, the open balloting revealed that man after man who had been paid in good hard cash to work for George Etienne Cartier had actually been in the secret service of the enemy all the while.

George McMullen's blackmail

ALL THAT AUTUMN, Sir John A. Macdonald was haunted by his secret promise to Allan. There was no way out of it. Senator David Macpherson remained utterly immovable and the Prime Minister realized he must form a new company without him. Like it or not, he had to keep his promise to the man who had been the biggest contributor to the Conservative coffers. At this juncture he ought to have entertained some doubts about Allan. On October 7, he was shocked to discover that the Montrealer, in spite of all his pious proclamations, had not actually broken off relations with McMullen and the others. Was this the man who ought to be heading up the greatest national venture?

There was nothing the Prime Minister could do. He had made a promise through Cartier and he would have to stick by it. But what actually *had* Cartier promised Allan? Macdonald realized that he himself did not know the exact details. Already there were rumours floating around Montreal about Allan's gifts to the Cartier campaign. When Macdonald learned from Allan the full extent of Cartier's financial dependence upon him, he was horrified.

In Chicago, George McMullen was also experiencing twinges of uneasiness as he studied Allan's expense accounts. In September, Allan informed him that he had paid out $343,000 and still had $13,500 to distribute. McMullen lost no time in getting to Montreal to confront Allan, who managed to mollify him. Then, on October 24, Allan, under Macdonald's goading, finally broke the news to his American associates that he would have to dump them. McMullen was in a state of rage. He had squandered more than a year of his time and tens of thousands of his and his associates' dollars and now it appeared that he had had no hope of success from the outset. Allan had deceived everybody. The apoplectic McMullen suggested that if the shipowner had a scrap of honour left he would either stick to the original agreement or step out of the picture. When Allan refused, McMullen set off to Ottawa with no less a purpose than to blackmail the Prime Minister of Canada.

The encounter, which occupied two hours, took place on New Year's Eve. McMullen came armed with Allan's letters to him, and he proceeded to read some compromising extracts. He talked mysteriously about political pay-offs. He said he could name names in that connection of persons "who are very near to you." Macdonald was inwardly aghast but, at moments like this, he knew enough to maintain a poker face. He denied that Allan had bribed the Government. In that case, McMullen replied smoothly, Allan must be a swindler – he had taken almost four hundred thousand dollars from the Americans on just that pretext. He urged Macdonald either to stick to the original agreement or to leave Allan out of the new company. Macdonald replied that he could do neither; if McMullen thought he was badly used, that was his problem. The Americans, said the Prime Minister, had been out of the company for some time.

Not so, replied McMullen, and he produced Allan's own correspondence in evidence. Again Macdonald was appalled, but he did not show it.

McMullen grew more threatening. He began to talk about what would happen politically if the public knew all the facts. Macdonald made no comment but asked for time to consult with Allan and his lawyer, Abbott. On that note the encounter ended, but McMullen was back in Ottawa three weeks later with more compromising correspondence. It must have been clear by now to the Prime Minister that Allan was an unfortunate choice to head the new company. For almost a year Macdonald had been telling his colleagues, his friends, his political enemies, and the country at large (as well as himself) that Allan was the only possible choice for the job – a man of business acumen, probity, sagacity, and experience who commanded the total respect of the financial community. Now he stood revealed as a conniver, a liar, a double-dealer, and, perhaps worst of all, a Yankee-lover – a man whose imprudence, in Macdonald's own words, "has almost mounted to insanity." And this was the man who would shortly be setting off for London on a mission of the greatest delicacy to secure the underwriting of the world's largest railway project! Clearly, if the financial community or the public at large knew what Macdonald knew, the railway scheme would collapse like a soap bubble.

McMullen would have to be bought off. The Prime Minister wrote to Hincks in Montreal and Hincks sought out Abbott, the lawyer. Abbott bargained McMullen down to $37,500 for the Allan letters, paying twenty thousand down and placing Allan's cheque for the rest in an envelope which he gave to Henry Starnes of Allan's Merchants' Bank. McMullen then placed the offending correspondence in another envelope and gave that to Starnes. The banker's instructions were to wait until ten days after the end of the coming session and then deliver the envelope with the money to McMullen and the envelope with the correspondence to Allan. This was the best arrangement that Abbott could make to keep the story from becoming public before Allan completed his negotiations in England and while Parliament was in session. But George McMullen did not bother to collect the second envelope from Henry Starnes, the banker. He had already received a higher bid from Macdonald's political enemies.

Lord Dufferin, the dapper new governor general, arrives at Parliament Hill for the opening of the Second Parliament of Canada – one of the most harrowing in Canadian history. But at this moment there was no hint of the storm that was gathering. The March sky was blue, the sun was bright, and, in Dufferin's words, the weather was "quite divine." Inside, the crimson Senate chamber had been cleared of chairs to accommodate the parliamentarians and their wives and daughters. Dufferin, who had served as a diplomat at St. Petersburg, Rome, and Paris, was "rather surprised to see what a high bred and good looking company they formed." He was as yet unaccustomed to the hurly-burly of Canadian politics, but in the days that followed he certainly had his fill of it, as the Pacific Scandal burst upon a startled nation.

Lucius Huntington's moment in history

BY THE TIME the first session of the Second Parliament of Canada opened on March 6, 1873, the Liberal Party was in on the secret and, as the session progressed, rumours began to flit around Ottawa about a coming political earthquake. On March 31, the Opposition's intentions were revealed when, at the opening of the day's proceedings, Lucius Seth Huntington rose to give notice of a motion to appoint a committee to inquire into matters generally affecting the Canadian Pacific railway. Huntington sat down amid Opposition cries of "Hear! Hear!" and a tingle of excitement rippled through the House.

Two days later, when Huntington prepared to make his motion, the corridors of the House were filled to suffocation, the galleries were crowded, the Treasury benches were full, and every Opposition seat was occupied. The Commons was silent and expectant. Seldom had any member faced such an attentive audience.

Huntington spoke that evening. He was a lawyer and politician of long experience, a polished speaker, resonant and melodious, but now there was a tremor in his voice and he talked so softly that the back-benchers had to lean forward to catch his words. He had reason to be nervous for he was putting his career on the line. If he could not prove his charges, he would certainly be forced to resign; if he *could* prove them, his name would go down in history.

His speech was astonishingly brief; it ran to no more than seven short paragraphs and was supported by no documentary evidence. Huntington charged that the Allan company was secretly financed by American capital and that the Government was aware of that fact, that Allan had advanced large sums of money, some of it paid by the Americans, to aid the Government in the elections, and that he had been offered the railway contract in return for his support. Huntington called for a seven-man parliamentary committee to inquire into every circumstance connected with the railway negotiations with power to subpoena papers, records, and witnesses. Then he sat down, "full of suppressed emotion," as a historian of the day recorded.

An oppressive silence hung over the House. Every eye had turned to the lean, sprawled figure of Macdonald, but the Prime Minister remained "inscrutable as stone." The silence was broken by the Speaker, asking for the question. The motion was lost by one of the largest majorities the Government had enjoyed that session. The Government press took the view that it was nothing more than a device to needle the ministry.

Macdonald, however, faced a rebellion from his own followers between sittings. Many felt that the Government had given the appearance of riding roughshod over its opponents and that its silence in the face of charges so serious could be taken as an admission of guilt. Accordingly, the Prime Minister rose a week later to announce the appointment of a select committee of five to investigate the Huntington charges.

Now Macdonald proceeded to set in motion a series of tactics of the kind that would eventually earn him the sobriquet – an affectionate one – of Old Tomorrow. His was to be a policy of delay. He agreed that the evidence should be taken under oath. But before the witnesses could be sworn, a bill had to be introduced into the House. Macdonald was reasonably confident that England, if prompted, would disallow such a bill. That would pave the way for a royal commission, whose members Macdonald himself could appoint.

Delay was dangerous to the Liberal cause. Telegrams could be destroyed in the interval; originals of documents and letters could disappear, and, indeed, did. The Liberal leadership belatedly realized that it had made a tactical error in not placing some of the evidence on the record when Huntington first made his charges. It is clear that he had

Lucius Seth Huntington, whose brief speech in Parliament touched off the Pacific Scandal. Huntington's information was based on documents rifled from John J. C. Abbott's safe by his confidential secretary and sold to the Liberal Party. At 46, Huntington was a lawyer of long experience and an eloquent speaker.

πολύμητις Οδυσσεύς

Αἰνείας Βουλημόρος

Δαΐφρος Ἕκτωρ

Πρίαμος μέγας

In April and May of 1873, immediately after the first hint of the scandal, the Illustrated News published a series of caricatures of leading politicians by its cartoonist, Jump, showing them attired as classical heroes. Macdonald was "the many-counselled Ulysses," Mackenzie was Aeneas, Edward Blake "the valiant Hector," and George Brown of the Globe was "great Priam." The drawings were accompanied by quotations from Pope's translation of the Iliad, which the News's educated readers could be expected to know. Weekly journals in those times were edited for the elite and not the masses.

seen copies of the Allan-McMullen correspondence and knew where the originals were stored. The evidence was to indicate that the Liberal Party had purchased Allan's indiscreet correspondence from McMullen for twenty-five thousand dollars.

Outwardly, the Prime Minister was totally in command. Inwardly, he was sick at heart. In May he suffered two blows. Allan's mission to England had been destroyed by the whispers of scandal from across the water, and so Macdonald's railway policy lay in tatters. The settlement of the North West, the knitting together of the disunited provinces, the building of a workable, transcontinental nation – all these remained an elusive dream.

And the partnership of Macdonald and Cartier was no more. Macdonald's political comrade-in-arms was dead in England of the kidney disease that had ravaged him for two years. At the nadir of his career, Macdonald had no one to turn to. Politically, he stood alone – weary, overworked, tormented, dispirited. He wanted out, but his party could not let him resign for there was no one to replace him. He turned, as he so often did in moments of stress, to the bottle; and for the next several weeks all who encountered him, from Governor General to hack reporter, were treated to the spectacle of the Prime Minister of Canada reeling drunk.

Yet his powers of recuperation were marvellous. He had the ability to pull himself together, even after days of drinking, when there was necessary business to attend to. And at the end of June, Macdonald needed his faculties; the Oaths Bill was officially disallowed just five days before the investigating committee was due to meet. Macdonald renewed his offer of a royal commission. Once again the Opposition had been frustrated in its attempts to get the evidence before the public. It was more than three months since Huntington had raised the issue and the country was in no sense aroused. There was only one course left open: the press.

Scandal!

ON THE MORNING OF July 4, the faithful readers of the Toronto *Globe* and the Montreal *Herald* opened their slim papers to the scoop of the decade. There, for column after column, was laid bare the correspondence of Sir Hugh Allan with his secret American backers. It was all in print for the country to ponder: Allan's detailed account of his victory over Cartier; Allan's long report on his coercion of the Quebec press and public; Allan's disbursements of $343,000; Allan's double game with his American associates. For the first time the public had something it could get its teeth into and the Pacific Scandal, as it was now universally called, became the major topic of the day.

At Macdonald's urgent behest, Allan, with Abbott's help, prepared a sworn affidavit to be published on July 6 in major Government newspapers. This lengthy document was designed to get the administration off the hook, and it largely succeeded. The statement was a masterpiece of tightrope walking. "He [Abbott] has made the old gentleman acknowledge on oath that his letters were untrue," Macdonald wrote gleefully to Lord Dufferin. It was clear that Macdonald's ministry, though bruised, was by no means broken. The weary Prime Minister felt that he could afford a short holiday at Rivière du Loup. It was while he was there, in his small cottage near the riverside, that the world crashed in on him.

The blow fell on July 17. A series of revelations appeared identically and simultaneously in the *Globe*, the *Herald*, and *l'Evénement* of Quebec and they were shocking.

The story took the form of a narrative by George McMullen. He claimed that Allan had lent Macdonald money. He identified the newspapers that Allan told him he had paid. He said that Allan had made an additional indefinite loan of ten thousand dollars to Hincks and had promised Hector

WHITHER ARE WE DRIFTING?

Louis Langevin, Cartier's successor, twenty-five thousand for election purposes, "on condition of his friendly assistance." There was worse to come. Appended to McMullen's narrative was a series of letters and telegrams which contained political dynamite. They had been buried at the end by design in an attempt to divert suspicion from the source from which they had been obtained. They had been rifled from Abbott's safe in the dark of the night, during the lawyer's absence in England, copied by his confidential secretary, and sold for hard cash to the Liberal Party.

Cartier to Abbott, Montreal, August 24, 1872: "In the absence of Sir Hugh Allan, I shall be obliged by your supplying the Central Committee with a further sum of twenty thousand dollars upon the same conditions as the amount written by me at the foot of my letter to Sir Hugh Allan on the 30th ult.

George E. Cartier

"P.S. Please also send Sir John A. Macdonald ten thousand dollars more on the same terms."

Terms? Conditions? What price Allan's sworn denials now?

Memorandum signed by three members of the Central Committee, J. L. Beaudry, Henry Starnes, and P. S. Murphy: "Received from Sir Hugh Allan by the hands of J. J. C. Abbott twenty thousand dollars for General Election purposes, to be arranged hereafter according to the terms of the letter of Sir George E. Cartier, of the date of 30th of July, and in accordance with the request contained in his letter of the 24th instant." *Montreal, 26th Aug., 1872*

Again, that damning word: *terms*. It was well for the Government that poor Cartier was dead.

Telegram: *Macdonald to Abbott at St. Anne's, Aug. 26, 1872:* "I must have another ten thousand; will be the last time of calling; do not fail me; answer today."

Reply: *Abbott to Macdonald from Montreal,*

Aug. 26, 1872: "Draw on me for ten thousand dollars."

The effect on the public of these revelations was incalculable. The Pacific Scandal became the sole topic of conversation in those late July days and continued so into the fall. All other news and comment were subordinated. The carnage among the party faithful was devastating. Many a loyal Tory was transformed, during that tempestuous summer, into a working Liberal.

In all his long career, nothing hit Macdonald so hard as the McMullen revelations. The news, as he said, "fairly staggered" him – it was "one of those overwhelming misfortunes that they say every man must meet once in his life." He had expected trouble but nothing so cataclysmic as this. He had certainly sent the telegrams, but he had never expected to be found out.

A royal commission was now an absolute necessity, preferably one that included "safe" judges. The indispensable Abbott was hurriedly called upon to assist in the negotiations. But at this point, with the crisis swirling around him, Macdonald took to the bottle and vanished from sight. No member of his cabinet could reach him or learn of his plans or purpose. The press reported that he had disappeared from Rivière du Loup. His wife had no idea where he was. The frantic Governor General, in the midst of a state tour of the Maritimes, could get no answer to an urgent and confidential letter. He followed it with an equally urgent telegram; silence. On August 5, the Montreal *Daily Witness* published in its two o'clock edition a rumour that Macdonald had committed suicide by throwing himself into the St. Lawrence. The story, concocted by his political enemies, vanished from the next edition but was widely believed at the time; it seemed to confirm the Government's guilt. Suicide or no, the fact was that for several days, in a moment of grave political crisis, the Prime Minister of Canada was on a drinking bout and could not be found by anyone. Dufferin finally unravelled

40

THE IRREPRESSIBLE SHOWMAN.

BARNUM WANTS TO BUY THE "PACIFIC SCANDAL."

"WE IN CANADA SEEM TO HAVE LOST ALL IDEA OF JUSTICE, HONOR AND INTEGRITY."—THE MAIL, 26TH SEPTEMBER.

Bengough accurately reflected the national feeling. The bitter quotation below is from a Conservative newspaper.

BLACKWASH AND WHITEWASH.

ILLUSTRATING THE RECENT GREAT OPPOSITION SPEECHES, AND THE DOINGS OF THE JOLLY ROYAL COMMISSION.

THE BEAUTIES OF A ROYAL COMMISSION.

"WHEN SHALL WE THREE MEET AGAIN?"

The cartoonist's comments on the Royal Commission mirror the general opinion that it was designed as a whitewash job, in which Macdonald himself would act as witness, judge, and prosecutor. The commissioners, carefully chosen by J. J. C. Abbott, contented themselves with publishing the evidence before them without comment.

the mystery and put it delicately in a private letter to the Colonial Secretary: "He had stolen away, as I subsequently found, from his seaside villa and was lying perdu with a friend in the neighbourhood of Quebec."

Macdonald's downfall

THE ROYAL COMMISSION began to take evidence on September 4. It was unsatisfactory on several counts. There was no commission counsel to cross-examine witnesses. The commissioners themselves did not seem to know what to ask them. Several of the principals declined to appear. Of the thirty-six witnesses called, fifteen contributed nothing whatsoever to the proceedings, nor were they pressed to contribute more. It was obvious from the beginning why Macdonald had opted for a royal commission. In Dufferin's words, "elderly judges have hardly the disembowelling powers which are rife in a young cross-examining counsel."

Day after day, for all of September, the public was treated to the spectacle of powerful business figures and important politicians, by nature and training supposedly men of precision, fumbling about on the stand, delivering fuzzy or evasive answers, testifying to receipts that were "lost" or missing, prefacing their remarks with such phrases as "I cannot remember," or "It is not very likely."

The tendency of the commissioners to take statements at their face value without further searching inquiry did not go unremarked. Macdonald's political enemy, George Brown, the former Liberal leader and publisher of the *Globe*, pounded this point home daily. Brown had just returned from England where he had dined with one of *The Times*'s chief editorial writers and other newspaper men. When Macdonald testified before the commission, the major British papers were ready to pounce.

It was Macdonald's testimony that the country was waiting for. The Prime Minister denied or qualified many of the statements in the McMullen account and also denied that Allan's election contributions had influenced the Government in any way. Further, he made it clear that the Government had never had any intention of allowing the Americans to control the railway. But there were two damning accusations that he could not and did not deny: he *had* asked Allan for election funds and he *had* promised Allan the presidency of the company.

Macdonald swore that he had not used one cent of Allan's money for his own election; but he was forced to make one other damaging admission: Allan's money had been spent in a manner "contrary to statute," in bringing voters to the polls and in "dinners and things of that kind." The Prime Minister's euphemisms and deliberate vagueness could not obscure in the public mind the obvious deduction that the money had been used to bribe the voters. In his second capacity of Minister of Justice, he had knowingly broken the law.

The British press came down very hard on the Prime Minister. *The Times* declared that his testimony had confirmed the McMullen revelations. The *Pall Mall Gazette* asserted that "the scandal of his conduct is without precedent" and called for his removal from office forever. All this was reprinted in the Opposition newspapers in Canada; George Brown's spade-work had paid off for the Liberal Party.

The final act was played out on Parliament Hill from October 23 to November 5 in what James Young, the parliamentarian-historian, called "one of the most remarkable and profoundly exciting debates of that period." Both sides were confident of success. Though the Opposition had the public on its side, the Government still had the votes. At this stage of political development, party lines were not yet tightly drawn. The Opposition was a loose amalgam of Reformers and Clear Grits, working under the umbrella of the Liberal Party. Many of those who supported Macdonald called themselves Independents. Nobody knew how the six members from the new province of Prince Edward Island would vote. Part of the parliamentary struggle, therefore, took place behind the scenes, as one side struggled to hold its supporters and the other strove to capture them.

At the close of the commission's hearings, Macdonald had estimated a Tory majority of twenty-five. By Monday, October 27, the number had dropped to eighteen and then to sixteen; some thought it as low as thirteen. But if the Prime Minister could hold the debate down to three or four days and make one of his powerful speeches early in the game, he could probably win the vote. Yet he did not speak. Day after day, the debate see-sawed back and forth but the Prime Minister remained silent. What on earth was wrong? His boasted majority was drifting away "like leaves in the Valley of Vallombrosa," in Lord Dufferin's phrase. His friends were full of angry entreaties. He *must* speak; only he could stem the tide. Stubbornly, the Prime Minister refused.

He had started to drink again. Haggard in appearance, he was weak with fatigue and ill with strain. It was assumed by many that he did not feel himself fit to take up the cudgels in his party's defence.

But this was not the case. Macdonald was waiting for Edward Blake to speak, for he was tolerably certain from hints in the Liberal press that the Opposition was holding some damning piece of evidence, some document of "a fatally compromising character," that Cartier had written. Or perhaps he himself had dispatched some damaging letter during the election; the appalling thing was that the Prime Minister could not be sure whether he had or not, he had been in his cups for so much of that period. He *must* have the last word. He could not afford to make his move and then have Blake follow him with such a *coup de grâce*.

It was only at the end of the week that the truth began to dawn upon him that, for once, he

The Liberal Party entrusted its final volley to Edward
Blake, the brilliant lawyer, who built his speeches,
brick by brick, on solid fact and hard evidence. A Blake
speech was considered short if it did not last five hours.

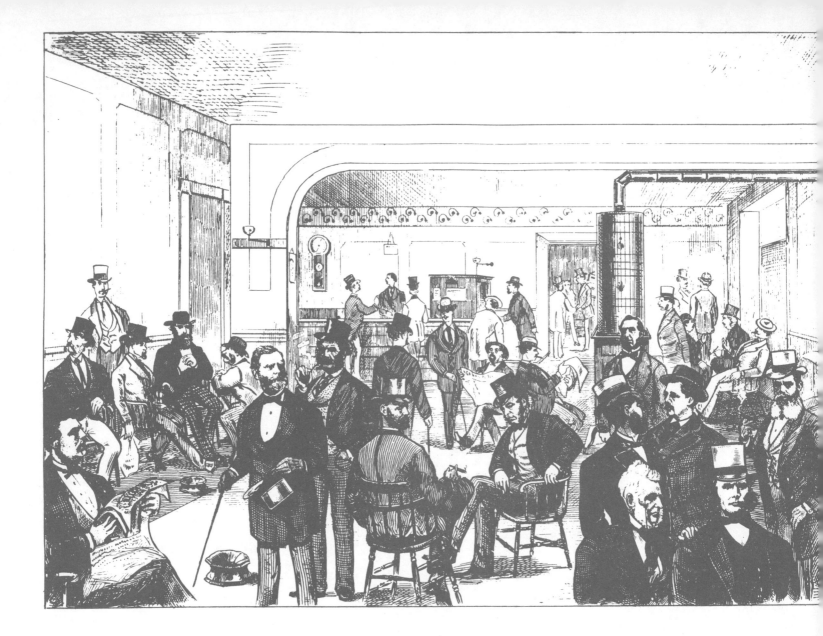

had been shamelessly outmanoeuvred. Blake was holding back on purpose, calculating that Macdonald's physical condition would deteriorate to the point where he could not speak at all. There would be no fresh revelations; the Liberals were waging a war of attrition.

Macdonald resolved at last to enter the arena on the evening of Monday, November 3. That night the corridors of the House were choked. Scores had missed their dinners in order to hold their places in the packed galleries. Even the back-benches were invaded by strangers. Every member, save the exiled Louis Riel, was in his seat as Macdonald rose slowly to his feet, pale, nervous, and haggard, "looking as if a feather would knock him down." Then, for the next five hours, he proceeded to electrify the House.

Those who were there would never forget it. Many felt it was the greatest speech Macdonald had ever made and some said it was the greatest they had ever heard. Even the vituperative *Globe* called it "extraordinary." Sick, dispirited, and

A contemporary engraving showing Members of Parliament gathering in the famous salon of the Russell House during the Pacific Scandal debate. This was Ottawa's "whispering gallery" in the 70's.

It was past 1.30 a.m. when Macdonald finished, but in spite of the late hour, the House continued to sit. Now Edward Blake hoisted his big frame from his chair and stood, erect and commanding, peering sombrely through his silver-rimmed spectacles at his adversaries. To this tousled lawyer with the powerful build and strange pallor the Liberal Party had entrusted its final volley. The speech Blake was about to give was exactly the kind the situation called for and exactly the kind at which he excelled. It was Blake's strength that he built his speeches, brick by brick, on solid fact and hard evidence and his weakness that he generally gave his listeners too much of both. Blake took nothing for granted. He verified every statement by reference to the original documents and long after he had proved his case conclusively he kept piling it on and on.

Blake spoke on until 2.30 that morning and then for another four hours the following afternoon and evening, building his case. To the faltering members, Blake's very lack of histrionics – no arm-waving, no rising inflections – added weight to his words. And when he said, "I believe that this night or tomorrow night will be the end of twenty years of corruption," there were ringing cheers. Macdonald was not present when Blake took his seat. He lay upon a couch in a committee room, half conscious, ill with fatigue.

Still the vote was in doubt. How effective had Blake been? Had he managed to cancel out the morale-building effects of Macdonald's passionate appeal? The Liberals had still not been able to force a vote; every man was in his place, waiting hour after hour for the division that would not come.

Finally it was the turn of Donald A. Smith to speak. The tough former fur trader, who was becoming a power in the Hudson's Bay Company and the Bank of Montreal, represented the riding of Selkirk, Manitoba. Smith usually supported the Government, but it was by no means certain how he would vote and Macdonald's supporters had been hesitant about approaching this frosty and im-

weary he might be; but somewhere within himself this homely, errant, and strangely attractive political animal had tapped a hidden well of energy. Some claimed it was the gin, which pageboys reportedly poured into the water glasses at his elbow, but Macdonald was driven by another, more powerful stimulation. He was fighting for his career; only he could salvage it. With a single speech, Macdonald solidified his hold upon the Conservative Party, a hold which had become increasingly weak and aimless. Without it he could scarcely have continued.

perious man. Finally, the Prime Minister was himself persuaded to talk to Smith. The meeting was not a success; when the Member was taken to Macdonald's office he found him drunk and belligerent. Nonetheless the feeling in the Government ranks was that Smith was on their side.

It was 1 a.m. on November 5 when Smith rose to an expectant chamber. His speech was brief but he managed to squeeze from it every possible ounce of suspense. His tone was bland: he did not consider, he said, that the Prime Minister took Allan's money with any corrupt motive. At that, the Government benches began to cheer; but Smith was not finished: he felt the leader of the Government was incapable of taking money from Allan for corrupt purposes. He would be most willing to vote for the Government – the cheers from the ministerial benches were now gleeful – *could he do so conscientiously* . . .

Consternation on the Conservative side! Cheers and laughter from the Opposition.

. . . It was with great regret, Smith said, that he could not do so: there was no corruption but "a very grave impropriety."

The Members skulked back to their seats as Smith sat down and with that the Speaker adjourned the House. There was a storm around Smith. The Prime Minister had always admired him. Now he felt betrayed. For most of the decade the name of Donald A. Smith would be anathema to the Conservatives.

It was, of course, all over. Macdonald did not wait for the ignominy of a vote. He resigned the following day and went, remarkably cheerfully, into opposition. Characteristically, he never again alluded to the subject; it was as if, to preserve his equilibrium, he had dismissed it from his mind.

The new leaders of the country did not. For most of the decade they would, on every possible occasion, taunt their opponents with the memory of the Pacific Scandal. It would influence their policies and their actions as it would influence those of the Conservatives. When, years later, a contract

"PROGRESSING FAVORABLY."

MISS CANADA (ANXIOUSLY).—"DOCTORS, HOW DO YOU FIND THE POOR DEAR PREMIER?"
DR. B N (FOR THE M.D.'s). "MADAM, WE'VE JUST HAD A CONSULTATION; THE SYMPTOMS ARE HOPEFUL. WE BELIEVE HE CAN'T SURVIVE OCTOBER!"

Though in retrospect Macdonald's defeat seems to have been a foregone conclusion, the issue was always in doubt, as these cartoons show. They also make clear the prominent part played by George Brown of the Globe (*wearing white sideburns*)

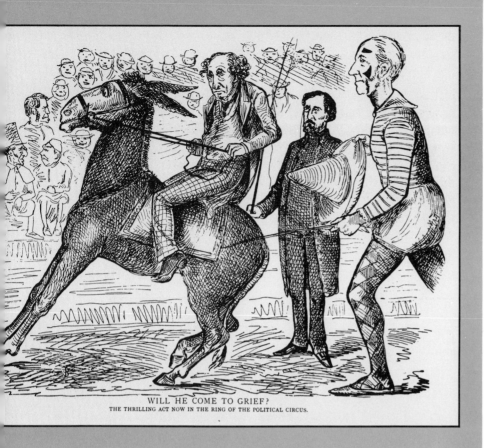

WILL HE COME TO GRIEF?
THE THRILLING ACT NOW IN THE RING OF THE POLITICAL CIRCUS.

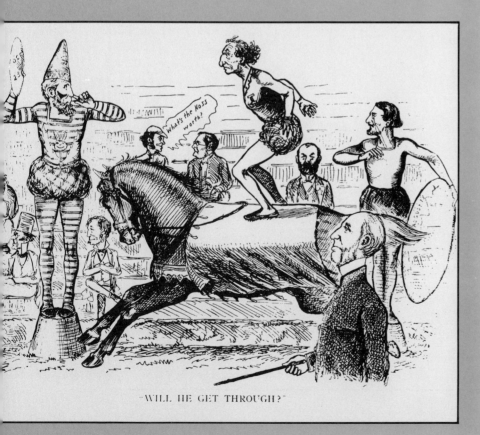

"WILL HE GET THROUGH?"

Donald Smith as he looked when he helped tumble the Tory government, an act that took the usually tolerant Macdonald more than a decade to forgive. Smith was only five years out of Labrador, where he had spent most of his adult life in the service of the Hudson's Bay Company. Now he was a power in both the fur company and the Bank of Montreal – aloof, outwardly unemotional, and totally unshakable. Pelted with rotten eggs in the election that followed, he did not bat an eyelid.

47

was finally signed for the construction of the Canadian Pacific Railway, the terms of the agreement, the choice of the principals, and their later relations with the Government would, in some degree, be affected by the events of 1873.

When Alexander Mackenzie went to the country early in 1874, he was returned in a landslide. It was generally agreed that Macdonald was finished and that he would quickly vanish from the political scene. The railway, it seemed, had been his nemesis. It had ruined his health, stained his honour, and wrecked his career. George Ross, the Liberal member for Middlesex, remembered thinking that a Macdonald revival would be a greater miracle than the passage of the Israelites through the Red Sea. He reckoned without the amazing recuperative powers of the most astonishing politician of the age.

THE CRUEL OBJECT OF "DISSOLUTION."

Bengough's Shakespearian phrase summed up Tory sentiments after Macdonald's defeat. Like most Canadians, he considered that John A. was finished politically and would slip quietly into retirement. The men in the sleigh, opposite, are (foreground) Lord Dufferin and Sir Richard Cartwright, with Blake, Brown, and Mackenzie standing. Cartwright, easily identifiable by his long white side-whiskers, joined the Liberals after the scandal disclosures and became Mackenzie's minister of finance. A bitter man, he never forgot the Pacific Scandal and never forgave Macdonald. Years later, when a statue of Canada's first prime minister was planned, Cartwright tried to have the scandal story engraved upon it.

" COMFORT NO MAN SPEAK;
'S TALK OF GRAVES, OF WORMS, AND EPITAPHS!"—Shakespeare.

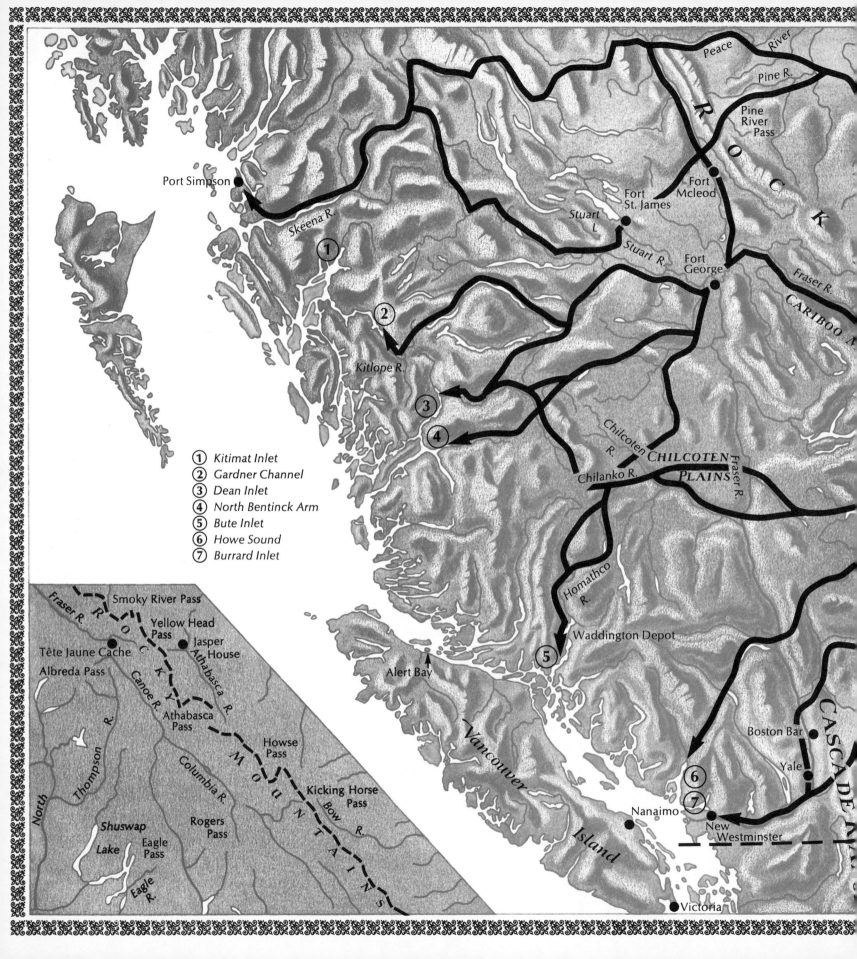

① Kitimat Inlet
② Gardner Channel
③ Dean Inlet
④ North Bentinck Arm
⑤ Bute Inlet
⑥ Howe Sound
⑦ Burrard Inlet

Port Simpson

Skeena R.

①

②

Kitlope R.

③

④

Peace River

Pine R.

Pine River Pass

ROCK

Fort Mcleod

Fort St. James

Stuart L.

Stuart R.

Fort George

Fraser R.

CARIBOO M

Chilcoten R.

CHILCOTEN PLAINS

Chilanko R.

Fraser R.

Homathco R.

Waddington Depot

⑤

Alert Bay

Vancouver Island

Boston Bar

Yale

⑥

⑦

Nanaimo

New Westminster

Victoria

CASCADE M

Fraser R.

ROCKY

Smoky River Pass

Yellow Head Pass

Jasper House

Tête Jaune Cache

Albreda Pass

Canoe R.

Athabasca R.

Athabasca Pass

Howse Pass

Kicking Horse Pass

North

Thompson R.

Columbia R.

Bow R.

MOUNTAINS

Shuswap Lake

Eagle Pass

Rogers Pass

Eagle R.

Fraser R.

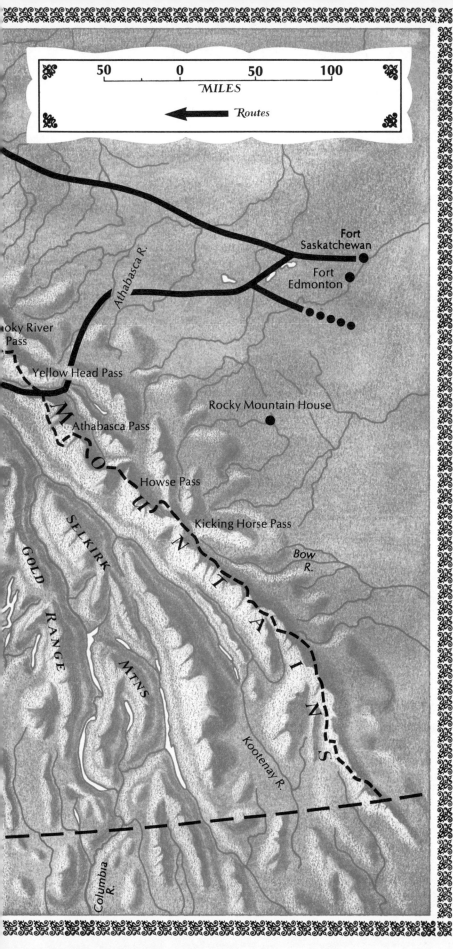

50   0   50   100

MILES

← Routes

Fort Saskatchewan

Fort Edmonton

Athabasca R.

oky River Pass

Yellow Head Pass

Rocky Mountain House

Athabasca Pass

Howse Pass

Kicking Horse Pass

Bow R.

SELKIRK

GOLD

RANGE

MTNS

M O U N T A I N S

Kootenay R.

Columbia R.

2

The Battle of the Routes

The map indicates the thoroughness of Sandford Fleming's surveys in British Columbia – and the dilemma faced by the government in trying to decide which route to follow and which terminus to choose. The surveys were probably too thorough, and some were almost certainly the result of procrastination. Unable to arrive at a politically acceptable decision, the government simply kept the engineers at work.

2076

1976

1876

WINTER QUARTERS M. DIVISION C.P.R.S. TÊTE JAUNE CACHE. BC

In the winter of 1876, a whimsical surveyor stationed near the
Yellow Head Pass whiled away the hours forecasting a day when
locomotives might actually steam through the Rockies. The balloon
craze was then at its height and he also predicted a time when
aircraft would replace trains — but not for another two centuries.

The pathfinders

ALL THIS TIME, while the political hurricane was gathering force in the settled East, hundreds of men were freezing, starving, sickening, and sometimes dying in the unexplored crannies of the new Canada, as they tried to chart a route for the railway.

No life was harsher than that suffered by members of the Canadian Pacific Survey crews. None was less rewarding. Underpaid, over-worked, exiled from their families, deprived of their mail, sleeping in slime and snowdrifts, suffering from sunstroke, frostbite, scurvy, fatigue, and the tensions that always rise to the surface when weary and dispirited men are thrown together for long periods of isolation, the surveyors kept on, year after year. They explored great sections of Canada, scaling mountains that had never before been climbed, crossing lakes that had never known a white man's paddle, and fording rivers not yet on any map. They walked with a uniform stride developed through years of habit, measuring the distances as they went, checking altitudes with an aneroid barometer slung around the neck, and examining the land with a practised gaze, always seeing in the mind's eye the finished line of steel. In the first six years of the Canadian Pacific Survey, forty-six thousand miles of Canada were reconnoitred in this manner.

Twelve thousand of these miles were then laboriously charted, foot by foot, by scores of survey parties. Axemen, tracing the pathfinders' blazes, hacked the lines clear of brush. The chainmen who followed meticulously divided the distances into hundred-foot sections, each marked by a stake. Behind the chainmen came the transit men, calculating the angle of each bend and estimating those distances which could not be measured by a chain. Behind the transits, the rodmen and levellers work-

ed, reckoning the altitudes and inscribing them on bench marks at half-mile intervals. By 1877 there were twenty-five thousand of these bench marks and more than six hundred thousand chainmen's stakes scattered across Canada from the Shield to the Pacific. At this point the surveys had cost three and a half million dollars and the lives of thirty-eight men.

Sandford Fleming took charge as engineer-in-chief in April, 1871. His task was not easy. A special kind of man was needed and it was impossible to find enough of them. Many could not endure the toil.

But even if enough good men could have been found, it is doubtful whether Fleming would have been able to employ them. Political considerations entered into the question: various sections of the country had to be considered, different nationalities and creeds had to be consulted, and there was a constant pressure to give jobs to friends or protégés of politicians. Often appointments were made over Fleming's head. The chief engineer found he had men of whom he had never heard working for him who could not be fired. Sometimes work had to be invented just to keep the political appointees busy.

After the first year of surveys, Fleming reported that it was impossible to obtain "the class of men required." That year two crews, working through the unexplored and impenetrable country between Ottawa and Fort Garry, simply gave up the ghost. There was a seller's market in survey labour and, like it or not, Fleming and his staff had to retain incompetents.

"I wish you would find out what Walter Dewdney is doing," Marcus Smith, in charge of surveys in British Columbia, wrote to a subordinate in May of 1875. "I heard last week that [he] was seen on

In 1874, a survey crew bridging a prairie river paused briefly as its photograph was snapped. Men strong enough to endure both the heavy labour and the isolation were hard to come by. Fleming admitted that "many of the men we were obliged to take, subsequent events proved, were unequal to the very arduous labour they had to undergo, causing a very considerable delay in pushing the work."

the wagon road blind drunk and making an ass of himself." Since Dewdney's brother Edgar was Member for Yale and a strong political power in the province, the erring Walter could scarcely be dismissed.

The wonder was that anyone worked on the surveys at all. It was a lonely, remote existence the surveyors led in the field, cut off from news of family, friends, or the world at large. There was little long-term job security, even for experienced engineers. Crews were discharged at the end of the summer and re-engaged the following spring. When the work began to diminish towards the end of the decade, there was real hardship.

In the field, the privations were appalling. In the Lake Nepigon area, J. H. E. Secretan was reduced to eating rose haws washed down with swamp water. Near Jackfish River, seven men perished as the result of a forest fire so hot that the very soil was burned away. Near Long Lake,

William Kirkpatrick had to take his party off surveying to pick blueberries to save their lives. And in central British Columbia, Roderick McLennan's survey party lost almost all of its pack animals; eighty-six died from cold, hunger, or overwork. All these incidents took place in the winter of 1871-72.

An even worse winter expedition was the exploration launched in 1875 by E. W. Jarvis, who was charged with examining the Smoky River Pass in the Rockies. Fleming had already settled on the Yellow Head as the ideal pass for the railway, but this did not prevent him from carefully examining half a dozen others. Jarvis set off in January from Fort George with his assistant, C. F. Hanington, Alec Macdonald in charge of dog trains, six Indians, and twenty dogs.

Both Jarvis and Hanington left graphic accounts of the ordeal. The party travelled through unmapped country with only two blankets per man and a

Sandford Fleming, posing with his engineering staff, is the most bewhiskered member of a generally shaggy assembly. Directly across the table, facing him, is his deputy and later adversary, "that old devil," Marcus Smith.

single sheet for a tent. Much of the time they had no idea where they were. They camped out in temperatures that dropped to 53 below zero. They fell through thin ice and had to clamber out, soaked to the skin, their snowshoes still fastened to their feet. They stumbled down box canyons and found the way blocked by frozen waterfalls, two hundred feet high. One day they experienced a formidable change of temperature – from 42 below zero to 40 above – and this produced a strange exhaustion, as if they were suddenly plunged into the tropics. One morning, while mushing down a frozen river, they turned a corner and saw an abyss yawning before them: the entire party, dogs and men, were perched on the ice ledge of a frozen waterfall, two hundred and ten feet high; the projection itself was no more than two feet thick.

By March, the dogs were dying and the Indians were "in a mournful state of despair, declaring that they . . . would never see their homes again and weeping bitterly." Hanington himself felt a sense of despair: "I have been thinking of 'the dearest spot on earth to me' – of our Mother and Father and all my brothers and sisters and friends – of the happy days at home – of all the good deeds I have left undone and all the bad ones committed. If ever our bones will be discovered, when and by whom. If our friends will mourn long for us or do as is often done, forget us as soon as possible. In short, I have been looking death in the face. . . ."

Jarvis described "the curious sensation of numbness, which began to take hold of our limbs" as they pushed slowly forward on their snowshoes, giving the impression of men marking time in slow motion. Yet they made it. Hanington had lost 33 pounds; Jarvis was down to a bony 125. The food

---

Charles Horetzky, the photographer who accompanied Fleming and Grant on their journey "from ocean to ocean," photographed this survey camp on the elbow of the Saskatchewan River when the chief method of transportation was still by Red River cart or foot.

given them when they finally reached Edmonton produced spasms of dysentery and vomiting. Still they kept on, setting off once more across the blizzard-swept prairie for Fort Garry. All told, they spent 116 days on the trail, travelling 1,887 miles, 932 of those miles on snowshoes and 332 of them with all their goods on their backs, the dogs being dead.

Why did they do it? Why did any of them do it? Not for profit, certainly – there was little enough of that – nor for adventure: there was too much of that. The answer seems clear from their actions and their words: each man did it for glory, spurred on by the slender but ever-present hope that some day his name would be enshrined on a mountain peak or a river or an inlet, or – glory of glories – would go into the history books as the one who had bested all others and located the route for the great railway.

Moberly's folly

ONE MAN who thought he had the route and who spent the twilight of his life recalling, with increasing bitterness but not always with great accuracy, the attempt to "humbug" the route away from him, was Walter Moberly.

Moberly was working in Salt Lake City in 1871 when the news came of the pact with British Columbia. He went immediately to Ottawa where Lady Macdonald, an old school friend, introduced him to the Prime Minster. The weathered surveyor insisted, with superb confidence, that he could tell Macdonald exactly where to locate the line from the prairies to the seacoast. Not only that but "you can commence construction of the line six weeks after I get back to British Columbia."

"Of course," Moberly added, "I don't know how many millions you have, but it is going to cost you money to get through those canyons."

Macdonald was impressed. Moberly had once been assistant surveyor general for British Columbia. In this role he discovered the Eagle Pass in the Gold Range (later called the Monashees) by watching a flight of eagles winging their way through the mountains. Moberly knew that eagles generally follow a stream or make for an opening in the alpine wall. Eventually he followed the route of the birds and discovered the pass he was seeking through the Gold Range. According to his own romantic account, he finally left his companions after a sleepless night and made his way down into the valley of the Eagle River, where he hacked out a blaze on a tree and wrote the prescient announcement: "This is the Pass for the Overland Railway."

Moberly returned to British Columbia, with the Prime Minister's blessing, as district engineer in charge of the region between Shuswap Lake and the eastern foothills of the Rockies. He was in his fortieth year – a man of legendary endurance, egotistical, impulsive, stubborn, and independent of spirit. He could not work with anyone he disagreed with, and he disagreed with anyone who believed there was any other railway route to the Pacific than the one that had been developing in his mind for years. Moberly had been thinking about the railway longer than most of his colleagues, ever since his explorations in 1858. Now, thirteen years later, he set out to confirm his findings. He began his explorations on July 20, 1871, the very day the new province entered Confederation.

He took personal charge of his favourite area bounded by the Eagle Pass of the Gold Range and the Howse Pass in the Rockies, just north of the Kicking Horse. Between these two mountain chains lay an island of formidable peaks – the apparently impassable Selkirks. It was in the hairpin-shaped trench around this barrier that the Columbia flowed, first northwest, then southeast again, until it passed within a few miles of its source. It was Moberly's theory that the railway would cut through the notch of the Howse Pass, circumvent the Selkirks by following the Columbia Valley, and

Walter Moberly and the heads of his British Columbia
survey parties, photographed in Victoria. Moberly, in
grey beard and salt-and-pepper suit, is seated centre,
facing left. Supple as a willow and tough as steel, he had a
passion for dancing but a legendary staying power that
allowed him to carouse all night and plunge next day into
the wilds without apparent loss of energy. He survived
several brushes with death and when this photo was made
had not yet lived out half of his long life.

then thread through the Gold Range by way of the Eagle Pass, which led to Kamloops and the canyons of the Fraser.

Moberly spent the next eight months in the mountains and trenches of British Columbia. He travelled down the olive-green Columbia with a crazy flotilla of leaky boats and bark canoes, patched with old rags and bacon grease. He trudged up and down the sides of mountains, clinging to the reins of pack horses, accompanied always by a faithful company of Indians.

When winter began, he set off on snowshoes for New Westminster, a distance of more than four hundred miles, as casually as if he were heading off on a pleasant Sunday hike. He went straight over the top of the glacier-capped Selkirks, seeking a practical pass, and was almost buried by an avalanche en route. New Year's Day, 1872, found him all alone in a trapper's abandoned hut, scrawling in his diary that it was "the most wretched New Year's Day I ever spent." He could not find a pass through those pointed peaks.

When Moberly emerged from the mountains, he had so convinced himself that his route was the only conceivable one that he determined to take it upon himself to push forward immediately locating the actual line through the Howse Pass. He would get permission later. He set about hiring extra men for the 1872 season, engaging trains of pack animals and buying thousands of dollars worth of supplies, great quantities of which he had cached at Eagle Pass since he reckoned his men would spend two seasons locating the line and would stay out all winter.

Four hours before Moberly and his party were scheduled to leave Victoria for the hinterland, he received a staggering blow. Fleming wired him that the Yellow Head Pass had been officially adopted for the route of the Canadian Pacific railway and that the Howse Pass survey was to be abandoned. He was to move his men north and take charge of a survey through the Yellow Head. All of Moberly's dreams dissolved at that moment. "His" route was not to be *the* route, after all.

WALTER MOBERLY'S COUNTRY

Bitterly disappointed, the surveyor rushed to Portland, Oregon, where he tried to buy his way out of his costly contracts. But most of the supplies had already been dispatched to remote mountain areas where they could never be used. Seven thousand dollars' worth were abandoned forever at the Eagle Pass.

He set off, first through Oregon by stagecoach (which broke down) and by steamboat (which sank), and then up through Washington Territory on horseback into British Columbia where he managed to intercept the packers he had hired. Then, with a heavy heart, he began moving his men north towards the despised Yellow Head Pass where Fleming had arranged to meet him on his trip with Grant from ocean to ocean. "Move" is scarcely an adequate verb to describe Moberly's transit: the pack trail had to be carved, foot by foot, out of the tangle of fallen cedars that barred the way up through the cavernous valleys of the Columbia, Thompson, and Albreda rivers.

Moberly himself reached the Yellow Head in early September. In Grant's *Ocean to Ocean* there is no hint of the disagreeable encounter that took place between the engineer-in-chief and his errant British Columbia deputy, but it must have been a painful one. Fleming was taken aback at the slow progress made on the surveys and by Moberly's reckless spending. Tons of supplies left at Eagle Pass! And four hundred pack horses! The chief engineer could not understand the need for so many. At that point his impulse was to fire Moberly. He could not afford to: somebody had to take charge at the Yellow Head and push the surveys forward.

Moberly's attitude to Fleming's verbal spanking was one of disgust, not with himself but with Fleming for his "unpatriotic action" in abandoning his own pet line. To Moberly, the decision to use the other pass was little short of treason. By his own account, he was on the point of leaving the service.

As Moberly took his leave of the Fleming party, he was himself plagued by worry over the slow progress of the surveys under his command. Ill fortune seemed to dog his footsteps; the survey parties were taking an unconscionable time to arrive from the Howse Pass. Actually, with Moberly so long gone they had simply settled down to wait out the winter. Moberly got them moving again: it would be touch and go if they could get through the high Athabasca Pass before the blizzards blocked it and cut them off from their work at the Yellow Head.

Another party had lost six precious weeks because its supplies had unaccountably failed to reach it from Victoria. It later turned out that the purveyor and accountant there – another political appointee – was incompetent. Moberly, as the man in charge, took most of the blame.

By this time Fleming had lost all confidence in Moberly. He sent him a message by Indian runner ordering him back to Kamloops. Fleming was convinced that this raw tactic would force Moberly to quit the service, but his stubborn deputy decided simply to ignore the order and press on with the survey of the Yellow Head come hell or blizzard.

Fleming tried again after the new year. In another message he informed Moberly that Marcus Smith had superseded him and would be in charge of all exploratory surveys in British Columbia. Moberly finally quit the service and left for Ottawa where he was "very coldly received by the Engineer-in-Chief." He lingered in the capital waiting for Fleming to sign his expense accounts. Fleming rejected the first audit and passed the accounts on to a second auditor who went over them again. They were passed at last, but not until the frustrated Moberly had been forced to borrow money to pay for his room and board.

Disheartened, Moberly moved to Winnipeg where, presently, he busied himself at the comparatively prosaic job of building the city's first sewers. For all of his life he complained bitterly about the treatment he had received at the hands of Fleming, but he did enjoy one moment of triumph: twenty years after he discovered the Eagle Pass, the last spike of the CPR was driven almost on the very spot where Moberly, in a moment of clairvoyance, had chalked on a blazed tree his prophecy that the overland railway would have to come that way.

That "old devil," Marcus Smith

MARCUS SMITH, who took over all surveys in British Columbia in the spring of 1873, was without doubt the most controversial figure that the Canadian Pacific Survey produced. No two men in the service seemed to agree about him. Moberly liked him. C. F. Hanington wrote that he was a wonderful man. Harry Armstrong, who worked first in Smith's drafting room in Ottawa and became his friend, described him as "a very crabbed and impatient man, though withal very kind of heart." But some of the men who worked under Smith used harsher terms. Robert Rylatt, a member of Moberly's Howse Pass survey party, wrote in a fury that Smith was "a hard, unjust and arbitrary wretch." In the summer of 1872, a young rodman named Edgar Fawcett, toiling in the Homathco country, called him "an old devil" and wrote in his diary: "I did not come here to be blackguarded by Mr. Smith for $45 a month." And when Smith announced he was leaving the party and moving on, another member wrote in *his* diary that it was "the best news we [had] heard since we left Victoria."

Smith was a pretty good hater himself. He referred to Henry J. Cambie as a sneak and a toady. Fleming was subjected to an entire lexicon of epithets. Fleming's successor, Collingwood Schreiber, was "mean and inferior," Major A. B. Rogers was "a thorough fraud," and Charles Horetzky was "a crazy, conceited fellow." Smith was suspicious of all politicians: Alexander Mackenzie was dishonest, in his view; the Governor General, of all people, he suspected of railway land speculation; and John A. Macdonald would "sacrifice anything or anybody to smooth down difficulties."

Smith reserved his most withering contempt for those who dared to oppose the route to the Pacific in which he had come, by 1877, to believe. This route led from the Pine Pass southwest through Fort George, across the Chilcoten Plains to the headwaters of the Homathco, and thence down that turbulent river to its mouth at Bute Inlet. Smith quarrelled bitterly with anyone who favoured any other line for the railway and employed every device he knew to force the government to accept the Pine Pass–Bute Inlet route. In 1872, when he first entered the long fiord of Bute Inlet and then made his way up the Homathco – "a scene of gloomy grandeur, probably not met with in any other part of the world" – it was love at first sight, as it had been with Moberly and all the other enthusiasts, including the chief engineer himself, who championed a line of route.

In his diaries and official reports, he waxed positively lyrical about the region. His description of the "charming" mile-wide valleys of the Chilcoten and Chilanko rivers had the ring of a hopelessly infatuated suitor composing a paean to his intended. He wrote of the bottom lands, ripe and mellow with bunch growth, with the clear streams meandering through them in graceful curves, of the pale, greyish-green of the grasses "in agreeable harmony with the dark foliage of the spruce," and of the "picturesque irregularity of the evergreens," the whole "forming a scene of pristine beauty rarely to be met with." Compared with the routine prose of some of his colleagues, Smith's seemed almost sensual on occasion.

He had just turned fifty-six – a stubby man with a barrel chest, tough as shaganappi and bristly as a wart-hog – when he first clambered up the dripping cliffs of the Homathco. He was a Northumberland man who had been a land surveyor all his life, and like so many surveyors, he was a hard drinker. On the prairie surveys, where prohibition reigned, his keg of "lime juice" contained straight whiskey. He was not an easy man to work under for he did not suffer incompetence, fatigue, or any kind of human frailty. Young Edgar Fawcett, the rodman on the Bute-Homathco survey, was toiling

Marcus Smith had worked for Sandford Fleming on the Intercolonial. Totally self-confident and more than a little proud, he employed every device he knew to force the adoption of his favourite railway route.

The entrance to the Homathco canyon—a scene of gloomy grandeur, probably not met with in any other part of the world," in Marcus Smith's description. The photograph was made during C. H. Gamsby's survey in 1875. Note the wooden framework built around the walls of the canyon, which drop sheer to the water.

up a steep, rock-strewn hill in June, 1872, when a tumbling boulder struck him a blow that knocked him insensible. Smith took personal affront at the mishap: "That boy who could not keep out of the way of stones would have to be sent home."

Anything that interfered with the progress of the survey distressed him, as several entries in the diary of George Hargreaves, the leveller in the Bute survey party, reveal:

June 26, 1872: "Old Smith came to camp about 7.30 and boiled over, accusing us of putting obstacles in his way and saying he would carry through with the survey if he had to send 5,000 miles for men."

July 3: "Had a row with Old Smith for not bringing the levels through before stopping work. . . . Says he, 'what did you mean by saying you was through, you must be an idiot.'"

July 5: "It appears Smith had a big row with two or three of the men and also with Bristow, the Transit. Called him a Gd. dmd. fool and Idiot. . . ."

But if Smith was hard on others, he was equally hard on himself. When he was sixty years of age, he travelled for one thousand miles through the Lake Superior country by canoe, all in a single summer, making two hundred portages that varied from a few yard to four miles.

He must have seemed a superman, albeit a satanic one, to the young chainmen and rodmen who, at the end of each day, found themselves so exhausted they were ready to throw in the sponge.

"Yesterday I really thought I should have to give in," one of them wrote, "I felt so the loss of having eaten nothing all day but a bit of bread and fat pork in 12 hours. If this is surveying, I have had my bellyfull of it."

Yet here was the demonic Smith, a man twice their age, driving late into the evening, scaling the rocks and forging through the glacial waters with enough breath left in his barrel chest to shower curses and imprecations upon the stragglers.

The truth was that he was as exhausted as any. "Felt terribly used up," he wrote in his journal on July 9, 1872. But he would not give up that night until he had worked out the calculations of his travels across the mountains. Four days later, when he boarded the boat to Victoria, he was near collapse: "Fatigue set in after a month of excessive labour and anxiety and I lay and dozed the hours away, totally unfit for anything."

Sick or not, Smith was back a month later. He was tortured by cramps in his hip and left leg and by August 11 was so ill he could not rise until noon. But rise he did, saddled a horse, and headed off across a swamp. The horse became mired. Smith tried to spur it on. The saddle slipped off and Smith tumbled into the morass. He was too weak to resaddle the horse but he managed to crawl all the way to the head of a lake where he found two Indians who cared for him.

He was still at it, in the same country, in the summer of 1875. He was then in his sixtieth year and he confided to one of his surveyors that he had "less heart for this journey" than any he had undertaken. "I am far from well and very weak and the mountain torrents are very high."

When he wrote that letter, Smith was planning to force his way again from the Chilcoten Plains through the Cascade Mountains to Bute Inlet. He set off on foot with six Indians, struggling for two and a half days along the perpendicular cliffs of the canyons. Sometimes it took several hours to move a few yards, since they had to climb as high as fifteen hundred feet and descend again to circumnavigate the spurs of rock. At one point, unable to bridge a torrent, they were forced to detour by way of a glacier fifteen miles long, whose sharp ridges they crossed on hands and knees.

It was not the kind of summer excursion a doctor would prescribe for an ailing man of fifty-nine, especially as the bridges had been swept away by the mountain floods. It took Smith and his men seven hours to construct a fly bridge over the Grand Canyon of the Homathco; it "looked a fishing rod

Facsimile of a page
from George Hargreaves's
diary of 1872. Hargreaves's
boss, W. O. Tiedeman,
a Smith disciple, was
clearly prepared
to leave a lost member of
the party to die in
the wilderness rather than
delay the survey.
Reason prevailed, but the
rescued man was
given extra work for
losing two days.

The grand canyon of the
Homathco (right), where,
in Marcus Smith's words,
"the awful grandeur of
the mountains, the roar
of the waters, and the
constant sense of danger
kept the nerves strong
and the mind active."
Smith was one of the
few surveyors who waxed
lyrical about the
scenery around him. Many
of his descriptions
are positively sensuous –
a fact that goes a long
way towards explaining
his love affair with
the wild land he chose
for the railway route.

157

and line hanging over the torrent." Smith crept gingerly over this precarious filament, dropped heavily to the rocks below, and then spent six hours scrambling over tangled creepers, huge deadfalls, and masses of detached rocks before reaching camp.

Smith's love-hate relationship with this strangely compelling land of grim canyons and smiling meadows had, to borrow his own phrase, used him up. Would all this travail be in vain? Survey parties were crawling over the rumpled face of British Columbia and probing the ragged fiords of the coastline, seeking a feasible method of reaching the Pacific. Sandford Fleming was contemplating no less than eleven different routes leading down from the mountain spine to salt water. Only two led through Smith's country. What if another route should be chosen? What if all those ghastly days in the numbing bogs and among the brooding crags should end in defeat? Marcus Smith was not a man to contemplate defeat; and he had not yet begun to fight.

THE PREMIER'S MODEL;

OR, "IMPLEMENTS TO THOSE WHO CAN USE THEM."

CANADA "WELL AND BRAVELY DONE, MACKENZIE; NOW STAND BY THAT POLICY, AND I'M WITH YOU ALWAYS!"

The prevailing attitude to Mackenzie and his new regime was distilled in this Bengough cartoon after the election. As a stonemason, the new prime minister had once created fortifications, canals, and court houses.

The noble man

"I WILL LEAVE the Pacific Railway as a heritage to my adopted country," Alexander Mackenzie is said to have declared in his dry, Gaelic accent, when Donald A. Smith, the Member for Selkirk, tried to argue the merits of using a private company to build the line. Smith, nonetheless, remained in Mackenzie's camp. "He is a noble man," Smith said of him, and the voters, who returned him with a landslide early in 1874, seemed to agree.

Though not immune to the pressures of nepotism and patronage, Mackenzie appeared to be a man of probity. The public had reduced Macdonald's following in the House to a corporal's guard, as he ruefully remarked, and placed his antithesis on the pedestal. With his metallic voice, his rigid attitudes, his Baptist teetotalism, and his blunt manner, Mackenzie was the exact opposite of the rounded, soft-spoken, tolerant, and indulgent politician whom he replaced.

As a Liberal, he stood for a retrenchment of government spending. He could not stomach the grandiose schemes of the Conservatives which all too often seemed to him to be designed as much for profit and patronage as for empire building. To Mackenzie and his followers, Macdonald's Pacific railway scheme was precipitate, rash, and spendthrift. The Tories, with their big business connections, were temperamentally attuned to taking chances; but Mackenzie's political base was in the sober farming districts and small towns of Ontario.

During Mackenzie's term of office, only a few miles of the CPR were built; but it is probable that Macdonald, in those lean years, could not have done much better. Mackenzie was unlucky. For the whole of his term the country was in the grip of a serious continental depression.

Like so much else, the depression was imported from the United States—touched off by the spectacular failure of Jay Cooke's Northern Pacific. It

67

was an accident of history that it neatly bracketed the Mackenzie regime; the new prime minister was shackled financially. Yet it is doubtful whether given prosperity he would have accomplished any more than he did. He did not see his country as a great transcontinental nation, settled for all of its length from sea to sea. Canada, to Mackenzie, lay east of the Shield; far off were two small islands in the Canadian archipelago: the Red River settlement and British Columbia. These were necessary nuisances. In addition, Mackenzie could not refrain from the kind of wild remark that filled British Columbians with dismay and goaded them into retaliation. As late as 1877 he was still using the word "insane" to describe the pact with the Pacific province.

Clearly his predecessor had saddled Mackenzie with an impossible burden. The policy was scarcely insane, but some of the terms were certainly foolhardy. In the prosperous glow of 1871, Macdonald had blithely promised the British Columbians that he would commence construction of the line in two years. *Two years!* In the spring of 1873, with the surveyors bogged down in the bewildering mountain labyrinth, Macdonald realized he must pay lip service to his incautious pledge. A few days before the deadline he recklessly picked Esquimalt, the naval harbour on the outskirts of Victoria, as the terminus of the Canadian Pacific Railway.

In practical terms, this meant that the railway would run to Bute Inlet on the mainland; it would then thread its way down for fifty miles from the head of the inlet through the sheer, granite cliffs of the coastline, leap twenty-nine miles across the Strait of Georgia to Nanaimo on Vancouver Island, and follow the east coast of the island to Esquimalt. It would require eight miles of tunnelling and untold rock cuts to negotiate those sea-torn precipices. Then the track would have to hop from island to island over six deep channels through which the rip tide sometimes tore at nine knots; that would require eight thousand feet of bridging and in two instances the spans would

THE NEW MASTER; OR,
A LESSON IN ENGINEERING.

Mackenzie was Minister of Public Works as well as Prime Minister. Henri Julien's cartoon shows him laying down the Liberal's new policy to Sandford Fleming (in beard and parka) and colleagues.

have to be thirteen hundred feet in length. That was greater than any arch then existing anywhere in the world.

This, then, was the *fait accompli* Mackenzie faced: a deadline determined, a terminus established, and a province militant. In this fertile ground were sown the seeds for the uneasy relationship between the Pacific province and central Canada that was to be maintained into the nation's second century.

During the election Mackenzie had been at pains to water down Macdonald's impossible dream. He talked about a land and water route across the nation, with the rail line to be built piecemeal. There was no real hope of attracting private capital during the depression. If the railway was to be commenced, it would have to be built in sections as a public work. The first, a line from Lake Superior to the Red River, and the second, a branch line in Manitoba from Selkirk to Pembina on the United States border, would, it was hoped, give the Red River its long desired connection with the outside world. After that, as funds were available, other sections would be built – but scarcely within ten years. That was not good enough for British Columbia whose premier, George Walkem, jumped with both boots into the heated Battle of the Routes, which was to last the rest of the decade.

In spite of Macdonald's choice of Esquimalt, the engineers had not made up their minds about the location of the terminus. At the close of 1873, Sandford Fleming was considering seven alternative routes to the coast. No fewer than six passes in the Rockies were being explored. By mid-decade, Fleming was able to report on twelve different routes through British Columbia to seven different harbours on the coastline.

But as far as British Columbia was concerned, there were only two routes that really mattered. One was the fur traders' trail through the Yellow Head Pass and down the Fraser Canyon to Burrard Inlet; if chosen it would guarantee the prosperity of Kamloops, Yale, and New Westminster. The mainland of British Columbia fought for this route.

PACIFIC PASTIMES; OR, THE "HARD ROAD TO TRAVEL."

Bengough's cartoon in Grip *of May 12, 1874, was a comment on Mackenzie's "sensible" railway policy of building the CPR by gradual steps. The new prime minister planned a route that would use both land and water—a mixture that Macdonald quipped, "generally produces mud."*

The other would lead probably from the Yellow Head through the Cariboo country and the Chilcoten Plains to Bute Inlet, then leap the straits to Nanaimo and thence to Victoria; it would guarantee the prosperity of the dying gold region and of Vancouver Island.

The Premier, a Cariboo man who knew a political issue when he saw one, opted instinctively with the Island interests for the Bute Inlet route and decided to go over the Prime Minister's head to the Crown itself. The Crown, in the person of Lord Carnarvon, the Colonial Secretary, offered to arbitrate the dispute between the province and the federal government.

Mackenzie's immediate thought was to reject the offer; here was the Colonial Office interfering in the domestic affairs of an independent dominion! But the Governor General persuaded him to accept arbitration. Under the resultant "Carnarvon Terms" of 1874, it was agreed that a railway would be built on Vancouver Island, the surveys would be pushed, and, when the transcontinental line was finally launched, the government would spend at least two millions a year on its construction. In return, the province accepted an extension of the deadline to December 31, 1890.

Now the stoic ex-stonemason began to suffer under the millstone of office. He was plagued with intestinal inflammation and insomnia, both the products of political tensions. On one side he felt the pull of the upstart province on the Pacific, holding him to another man's bargain. On the other, he felt the tug of the implacable Edward Blake, the rallying point for the anti-British Columbia sentiment and a popular alternative as Prime Minister.

The rebellious Blake had left the Cabinet and in October, 1874, delivered himself of the decade's most discussed public speech at Aurora, Ontario. In a section devoted to railway policy he dismissed British Columbia as "a sea of mountains," and attacked the railway scheme as foolish and costly. If the British Columbians wanted to separate from Canada, Blake said in effect, then let them. To get

Premier George Walkem of British Columbia. Mackenzie tried to placate him over the railway issue but Walkem rudely rebuffed his emissary and went straight to the British crown. The Premier was a shrewd politician and an accomplished crayon artist with a propensity for drawing lions – a hobby that may have had Freudian overtones.

THE NEW DEPARTURE.

Blake leaving the Cabinet, as portrayed by Bengough. The painting on the wall is entitled "Resignation."

Blake back into the Cabinet, Mackenzie was forced to add a hedge to the Carnarvon Terms; they would be carried out *only* if that could be done without increasing taxes. Blake returned in May, 1875, as Minister of Justice. Together, he and the Prime Minister worked out a compromise offer to British Columbia: in lieu of the Island railway, the government was prepared to pay the province $750,000.

Opinion in the rest of Canada was solidly behind Blake. In April, 1876, when Parliament passed the taxation declaration that he insisted upon, the vote was 149 to 10. Only the Island members opposed it. The Government of Canada had resolved to go its own way in the matter of the railway and to stop trying to conciliate British Columbia. If that meant separation, so be it.

CANADIAN
Illustrated News

Vol. XIV.—No. 9.   MONTREAL, SATURDAY, SEPTEMBER 9, 1876.   { SINGLE COPIES, TEN CENTS. / $4 PER YEAR IN ADVANCE.

BRITISH COLUMBIA IN A PET.

Uncle Aleck:—Don't frown so, my dear, you'll have your railway by and bye.
Miss B. Columbia:—I want it *now*. You promised I should have it, and if I don't, I'll complain to Ma.

This cover cartoon, which appeared immediately after Lord Dufferin's western trip, accurately captured the eastern feeling towards B.C.

Lord Dufferin, photographed in costume at a vice-regal ball in 1876. His Excellency was a bit of a ham.

The "horrid B.C. business"

FREDERICK TEMPLE BLACKWOOD, Viscount Clande-boye and Earl of Dufferin, was chafing, meanwhile, with inactivity. He longed to get away on a voyage of conciliation for which he felt his undoubted gifts as a diplomat superbly qualified him. Specifically, he wanted to go out to British Columbia as both a spokesman of the federal government and an agent for the Colonial Secretary.

Mackenzie, Blake, and Richard Cartwright, the Minister of Finance, greeted His Excellency's proposal with something akin to terror – at least that was the word the Governor General used. The idea of the Queen's representative, especially *this* Queen's representative, plunging into the most delicate problem in Canadian dominion politics did not make them rest easily. Dufferin loved making speeches; he made them on every possible occasion. He would undoubtedly make speeches all over British Columbia. His speeches were full of Irish blarney and could be calculated to butter up his listeners to the point of embarrassment. Would he unwittingly inflate the expectations of the people to the point where a revival of understanding would be more impossible then ever? The three called on the Governor General on May 26 and "there ensued a long and very disagreeable discussion." Finally it was agreed that Dufferin would make a state visit to British Columbia but must maintain the traditional vice-regal attitude of strict neutrality.

The Governor General and his countess went by rail to San Francisco and there embarked by naval vessel for the "nest of hornets," as Dufferin called Victoria. They debarked from HMS *Amethyst* at Esquimalt harbour on August 16, 1876, and drove through the streets of the capital, cheered on by the entire populace – canoe-loads of Indians, Chinese in pigtails, Cariboo miners, scores of little girls in private-school uniforms, old Hudson's Bay hands and, most of all, hundreds of loyal English men and women – retired army officers, former civil servants, newly arrived immigrants.

As a newcomer, Dufferin was able to see Canada whole and not as a loose collection of self-centred and often antagonistic communities. The petty provincialism of the Canadians bothered him, and he tried throughout his term to encourage in them a feeling of common pride. But in Victoria he was dismayed to find no flicker of national feeling. The Island town was in every sense a little bit of Old England. Most of the residents had been born in Britain and "like all middle class Englishmen, have a vulgar contempt for everything that is not English." Not only did the capital consider itself separate and distinct from Canada, but it also considered itself apart from the rest of the province.

Dufferin's preconceived notions about the greed of British Columbians for the money the railway would bring in were largely confirmed in the remarkable week that followed. Day after day, beginning at nine in the morning and continuing without interruption until seven at night, he found himself receiving delegation after delegation to discuss the most controversial question in the country. "Lord Dufferin," his private secretary wrote to Mackenzie, "bids me add that he finds great difficulty in keeping his temper with these foolish people." At that point, the Governor General had spent seven days, ten full hours a day, "listening to the same old story, abuse of Mackenzie, of Canada, of Sir John Macdonald and the absolute necessity of bringing the Pacific Railway via Bute Inlet to Esquimalt."

Triumphal arches bedecked the route of the Governor General's procession through the streets of Victoria. The parade took two hours and a half to pass through the centre of town to Government House where one hundred young ladies were waiting to strew the viceregal path with flowers. In the procession were a personal escort of green-clad archers, an army of flag-carrying boys, and three hundred Indians recruited from twelve coastal tribes.

Lord Dufferin refused to pass through the arch at left, with its inflammatory slogan. He suggested that "S" in "Separation" be replaced by "R," but this was rejected. An attempt was then made to force his carriage forward, but it wheeled about in time, at which point, as Lady Dufferin noted in her journal, one man "jumped about as if he were mad, and when he met us above the arch he jumped again and shrieked, 'Three groans for Mackenzie.'" As the Governor General was to learn, Victoria's desire to be the CPR terminus was a desperate one.

All along the viceregal route there were signs like this one urging an immediate start on the Pacific Railway. Other signs read: "Our Railway Iron Rusts," "Railroad, the Bond of Union," "The Iron Horse, the Civilizer of the World," "United without Union," and "Confederated without Confederation." The bitterness against the East was all-embracing. Lord Dufferin wrote that "the perfidy with which they consider themselves to have been treated has filled the entire community with a sentiment of genuine contempt for everything and everybody East of the Rocky Mountains."

This was one of three arches erected by the Chinese community in Victoria for the Dufferin visit. Another read, somewhat wistfully, "British Laws Are Just." Not far away, a rival arch cried: "Chinese Must Go." Under that slogan the Governor General also refused to pass.

But then, Victoria was literally fighting for its life. The depression had dealt the community a blow more staggering than that which the rest of the country had suffered. The cost of living remained astronomical because of the town's isolation. As Dufferin reported to Carnarvon, "In Victoria the one idea of every human being is to get the railway to Esquimalt. It is upon this chance that the little town must depend for its future . . . most of its inhabitants have wildly speculated in town lots. . . . You can therefore imagine the phrensied [*sic*] eagerness with which Victoria grasps at every chance of making itself the terminus of the great transcontinental railway."

When he reached the mainland, it was the same story. "The location of the Canadian Pacific Railway, and its terminus along such a line, and on such a spot as may enhance the value of his own individual town lot, or in some other way may put money into his pocket, by passing as near as possible to where he lives, is the common preoccupation of every Columbian citizen."

Yet in spite of the constant pressure upon him, he returned to Ottawa with considerable sympathy for the British Columbians. He suspected that Mackenzie, pushed by Blake and Cartwright, was trying to wriggle out of his commitments. As a result, the "horrid B.C. business," as Lord Dufferin branded it, touched off an extraordinary scene at Rideau Hall. Here, for the first and only time in Canadian history, a governor general and his two chief advisers came perilously close to fisticuffs.

Dufferin was convinced that Lord Carnarvon should re-enter the picture to arbitrate the question of the Island railway, which Victoria continued to claim was part of the main line of the CPR and which Mackenzie insisted was a local project only. The Governor General even suggested raising the $750,000 offered in lieu of the line to an even million: any reasonable sacrifice was worth while, if Confederation was at stake.

On Saturday, November 18, he met with Blake and Mackenzie at Rideau Hall. Both men were

THE TRANSPARENT FACTS.

IN THE MATTER OF THE "CARNARVON TERMS."

stubbornly opposed to him and the scene that followed was stormy and disagreeable. They "nearly came to blows . . . Mackenzie's aspect was simply pitiable and Blake was on the point of crying as he very readily does when he is excited."

The day after this extraordinary encounter, everybody cooled off and a face-saving formula was evolved, hoisting the matter for eighteen months until the surveys could be completed and a route fixed; failing that, Mackenzie cautiously agreed to some sort of London meeting under Carnarvon's auspices.

With that the importunate Dufferin had to be content. He had pushed his ministers as hard as any governor general could or ever would; he undoubtedly felt he had been successful; but the hard fact was that he had battered his noble head against an unyielding wall of granite.

The Battle of the Routes

By 1877, the Battle of the Routes had reached the stage of a pamphlet war, and still Sandford Fleming had not chosen a pass through the Rockies or a terminus along the coastline. Some of this apparent dallying had to do with the nature of the country itself, but much of it was clearly political procrastination.

Fleming's own opinions in his massive report of 1877 were clouded in ambiguity. By 1875 there was a general understanding that Bute Inlet would probably be the terminus. Then, in November of 1876, it occurred to Fleming, rather tardily, that the Admiralty might be asked its views on the various harbours along the coast. The opinion of the seamen was overwhelmingly in favour of Burrard Inlet.

In spite of that, Fleming still could not make up his mind. Obviously he felt the final decision was up to the politicians; and in case they could not decide, he had a suggestion: there was another choice

at the mouth of the Skeena River, a harbour five hundred miles closer to the Orient than the other two.

Fleming at that time was an absentee engineer-in-chief. He had been a robust man who thought nothing of warding off a bear with an umbrella or unrolling his blankets in two feet of snow, as he had done on his twenty-fourth birthday, but by 1876, in his fiftieth year, he was exhausted. Between 1871 and 1876 he had held two man-killing positions as chief engineer of both the Intercolonial and the Canadian Pacific. When the Intercolonial was completed in 1876, Fleming's doctors ordered a complete rest. He was granted a twelve-month leave of absence and went off to England but was twice recalled by the government, once to write the monumental 1877 report and again to deal with his deputy, the bristly Marcus Smith. The leave stretched out over a two-year period.

For nineteen months, between the spring of 1876 and the beginning of 1878, Fleming was absent and Marcus Smith was in his place. Smith had the job but he did not, apparently, have the authority. During his visits back to Canada, Fleming would countermand his deputy's instructions or disagree with his views. Much of this was due to Smith's furious championing of a single railway route through British Columbia from the Pine Pass to Bute Inlet.

Smith would not give up on Bute Inlet. The obvious impracticality of a causeway across the strait had not cooled his ardour for "his" route. A steamboat, he insisted, could move an entire train across to the island. He had also become disenchanted with the Yellow Head Pass, which his absent chief favoured. By 1877 there had taken shape in the back of that mysterious mind a preference for the Pine Pass which lay farther to the north. In April of 1877 he asked Mackenzie for permission to probe the pass with three survey parties, adding that he himself would like to go along. Mackenzie, who was trying to slash expenses in the department, turned him down, whereupon the irrepressible Smith determined to go ahead secretly without authority.

He wrote to Henry Cambie, who had replaced him as chief of surveys in British Columbia, to send Joseph Hunter to the Pine River country with two or three men and some packers. The trip was to be completely confidential. Snoopers were to be told only that Cambie was extending his explorations of the Skeena country. Meanwhile Smith went out to British Columbia himself on a tour that took on some of the aspects of a political campaign.

Smith accelerated his behind-the-scenes manoeuvres. He instructed Hunter to leak some information unofficially to the press about his Pine Pass explorations. Smith actually composed a press release about it, praising the Pine Pass as shorter and lower than the Yellow Head.

Meanwhile, Henry Cambie in British Columbia had been caught up in the intrigue. Mackenzie, unable to budge Smith, had gone around him and wired direct to Cambie to commence the survey of the Fraser, which the Governor General had so urgently recommended on his return. When Smith returned from the West, he found himself snubbed. Mackenzie asked Cambie to report to him directly.

The strange spectacle of a cabinet minister (and Prime Minister to boot) trying to circumvent his own department head in order to obtain information from a subordinate continued all that month. Mackenzie kept on ignoring Smith and meeting secretly with Cambie. For the wretched Cambie, the squeeze was getting tighter. He kept putting off his written report to Mackenzie. Mackenzie kept demanding it. He did not, however, ask for any special report from Marcus Smith. "He shall get one nevertheless whether he likes it or no," Smith remarked grimly. He firmly believed that Cambie was being used as a tool by Fraser Valley speculators to push the Burrard route.

Quite clearly, the Prime Minister had settled on Burrard Inlet as the railway terminus. There were many reasons for his decision: the Admiralty report; the skilful advocacy of the mainland Members of Parliament; Lord Dufferin's own opinion; the new surveys by Cambie; and, finally, Smith's

bull-headed intransigence. The acting chief engineer had got his minister's back up. By March, 1878, Mackenzie had ceased to consult him or even speak to him.

On March 29, Smith sent in his own official report. Predictably, he advocated the Pine Pass–Bute Inlet route, but suggested another year's delay to settle the final location of the line. This presented Mackenzie with a new dilemma. He could scarcely decide on Burrard Inlet in the face of the direct and public opposition of his acting chief engineer. There was only one thing to do: without telling Marcus Smith, he sent for Fleming who for the second time found his sick-leave in England interrupted.

Fleming returned to find his department in an uproar. Mackenzie had determined that Smith must go and told Fleming that he must no longer consider Smith an officer of the department. This resulted in a curious situation: there was the peppery Smith, still fuming away in his office, still, apparently, on the staff, but stripped of his powers. "He did not receive his dismissal but he was as good as dismissed," Fleming later recounted. No doubt Fleming expected Smith to resign, but Smith hung on stubbornly.

Fleming, meanwhile, set about writing his own report. In this he was finally forced to a conclusion: if engineering decisions alone were to govern the selection of a route, and if that selection could not be postponed further, then the Bute Inlet route should be rejected and the Burrard Inlet route selected. He left the question of a pass open. He thought there should be more extensive surveys in the region of the Peace River Pass in case it proved to be less expensive than the Yellow Head.

On July 12, 1878, the government settled officially on the Fraser River–Burrard Inlet route and prepared to call for tenders for the construction of the railway through the dismal canyon of the Fraser. That seemed to be the end of the horrid B.C. business. It was not. Party lines had already been drawn around the opposing routes. The Pine Pass–Bute Inlet route, thanks in part to Marcus Smith's

The jubilant spirit of the people of Winnipeg over the arrival of an actual locomotive was reflected in the decision of the tiny Manitoba Free Press to rush an extra into print – even though the engine would be used only to pull a work train on a half-finished railroad.

FREE PRESS EXTRA.

MONDAY, OCT. 8, 1877.

The First Locomotive in the North-West!

To Arrive this Afternoon!

Celebration of the Event!

Intelligence has just been received that the first locomotive and tender, with a caboose and six flat cars, which are being brought down for the Pembina Branch by Mr. Joseph Whitehead, will arrive here this afternoon at about four o'clock by the steamer Selkirk.

Notwithstanding the short notice, we understand that a fitting reception will be tendered; and the mayor and corporation, it is understood, will take the necessary steps for the proper recognition of this important event in the history of the North-West.

The steamer will probably stop at No. 6 warehouse, foot of Post-office street.

Let there be a grand rally of citizens on the occasion!

importuning, had become a Tory route. As for Smith, he was still around. Two years later, in a new job and under a new administration, he would still be, in his own eyes at least, "the *Bête Noir* [*sic*] of the Govt."

The first locomotive

ON THE MORNING of October 9, 1877, the citizens of Winnipeg were awakened by the unaccustomed shriek of a locomotive whistle. For the generation to follow, this would become the authentic sound of the prairie, more familiar than the laugh of the loon or the whine of the wind in the wolf willow. But on this crisp October day it was something totally new. There were many there that day who had never heard a train whistle and for some of these, the Indians and Métis, it was as symbolic in its sadness as it was for the white community in its promise.

She was a Baldwin engine – the *Countess of Dufferin* – and she came complete with six flat-cars and a van; but she could not arrive under her own steam. She had to be floated down the river because the railway to the boundary was not finished. Even if it had been, there was nothing yet on the other side of the American border with which it could connect.

But a locomotive was still a marvel, and the entire town streamed to the dock to inspect it and to cheer the massive contractor, Joseph Whitehead, who was in charge and who as a boy had worked on horse-drawn railways in England. Whitehead, who was laying track on the line between St. Boniface and Selkirk, had imported her as a work engine. For the white community, at least, she was a promise of things to come, an end to the maddening isolation of half a century and a tangible response to the pleas for a railway which had been issuing from Red River since the beginning of the decade.

This isolation was real and terrible and could

The Countess of Dufferin *arrives at St. Boniface.*
After this photograph was taken, track was laid to the water's
edge and the locomotive debarked under its own steam.

The Selkirk, *which brought the first locomotive into the Canadian North West, was Jim Hill's steamboat.*
A student of transportation and forwarding techniques, he built her secretly in the winter of 1870-71.

be translated into concrete terms. At the beginning of the decade a keg of nails cost at least ten times as much at Red River as in Ontario; small wonder that Red River carts were held together with shaganappi!

The steamboats, which began to arrive on the river in the late sixties, did not appreciably lower prices save during those brief periods when rival lines fought for control. The Hudson's Bay Company held a monopoly of the Red River traffic with its rickety *International* until one spring day in 1871, when a strange vessel loaded with 125 passengers and 115 tons of freight steamed into Fort Garry. This was the *Selkirk*, operated by James Jerome Hill, a one-eyed ex-Canadian with a razor-sharp mind, now operating out of St. Paul. Hill had

unearthed an old United States law providing that all goods crossing the border from American territories into Canadian ports must be bonded. He quietly built the *Selkirk*, had her bonded, and persuaded the customs officials at Pembina on the border to hold up all unbonded vessels plying the river. The *International* was legally beached and Hill had a transportation monopoly of the Red River valley. It was said that he paid off the entire cost of constructing his new steamboat with the profits of that first voyage.

Jim Hill had had the audacity to challenge the monopoly rule of the Hudson's Bay Company, which for two centuries had enjoyed the mastery of the North West. Donald A. Smith, the company's chief commissioner, struck back. He had the *International* bonded by assigning the steamer

The International, *photographed in 1874, loaded with Mennonite immigrants. "Her engines," wrote William Francis Butler, "were perfect marvels of patchwork – pieces of rope seemed twisted around the crank and shaft – mud was laid thickly on boiler and pipes, little spurts of steam had a disagreeable way of coming out of places not supposed to be capable of such outpourings."*

to Norman Kittson, a respected Minnesota fur trader who was the Hudson's Bay agent in St. Paul. Then he leaped into battle with Hill.

They were evenly matched adversaries and, in many respects, remarkably alike – short, fierce-eyed, muscled men with backgrounds crammed with adventure and romance. They knew and respected one another, having met quite by accident on the bald, snowswept prairie in February of 1870. Since it was axiomatic that neither would give way, the two at last agreed to join forces in secret. On the face of it, both retired from the steamboat business, leaving it in the hands of Norman Kittson's Red River Transportation Company. In actual fact, the Kittson Line was a joint venture of Hill, Kittson,

and the Hudson's Bay Company. The company's shares were in Smith's name, but he agreed in advance to transfer them to whoever succeeded him as chief commissioner. The Kittson Line gave the Hudson's Bay Company a one-third discount on all river freight and thus a commanding edge on its competitors.

No sooner was this secret arrangement completed than the freight rates shot skyward. In the winter of 1874-75 a group of Winnipeg and Minnesota merchants, incensed at the monopoly, launched a steamboat line of their own. They built two rival boats, the *Minnesota* and the *Manitoba*, and another battle was soon in progress. Norman Kittson launched a rate war, bringing his own

When the Manitoba *steamed into Winnipeg on May 14, 1875, an impromptu saturnalia took place as local merchants celebrated their release from "the dreaded monopoly."*

prices down below cost. Through friends in the Pembina customs depot, he arranged that the *Manitoba* be held indefinitely at the border. When it was finally released in July, he charged it broadside with his *International*, rammed it, and sank it with its entire cargo. No sooner was it back in service than it was seized for a trifling debt. The same fate awaited its sister ship, south of the border. The merchants sold out to Kittson in September. And the rates soared again. Kittson and his colleagues shared a dividend of eighty per cent and the rising wrath of the Red River community.

Meanwhile, in September, 1874, the first sod had been turned on the long-awaited railway – a branch of the future CPR – that was to run from Selkirk through Winnipeg's neighbour St. Boniface down to Pembina to connect, it was hoped, at the border with a United States line, as yet uncompleted. The construction moved at an unbelievably leaden pace. After the grading was completed, all work stopped: there was no point in building a railroad to nowhere – and construction of the American line had halted ninety miles below the border. The contract for laying steel was not let for another three years until it became clear that the moribund St. Paul and Pacific, reorganized and renamed the St. Paul and Manitoba, was actually going to reach the border (as it did late in 1878).

By the time the last spike of the Pembina Branch was driven in November, 1878, the population of Winnipeg had reached six thousand. A gala excursion load of citizens was taken by train to Rousseau for the ceremony. With a single blow, Mary Sullivan, the strapping daughter of an Irish section boss, drove the spike home, to the cheers of the assembly. The cheers, however, did not last long. The rails had been laid, but to describe the Pembina Branch as a railway was to indulge in the wildest kind of hyperbole. Under the terms of the contract, the builders had until November, 1879, to complete the job and turn the finished line over to the government. They determined, in the meantime, to squeeze the maximum possible profit out of it by running it themselves while they continued to build the necessary sidings, station houses, water towers, and all the requisite paraphernalia that is part of a properly run railroad.

In the months that followed, the Pembina Branch became the most cursed length of track on the continent. To travel it required nerves of steel, a stomach of iron, and a spirit of high adventure. A man from *The Times* of London reported that he and his party were more seasick on the Pembina Branch than they had been crossing the stormy Atlantic. One of the company, so *The Times*'s man said, had not really said his prayers in a long, long time but was so shattered by the experience that he reformed on the spot, took to praying incessantly and, through sheer terror, managed to scare up some extra prayers that had lain forgotten in the dim recesses of his mind since childhood. The Pembina railroad shook them loose.

In Winnipeg, the citizenry could only wait and hold their breath and listen to the faint sounds of activity in the East where, piece by piece, the railway was being built on Canadian soil from the head of Lake Superior.

Adam Oliver's favourite game

ON THE AFTERNOON of June 1, 1875, a spirited ceremony took place near Fort William on the left bank of the Kaministiquia River, about four miles from its mouth on Thunder Bay, Lake Superior. Here was turned the first sod of the main line of the Canadian Pacific Railway. The affair was sponsored by the firm of Sifton and Ward, which had secured the contract to grade the first thirty-two miles of roadbed for a line that the government intended to build in sections between Fort William and Selkirk, Manitoba. Like so many contractors in those days, John Wright Sifton and his brother Henry were up to their sideburns in politics, being close friends and supporters of the Prime Minister.

John Wright Sifton, shown here in his garb as Speaker of the Manitoba Legislature, could expect favours from the government. He hailed from Mackenzie's riding of Lambton and had been reeve of the municipality.

With a crowd of five hundred in attendance, Judge Delevan Van Norman announced the beginning of the actual construction of the Canadian Pacific Railway. Soon, the Judge declared, an immigrant with his family might "with celerity, safety and certainty examine the country from Cape Breton in Nova Scotia to Vancouver's Island in British Columbia, in the meantime passing over a space as vast as the great ocean that divides and separates the old world from the new."

As the applause for the Judge's speech died, Adam Oliver, who had been one of those instrumental in securing the terminus for Fort William, rose. He was known as an impassioned player of euchre, whose several variations include "Railroad Euchre" and "Cutthroat Euchre"; Oliver, as events were to prove, certainly knew something about the cutthroat aspects of the railroad game. He and his partners, Joseph Davidson and Peter Johnson Brown (a former reeve of the township), owned forty thousand acres of good timber in the Fort William area together with considerable property and a lumber mill. They already had one government contract – to build the telegraph line accompanying the railroad to the Red River – and were about to sign another for the construction of an engine house. Oliver, like the Siftons, was a prominent Liberal and also a member of the provincial legislature. As a Senate inquiry tardily discovered, the three partners, Oliver, Davidson, and Brown, were planning to make a killing at the taxpayers' expense. The story did not leak out until the summer of 1877, when it was revealed that Oliver and his Liberal friends had been selling their land to the government at fancy mark-ups. Worse than that, they had actually put up part of a building – the Neebing Hotel – on land already appropriated for the railway and had managed to sell it to the Crown at an inflated price.

Just how much political muscle Adam Oliver had with the Mackenzie administration came to light in 1880 when a royal commission began investigating various contracts awarded along the

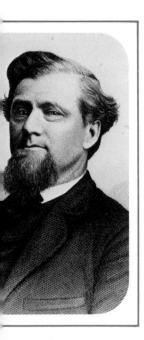

Adam Oliver had been a Liberal MPP in Ontario until he was unseated for bribery and corruption. His party connections made him privy to inside information and his pull at Ottawa helped get him a lucrative contract at an inflated price.

THE NEEBING ROOKERY.

A GREAT BOON TO THE OPPOSITION CROWS.

Bengough's cartoon shows the Tory birds, driven off by the scarecrows of their own peccadillos, roosting gratefully on Oliver's Neebing Hotel. A strong Liberal, Bengough did not believe there was any substance to the Neebing charges.

north shore of Lake Superior. The circumstances under which Oliver, Davidson and Company secured a quarter-million-dollar contract to build the telegraph line from Thunder Bay to Winnipeg were as astonishing as they were suspicious.

Tenders for the line were opened in August, 1874, but the actual contract was not awarded until the following February. The intervening months were spent in what a later century was to brand as "wheeling and dealing." The lowest bid was passed over in a fashion that the Royal Commission described as "peremptory." The next two lowest bids were both entered, in effect, by one Robert Twiss Sutton of Brantford, who clearly had no intention of fulfilling the contract. He had entered the contest in order to be bought off by his competitors, a fairly common practice in those days. In December, Adam Oliver arrived in Ottawa to do the buying off.

Oliver expected to be able to buy up the lower of the two Sutton bids. But once in the capital he discovered that for mysterious reasons he could actually be awarded the higher one. Oliver promised Sutton a quarter of the profits; Sutton paid off a silent partner (another front man); and Oliver's firm ended up with the coveted contract. It was fifty-three thousand dollars fatter than it would have been had the lowest tender been accepted.

Apart from the cavalier treatment of the lowest bidder, there was never any explanation of how the higher of the two Sutton bids came to be accepted, rather than the lower one. But one thing did develop from the testimony. It was Mackenzie himself who handled the entire business and not one of his underlings, as was the general practice. And all the dealings with the Minister were in the hands, not of Robert Sutton, the official tenderer, but of Adam Oliver. To achieve the kind of financial miracle that Oliver managed required a detailed knowledge of all the tenders for the contract – information that was supposed to be secret.

In Adam Oliver's favourite game, the maker's side must win at least three tricks to avoid being euchred. Oliver had won them all: he had wangled the terminus for Fort William, he had sold property to the government at extortionate prices, and he had gained a telegraph contract at a bonus rate. He was not quite so successful as a builder. The complaints about the state of the line were continual. Poles, badly anchored, kept toppling. Wires stretched over trees in lieu of poles strangled and killed them; the roots decayed, and the trees fell over, taking the wires with them. Sometimes it took a message as long as a month to reach Winnipeg on Adam Oliver's expensive telegraph line.

David Glass, a former mayor of London, suddenly became a successful contractor after defecting to Mackenzie's party during the scandal.

The stonemason's friends

THE STRAINS OF OFFICE were beginning to tell on Mackenzie's temper and health; it was the railway that was chiefly to blame. Not only was he Prime Minister, but he had also chosen to assume the burden of the Ministry of Public Works, the most sensitive of cabinet posts in that era of railway contracts. Like most politicians of the time, Mackenzie undoubtedly played favourites. His government awarded eleven contracts west of Lake Superior for grading, track-laying, and telegraph lines. Eight of the largest contracts – amounting to ninety-five per cent of the total sum paid – went to prominent Liberal wheel-horses, men who in every case were members of a federal or provincial parliament, past, present, or future.

Mackenzie took over the Department of Public Works with the memory of the Pacific Scandal haunting him, determined to establish an inflexible method of handling tenders on public contracts. The lowest bidder *must* be given the job. But political friends were able to obtain special favours. For them, in instance after instance, the department found a way to depart from its policy. One such firm was Sifton, Glass and Company, which managed, in 1874, to acquire a lucrative contract for telegraph construction west from Fort Garry along the proposed right of way. The active partner in this firm was Mackenzie's friend and fellow Liberal, John Wright Sifton. The front man, who did the talking in Ottawa, was David Glass.

Glass was not a contractor at all, but a trial lawyer in London, Ontario. He was also the first Tory to turn against Macdonald in the Pacific Scandal debate of 1873. Now he was a Liberal with a special claim to Mackenzie's gratitude.

That gratitude was not long in appearing. The firm was allowed to enter a tender so ambiguous that Mackenzie and other members of the department appeared to misunderstand it. They not only passed over a better offer, but they also allowed Sifton and Glass to renegotiate the original tender to their considerable advantage. The partners tendered on the basis of the entire line but were awarded the contract for only part of it – the easy part; yet they were allowed to charge for the work as if they were building the difficult parts as well. In short, they were paid an inflated price. Theirs was by no means the lowest bid: two lower bidders mysteriously dropped out and a third firm was passed over on a flimsy excuse.

The resultant telegraph line was almost totally unsatisfactory. The poles were badly set, so that they often fell into the swamps and muskegs, and, since they were made of the cheapest available wood, quickly rotted and fell away. The contractors, however, pocketed a sizable profit, having received, in the commission's words, "that to which they were not entitled." But a political debt was a political debt and David Glass could not say that his bold support of the party in 1873 had not been recognized in the contract of 1874.

Another political friend was Joseph Whitehead, former mayor of Clinton, Ontario, and a Liberal member of Parliament from 1867 to 1872. Whitehead knew how to buy his way into newspapers or the goodwill of newspapermen, how to peddle influence, how to purchase contracts, and how to deal with politicians. The machinations by which he secured the contract for Section Fifteen of the Thunder Bay–Selkirk line give an insight into the relationship between politics and business in the Mackenzie era.

Section Fifteen was a thirty-seven-mile stretch of right of way that ran through muskeg country between Cross Lake and Rat Portage, near the border between Ontario and Manitoba. Whitehead tendered on the contract for grading and laying track, but when the bids were opened on September 20, 1876, his was certainly not the lowest. The lowest tender withdrew from the contract; accordingly, the next lowest bidder was awarded the job. Whitehead, of course, knew exactly who had bid and how much had been bid. He also knew whom to pay off. He borrowed twenty thousand dollars from his brother-in-law, Senator Donald McDonald, and paid it to the successful bidder, who obligingly withdrew. Mackenzie awarded the contract to the next highest bidder whom Whitehead bought off for another ten thousand.

Thus did Whitehead secure a contract worth a million and a half dollars. But this, he figured, would be only the beginning; the area through which Section Fifteen would run had been subjected to the skimpiest of surveys; there would be unavoidable extra charges, not subject to competitive bidding, for which he could bill the government. Before Whitehead was through, these extras, none of them officially authorized by the department, had come to $930,000.

Another firm that obtained extraordinary favour in the fall of 1874 was Cooper, Fairman and Company, a hardware company in Montreal. The Department of Public Works showed an astonishing preference for this concern in its purchases of steel rails, nuts, bolts, and fishplates, bending or breaking the rules in its favour in several instances.

The silent partner in this company was the Prime Minister's brother, Charles Mackenzie, a Sarnia hardware merchant. In 1873 he had put fifteen thousand dollars into the firm – more than the other two partners combined. He was to receive a third of all profits in return. There was little business until the government contracts began to roll in. Mackenzie left the company officially in May, 1875, after the story leaked out, but there is no doubt he was very much a part of the firm for at least a portion of the period when his brother's department was granting it extraordinary public favours.

In the end, it developed that not all the steel rails contracted for were really needed. They had been purchased prematurely, apparently because both Fleming and Mackenzie believed they were getting a bargain. The purchase was a disaster for all but Mackenzie's brother's firm. At most, twenty thousand tons were needed for the work in progress. But having purchased that amount, Mackenzie ordered an additional thirty thousand tons, even though the price was higher. Half of this extra order was supplied by Cooper and Fairman at double the going rate. After that, to everyone's discomfiture, the bottom dropped out of the market. The rails rusted for years, unused, while the price of new rails went lower and lower and the interest mounted on the original investment. It was beginning to be apparent to the country at large that the government's venture into the railway business was as disastrous as that of Sir Hugh Allan.

"That fellow Smith"

FROM HIS POPLAR-SHADED MANSION of Silver Heights, high above the Assiniboine, Donald A. Smith was contemplating with more than passing interest the future of the Pembina Branch line. He was a member of a syndicate which by 1878 was establishing rail connection from St. Paul to Pembina on the border. If the same group could lease the government road into the Red River Valley it would have a through line to Winnipeg. It was left to Smith to handle the matter politically. As the man who had laid the last straw on the camel's

back in the Pacific Scandal debacle of 1873, he had considerable pull with the Mackenzie government. In Winnipeg he was admired, hated, feared, respected, but scarcely loved. His political support came from the fur traders, many of whom were shunted across constituency lines at Hudson's Bay Company expense on election day. Thus, for all of his days in Winnipeg, Donald A., as he was called, was a figure of controversy. Seldom quoted in the newspapers, he was constantly attacked in them, especially after he shifted his political loyalties in 1873. But the laird of Silver Heights remained imperturbable.

The rail line to the border, which Smith and his partners coveted, was officially a branch of the almost non-existent CPR. Early in 1878 Smith's cousin, George Stephen, arranged with Alexander Mackenzie for a ten-year lease of the government line to the syndicate, which was building the connecting line from St. Paul. That would require an amendment to the Canadian Pacific Railway Act of 1874. On March 18, Mackenzie rose in the House to introduce a bill which would empower Parliament to lease the Pembina Branch to unspecified parties. No mention was made of Donald A. Smith's interest; indeed, the Prime Minister was at considerable pains to conceal it, for Smith's name was an abomination to the Conservative opposition. If, in 1878, the Member for Selkirk had risen in the House to support motherhood, it is conceivable that Macdonald and his followers would have been strongly tempted to opt for matricide.

When the debate began on the Canadian Pacific Railway Act Amendment Bill, at the time of its second reading on April 4, 1878, the Conservatives were ready with sharpened claws. Macdonald referred to "the indecent spectacle of an honourable gentleman coming into the House as an advocate and pressing this lease in his own interest . . . he advocated more warmly and strongly this Bill, which was in his own interest, and which would put money in his own pocket, than the Minister who introduced it."

EATING THE LEEK;

OR, "HENRY V." AS LATELY PLAYED IN THE COMMONS.

FLUELLEN.—MR. MACKENZIE.   PISTOL.—DR. TUPPER.

The Liberal press quickly accepted Mackenzie's explanation of why he purchased so many steel rails and his insistence that his brother, Charles, was not implicated in favours granted to a firm he had secretly financed.

But in the acrimonious set-to that followed, Smith at no time admitted to his own substantial interest in the company, even when pressed and taunted by the Opposition – though it was clear to all that he was deeply involved.

It was inevitable that the bill should pass; the Government's majority saw to that. But it was a different story in the appointed Senate, where the Tories, who still had a preponderance of votes, threw the bill out.

On May 9, the day before the end of the session, Mackenzie took occasion to reprimand the Senate for its actions. This allowed Macdonald to return to the attack. The Senate, he said, put a stop to the Government's bargain with Smith "to make him a rich man, and to pay for his servile support." That sally provoked the most explosive and perhaps the most harrowing scene in the history of the House of Commons.

The House was scheduled to dissolve. The members were in their seats at 3 p.m. on May 10, awaiting the traditional knock of the Gentleman Usher of the Black Rod, when Smith rose on a question of privilege. After denying that he had ever admitted being a member of the St. Paul syndicate, he began to attack Charles Tupper for some remarks Tupper had made the previous summer.

Tupper, seeing Black Rod at the door (the signal that the session was at an end), realized that he would have no opportunity to answer. "The Cumberland War Horse" had no intention of allowing that. He rose at once on a point of order, and a shouting match followed. It was some time before the Sergeant-at-Arms managed to announce "a message from the Governor General," and by this time the House was in an uproar. The Speaker tried to say that he had "very much pleasure in informing the House it now becomes my duty to receive the Messenger." Then Tupper's powerful voice was heard, over all, bellowing, "Coward! Coward!" at the imperturbable Smith.

Smith held his place.

"Coward! Coward! Coward!" Tupper boomed,

91

"... mean, treacherous coward!"

"Who is the coward?" Smith retorted. "The House will decide – it is yourself."

"Coward!" shouted Tupper once again. "Treacherous ..."

Smith began to speak again, but the harried Speaker interrupted him and asked that Black Rod be admitted.

It was Macdonald who got in the last word, surely the most unparliamentary expression ever to appear in Hansard.

"That fellow Smith," he cried "is the biggest liar I ever met!"

The Gentleman Usher was admitted to "as excited a mob as ever disgraced the floor of a Parliamentary chamber." Tupper and Macdonald and some other Tories, enraged beyond endurance, rushed at Smith, bent on physical assault. Several tried to strike him. Macdonald had to be pulled away from Smith, crying that he "could lick him quicker than hell could scorch a feather." The disorder was so great that the Speaker could not at once leave the House because of the throng at the door. Finally he was allowed to proceed to the Senate chamber, followed by the dishevelled crowd. Thus did the Mackenzie regime come to an end, not with a whimper but a bang. It could not accommodate Donald A. Smith and his colleagues with an exclusive lease of the Pembina Branch but it could grant running rights for ten years over the line and it did just that in August. That was one of its last official acts.

PARLIAMENTARY LANGUAGE PROHIBITED

Bengough, in Grip, *made game of the Tory leaders' indiscretions in the House in a cartoon that showed Macdonald and Tupper being reprimanded by a saloon-keeper for using "Parliamentary Language" in a respectable establishment: "This isn't the House of Commons!"*

3

The Birth Pangs of the CPR

"A New Era in Railway"
was the title of this
cartoon in the Illustrated
News *for July 24, 1880.*
It shows a triumphant prime
minister and the Quebec
premier, J.A. Chapleau.
Macdonald had just left
for London to negotiate a
Pacific railway contract.

O, OUR PROPHETIC SOUL!

(See last week's Cartoon.)

JOHN A. "I DON'T KNOW, BUT IT SEEMS TO ME THIS PICTURE OF YOURS, MY PROPHETIC FRIEND, NEEDS A LITTLE 'RE-ADJUSTMENT,' DON'T IT, HEY?"

Grip's cartoonist, Bengough, shared the general astonishment at Macdonald's victory and publicly ate crow in the first post-election issue, in which he reproduced several of his anti-Tory cartoons, including one that had appeared on election eve showing Mackenzie back in power. Macdonald had privately predicted the victory, but even he was surprised by its magnitude. As for Mackenzie, he wrote: "Nothing has happened in my time so astonishing."

The two cartoons at the right are comments on the National Policy that swept Macdonald into power. The promised tariff was designed to prevent Uncle Sam from dumping surplus products at cut-rate prices on the Canadian "slaughter market."

Resurrection

SEPTEMBER 17, 1878, was the day of a political miracle in Canada. Long before the election was called, it was clear that the Conservatives were on the rise; but nobody could be sure of the results. When they began to come in few could give them credence.

The polls closed at five and by seven it was clear that Macdonald had suffered personal defeat in Kingston. But this news was superseded by indications of massive Conservative gains. By nine, it was apparent that the Mackenzie administration had fallen; by eleven, that Macdonald and his party had scored a landslide of unprecedented proportions. In the session just past, the Liberals had held 133 seats to the Conservatives' 73. In the new parliament, the Conservatives would have 137 seats to the Liberals' 69. For Macdonald, who would soon win a by-election in Victoria, B.C., revenge was sweet.

For two years after his defeat, the Tory chieftain had kept his peace while the Liberal press continued to announce his imminent retirement. Then, during the session of 1876, Macdonald revived and the country became familiar with the phrase "National Policy."

In 1878, the National Policy was nothing more than a euphemism for a protective tariff. It was only in later years that it was seen as one leg of a three-cornered foundation on which the superstructure of the transcontinental nation rested. The other two legs were the encouragement of western settlement and the construction of the Pacific railway. The railway was the key: without it western settlement would be difficult; with it there would be more substantial markets for the protected industries. Macdonald himself saw this. "Until this great work is completed, our Dominion is little more than a 'geographical expression,'" he told Sir Stafford Northcote, the Governor of the Hudson's Bay

97

Company. "We have as much interest in British Columbia as in Australia, and no more. The railway once finished, we become one great united country with a large interprovincial trade and a common interest." As it turned out, the National Policy was to become the policy of the country and the future would extend it to include a variety of awkward, expensive, and contentious Canadian devices which, like the railway, would continue the horizontal development of the nation that Macdonald began.

Actually there was not much difference between the Macdonald government's railway policy and that of its predecessor. In the absence of any offers from private capitalists, the administration was forced to continue Mackenzie's policy of building the line in instalments: the 181-mile gap in the Lake Superior area would be completed; an additional two hundred miles would be contracted for, to run west of the Red River; and it would all be accomplished without raising taxes – or so Charles Tupper insisted.

Tupper announced in May of 1879 that the government considered the selection of Burrard Inlet to be premature. It wanted more time to survey the Pine and Peace River passes and Port Simpson on the coast. Marcus Smith's furious efforts had obviously not been in vain. In spite of this, the government felt compelled to let four contracts that year for 125 miles of railway in British Columbia.

One of the bidders on all four sections, though by no means the lowest, was a young American named Andrew Onderdonk, the scion of a prominent Hudson River family. Tupper was impressed by Onderdonk, who appeared to have almost unlimited means behind him from American financiers. In the muskeg country west of Lake Superior, Canadian contractors were running into difficulties. Some of the low bidders on the four British Columbia sections looked alarmingly shaky. Obviously, a man of experience backed by solid capital could build all the sections more cheaply and efficiently than four under-financed contractors working independently. Onderdonk was allowed to purchase the four contracts. He paid a total of $215,000 for the privilege, arrived at Yale on April 22, 1880, to a salute of thirteen guns, and by May was ready to begin construction. None of Macdonald's followers appeared to grasp the irony of a Conservative government awarding an important section of the railway to a Yankee contractor.

"ANTI-SECESH."

Meanwhile, Marcus Smith, who had been pronounced dead by both Fleming and Mackenzie, refused to lie down on the subject of the Pine Pass–Bute Inlet route. Indeed, he seemed to have gained a new lease on life with the advent of the new administration. There is something madly magnificent about Smith's furious windmill-tilting at this late date. On January 20, 1879, he sent Tupper a confidential memorandum detailing his differences

George Walkem, re-elected in British Columbia on a "fight Ottawa" platform, was threatening secession when this cartoon, titled "Anti-Secesh," appeared. To appease B.C., Macdonald awarded contracts along the Fraser.

Henry Cambie, chief of surveys in B.C., explored much of the northern half of the province seeking an alternative route. He later worked for Onderdonk at Yale.

with Fleming. He followed this up with another long memo asking Tupper to give him charge of a two-year survey of the Pine Pass section of the Bute Inlet route. In May he wrote to Macdonald asking him to intercede on his behalf to reinstate him as engineer of the British Columbia division.

In the meantime, Henry Cambie had taken a distinguished party of surveyors and scientists right across the uncivilized hinterland of northern British Columbia, from Port Simpson to the Peace River. Cambie returned on his own with a pack train and reached the top of the Pine Pass in a raging blizzard. He made his way back to civilization down the fast-freezing Fraser, shooting the rapids of the canyon himself, without a pilot. "Sham surveys" Smith called them when Cambie returned; but on the strength of his report the government, in October, 1879, finally gave up on the Bute Inlet route and announced that Burrard Inlet would be the official terminus after all. The Yellow Head, apparently, would be the pass through the Rockies.

Still Marcus Smith would not admit defeat. He wrote immediately to Senator David Macpherson, attacking the whole decision. Then he allied himself with General Butt Hewson, an American engineer resident in Canada who was preparing a pamphlet urging the adoption of the Bute Inlet–Pine Pass route.

All this pressure undoubtedly had some effect on public policy. On February 16, 1880, Tupper told the House that he still wanted more information on the Pine River–Peace River country before finally making up his mind about the choice of a pass through the Rockies. It was now the ninth year of the Canadian Pacific Survey in British Columbia and it seemed by this time that every notch in each of the mountain ranges and all the intervening trenches had been combed as carefully as a Japanese sand garden. Every pass had been argued over, reported on, discarded or, sometimes, resurveyed – every pass, that is, except the Kicking Horse, which lay to the south, neglected and unsurveyed, waiting to be chosen.

The line in British Columbia was begun at the most difficult of all locations – at Yale, near the entrance to the Fraser Canyon. Here Andrew Onderdonk made his headquarters in the spring of 1880, arriving to a salute of 22 guns. Tupper's reason for choosing to start at this unprepossessing location was that it would mean "the breaking of the backbone of the undertaking." The real reason was that no one yet knew where the railway route would be located – except along this gloomy gorge.

101

SANDFORD FLEMING's days as engineer-in-chief were numbered. The dissensions within his own department, as symbolized by the intractable Marcus Smith, the total identification with Mackenzie's sluggish and sometimes inept railway policies, the bills coming in from Lake Superior, far in excess of estimates, the expensive surveys in British Columbia – all these were laid at his door. In the spring of 1879 he had been given a hard time as a witness before the Commons Public Accounts Committee and it was clear that a royal commission would follow.

Macdonald intended that Fleming should go, but with as much honour as possible and with the government's blessing; one never knew when he might be needed again. Clearly, he was not the man to prosecute Macdonald's more aggressive railway policy.

He was eased out of office in February, 1880, before the Royal Commission commenced its hearings. The government provided for him handsomely with a bonus of thirty thousand dollars. It also offered him a titular post with the railway, but this Fleming declined for he did not care to be a figurehead.

When the Royal Commission finally made its report it came down very hard on the former engineer-in-chief, but by then the railway builders were at work in the swampy, half-frozen land west of Fort William.

As Harry Armstrong, a resident engineer along the half-completed Fort William–Selkirk line, wrote, "We began the work of construction of Canada's great highway at a dead end." It was true. One chunk of railway was begun at the Red River and ran hesitantly eastward towards the muskegs on the Ontario-Manitoba border. Another was built westward from Fort William, literally to nowhere. These two pieces were useless because they did not connect. The navvies were toiling in the empty heart of Canada without rail transportation to supply them, in a country scarcely explored. Four years later, when other contractors began to fill in the 181-mile gap between, every pound of supplies and heavy equipment had to be taken in by canoe and portage because the end of steel was still a good hundred miles from the water route. The distance between Fort William and Selkirk was only 435 railroad miles. But the barrier was so formidable that it took seven years before through rail communication was completed from the lakehead to the Red River.

Much of this country, smiling in the sunshine, gloomy in the frequent slashing rains, would one day become a tourist mecca; but in the seventies it was a hellhole for the contractors who saw their fortunes sink forever in the seemingly bottomless slime of the great muskegs.

The muskegs came in every size. There were the notorious sinkholes over which a thick crust of vegetable matter had formed. In such a morass near Savanne, north of Fort William, so legend has it, an entire train with a thousand feet of track was swallowed whole.

Worse than the sinkholes were the giant muskegs, like the Poland Swamp or the Julius Muskeg, the most infamous bog of all – a vast bed of peat six miles across, its depth unknown. From these deceptively level, moss-covered stretches the naked trunks of dead tamaracks protruded, their roots weaving a kind of blanket over a concealed jelly of mud and slime. The road was carried over them on log mattresses floated on top of the heaving bog – unwieldy contraptions of long, interlaced timbers, which would sometimes run for eight hundred feet. Later on the muskegs were filled in.

Then there were the apparently placid lakes that seemed so shallow, whose bottoms consisted of unfathomable muskeg which swallowed up tons of earth and gravel fill, month after month. The

Joseph Whitehead, according to a royal commission, had "a strong belief in the corruptibility of public men."

real lake bottoms were concealed by a false blanket of silt which had never been properly probed during the hasty surveys. Lake Macquistinah, for instance, devoured 250,000 yards of earth fill; and on Section Fifteen the hapless Joseph Whitehead saw his dreamed-of profits slowly pouring into the notorious Cross Lake in the form of 220,000 yards of gravel at a cost of eighty thousand dollars. And still the line continued to sink.

Cross Lake was to prove Whitehead's undoing. The contractor began work on it in 1879 and was still pouring fill into it when the government relieved him of his contract in March, 1880. Ton after ton of sand and gravel vanished into that monstrous gulf without appreciable results. Sometimes the embankment would be built up five or six feet above the water; then suddenly the lake would take a gulp and the entire mass of stone, gravel, and earth would vanish beneath the waves.

There seemed no end to the depth of these incredible swamps. In one muskeg, piles were driven ninety-six feet below the surface before any bedrock was found. Even after the muskegs were conquered, the roadbed tended to creep forward with every passing train. When a heavy engine, hauling thirty-five cars, passed over the track, the rails crept about two feet in the direction the train was moving. As a result track bolts broke almost daily. An actual series of waves, five or six inches deep, rippled along the track and was observable from the caboose.

Temporary trestles were filled by dragging giant ploughs along a line of flatcars loaded with gravel. The ploughs were designed on the spot by Michael J. Haney, the colourful Galway Irishman who took over the running of Section Fifteen for the government after Whitehead's downfall.

Haney was described by Harry Armstrong, the pioneer engineer, as "a rushing devil-may-care chap who did things just as he chose without regard to authority." He seemed accident-prone to an almost unbelievable degree – yet he managed to survive. His particular brand of derring-do was hard

103

*Michael Haney's giant plough: temporary trestles were
filled in by dragging it down a line of loaded flatcars
using a cable powered by a detached engine. Cataracts of
gravel descended from the bow, filling in the cut below.*

on him physically – after two years on Section Fifteen he was a sick man and his doctor ordered a complete rest – but it certainly got results. When he took over Section Fifteen there was a deficit of almost four hundred thousand dollars. Under his management a balance of $83,000 appeared on the black side of the ledger. Haney, of course, was a salaried man. The $83,000 was paid by the government to Joseph Whitehead.

Sodom-on-the-Lake

IN THIS DISMAL LAND west of Lake Superior, nature seemed to have gone to extremes to thwart the railway builders. When they were not laying track across the porridge of the muskegs they were blasting it through some of the hardest rock in the world. The major explosive was nitro-glycerine, an awesomely unstable liquid. The technique was to pour the explosive into drill holes, each about seven feet deep, and set it off by a fuse. In less than two years some three hundred thousand dollars were spent on nitro-glycerine on Section Fifteen, often with disastrous results. There was among the workmen an almost cavalier attitude to the explosive. Cans of nitro-glycerine with fuses attached were strewn carelessly along the roadbed in contravention of all safety regulations, or carried about with such recklessness that the fluid splashed upon the rocks. Whole gangs were sometimes blown to bits in the resultant explosions.

The number of men killed or maimed by accidental explosions was truly staggering. In one fifty-mile stretch Sandford Fleming counted thirty graves, all the result of the careless handling of nitro-glycerine.

In these circumstances the only real respite was alcohol. Prohibition was in effect all along the line, but this did not stop the whiskey peddlers who had kegs of liquor cached at points along the entire right of way. Since a gallon of alcohol, which was

Michael Haney

sold in the cities of the East for as low as fifty cents, could, when properly diluted, return forty-five dollars to an enterprising peddler on the line, business continued brisk in spite of the vigilance of the police. The peddlers hid out in the bush or on the islands that dotted the swampy lakes, moving into the work camps in swift canoes of birchbark and darting away again at the approach of the law. If caught, the peddler generally escaped with a fine, since these were the chief source of income for the struggling towns and villages that were springing up at the end of steel. A description of Christmas Eve, 1880, by the postmaster of Whitemouth, a railroad community midway between Winnipeg and Rat River, gives an idea of the role liquor played during the festive season:

"The demon of strong drink made a bedlam of this place, fighting, stabbing and breaking; some lay out freezing till life was almost extinct. The Post Office was besieged at the hours of crowded business by outrageous, bleeding, drunken, fighting men, mad with Forty-Rod, so that respectable people could not come in for their mail . . . . It is only a few days since in one of these frenzies a man had his jugular nearly severed by a man with a razor."

The one really permanent town along the half-constructed line and by far the largest was Rat Portage on Lake of the Woods. With true chamber of commerce fervour it called itself "the Future Saratoga of America." A less subjective description was provided by a correspondent of the Winnipeg *Times* in the summer of 1880:

"For some time now the railway works in the vicinity of Rat Portage have been besieged by a lot of scoundrels whose only avocation seems to be gambling and trading in illicit whiskey and the state of degradation was, if anything, intensified by the appearance, in the wake of these blacklegs, of a number of the *demi-monde* with whom these numerous desperadoes held high carnival at all hours of the day or night."

The town itself, in the words of one observer, seemed to have been "laid out on designs made by a colony of muskrats." Shanties and tents were built or pitched wherever the owners fancied and without reference to streets or roadways. As a result, the streets were run between the houses as an afterthought so that there was nothing resembling a straight thoroughfare in town.

With a floating population sometimes bordering on three thousand, the community was the headquarters for Section B. The expense of the administration was borne by the contractors, who built the jail and organized the police force. All fines, however, went to the government. Between April and November of 1880, six thousand dollars was collected in fines. The convictions – highway robbery, larceny, burglary, assault, selling illicit whiskey,

and prostitution – give a fair picture of Rat Portage as a frontier town.

In 1880 it was easily the roughest town in Canada; eight hundred gallons of illegal liquor poured into town every month, hidden in oatmeal and bean sacks or disguised as barrels of coal oil. So profitable was the business that there was a whiskey peddler for every thirty residents. Here, on a smaller and more primitive scale, was foreshadowed all the anarchy of a later prohibition period in the United States – the same gun-toting mobsters, corrupt officials, and harassed police.

It was reports of these conditions, seeping back to Winnipeg, that persuaded Archbishop Taché of St. Boniface that the construction workers needed a permanent chaplain; after all, a third of them were French-Canadian Catholics from Manitoba. He selected for the task the most notable of all the voyageur priests, Father Albert Lacombe, a nomadic Oblate who had spent most of his adult life among the Cree and Blackfoot of the Far West. In November, 1880, Lacombe set out reluctantly for his new parish.

He did not want to be a railway chaplain. He would much rather have stayed among his beloved Indians than have entered the Sodom of Rat Portage, but he went where his church directed. On the very first day of his new assignment he was scandalized by the language of the navvies. His first sermon, preached in a boxcar chapel, was an attack on blasphemy. "It seems to me what I have said is of a nature to bring reflection to these terrible blasphemers, who have a vile language all their own – with a dictionary of grammar which belongs to no one but themselves," he confided to his diary. "This habit of theirs is – diabolical!"

But there was worse to come: two weeks after he arrived in Rat Portage there was "a disorderly and scandalous ball," and all night long the sounds of drunken revelry dinned into the ears of the unworldly priest from the plains. Lacombe even tried to reason with the woman who sponsored the dances. He was rewarded with jeers and insults.

Rat Portage in 1880 consisted of a "lot of crooked winding trails that appeared to go nowhere in particular."
"Forty-Rod" (so called because it was said that it could kill a man at that distance) sold for the same price as
champagne did in Winnipeg from the illegal saloons operating on the islands that speckled Lake of the Woods.

"My God," he wrote in his diary, "have pity on this little village where so many crimes are committed every day." He realized that he was helpless to stop all the evil that met his eyes and so settled at last for prayer "to arrest the divine anger."

As he moved up and down the line, covering thirty different camps, preaching sermons as he went, celebrating mass in the mornings, talking and smoking with the navvies in the evenings and recording on every page of his small, tattered black notebooks a list of sins far worse than he had experienced among the followers of Chief Crowfoot, the wretched priest was overcome by a sense of frustration. The heathen Indians had been so easy to convert! But these navvies listened to him respectfully, talked to him intimately, confessed their sins religiously, and then went on their drunken, brawling, blaspheming, whoring way totally unashamed.

Ill with pleurisy, forced to travel the track on an open handcar in the bitterest weather, his eyes affronted by spectacles he did not believe possible, the tortured priest could only cry to his diary, "My God, I offer you my sufferings."

"Please God, send me back to my missions," he pleaded, but it was not until the final spike was driven that his prayers were answered. He had not changed many lives, perhaps, but he had made more friends than he knew. When it was learned that he was going, the workmen of Section B took up a large collection and presented him with a generous assortment of gifts: a horse, a buggy, a complete harness, a new saddle, a tent, and an entire camping outfit to make his days on the plains more comfortable. Perhaps, as he took his leave, he reasoned that his tortured mission to the godless had not been entirely in vain.

Father Albert Lacombe preferred Indians to railroad navvies. He was not above blackmailing the workmen in his flock by threatening to write home to their girl friends and report them if they sinned too deeply.

Two streaks of rust

ON ONE of those early trips to the Canadian North West in 1870, when he was planning his steamboat war against the Hudson's Bay Company, James Jerome Hill's single eye fastened upon the rich soil of the Red River country and marked the rank grass that sprang up in the ruts left by the wagon wheels. It was the blackest loam he had ever seen and he filed the memory of it carefully away in the pigeonholes of his active mind. Soil like that meant settlers – tens of thousands of them. Settlers would need a railway. With Donald Smith's help, Jim Hill meant to give them one.

There was a railway of sorts leading out of St. Paul in 1870. It was supposed to reach to the Canadian border but it had not made it that far. One of its branches ended at Breckenridge on the Red River, where it connected with the Kittson line of steamboats. Another headed off northwest to St. Cloud at the end of the Red River trail. An extension faltered north towards Brainerd, where it was supposed to connect with the main line of the Northern Pacific. But neither branch nor extension could properly be called a railroad. They had been built in a piecemeal fashion out of the cheapest materials. Unused piles of bridge timbers, railway ties, and other bric-a-brac littered the right of way, and the farmers along the line were helping themselves to whatever they needed. The rolling stock was incredibly primitive – the engines ancient and creaky, the cars battered and rusty.

The story of the St. Paul and Pacific Railroad is a case history in railway looting. Russell Sage,

Jim Hill lost one eye playing wild Indians as a child, but he kept the other one wide open. In St. Paul he was looked on as an eccentric and an overly talkative dreamer. Opinions changed after he bought a railway.

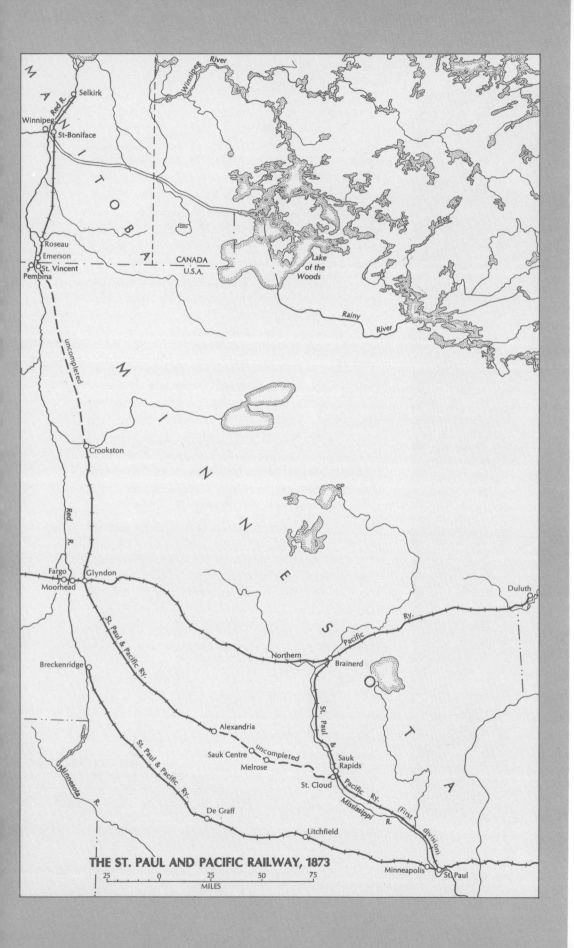

THE ST. PAUL AND PACIFIC RAILWAY, 1873

25   0   25   50   75
MILES

The baggage room of the St. Paul and Pacific Railroad, as photographed in 1870, was not exactly palatial and neither was the line it served. The rails were not even of steel but of iron – and fifteen distinct patterns of iron at that. By 1873 it was in such terrible condition that when the receiver in bankruptcy arrived to take it over, the single battered locomotive would not operate on the rails; he had to inspect what was left of the road by handcar.

a railway promoter, had corrupted the Minnesota legislature into handing over vast land grants and bond issues, the proceeds of which he and his cronies coolly pocketed. In just five years the road was bankrupt. The Sage group then reorganized the bankrupt company into two new companies, thereby ridding themselves of all their debts while keeping the valuable land grant. Then they proceeded to lobby for even more land and when they got it floated a bond issue of $13,800,000 in Holland. They diverted some eight million dollars of this sum to their own pockets and plunged the railroad into bankruptcy again.

In the early seventies the railway consisted of some five hundred miles of almost unusable track – "two streaks of rust and a right of way," as it was contemptuously called. One of its lines actually went from nowhere to nowhere, a phantom railroad lying out on the naked prairie with no town at the terminal end of iron and no facilities created to do business at the other.

Yet this was the line that Jim Hill coveted; and this was the line that would eventually make Jim Hill, Donald Smith, Norman Kittson, and George Stephen rich beyond their wildest dreams and gain them both the experience and the money to build the Canadian Pacific Railway.

Hill was the kind of man who could gaze upon an empty plain and visualize an iron highway. He took a look at St. Paul when it was only a hamlet and realized he was at one of the great crossroads of western trade. Accordingly, he set himself up as a forwarding agent. But in the early seventies, no one took Jim Hill seriously – perhaps because he talked so much. There he sat in his old chair in front of his coal and wood store, babbling away, his single black eye burning itself into the listener's consciousness and his insistent finger always gesticulating.

He was Canadian by birth and Celtic by heritage – half Scottish, half Irish. He was born in a log house at Rockwood, Ontario, and was much influenced by his teacher, the great Quaker educator William Wetherald, who taught him the value of books. For all of his life Hill remained a student; he studied scientific treatises, classical art, geology, finance – everything he could get his hands on. Rockwood could not hold him; at eighteen, his heart fired by the idea of adventure, he set off for the Orient. He got only as far as St. Paul, which was then at the very edge of the frontier.

For eight years, from 1856 to 1864, Hill worked at a variety of jobs in St. Paul, reading and studying all the while. He read voraciously, at all hours and in every setting. By the time he decided to try his hand at business, his knowledge was encyclopaedic and his memory prodigious. He had, it seemed, studied everything. One of the things he studied was the Toonerville operation out of St. Paul; and one of the things he learned was that whoever owned the railway could come into possession of two and a half million acres of the richest agricultural land in the American mid-west. The time would come, Hill reckoned, when the railway could be bought for a song. It was all a matter of waiting.

In Winnipeg, Donald A. Smith had a similar idea. The Red River needed a lifeline to the East. If such a line could be built from Selkirk to the border and if the bankrupt American line out of St. Paul could somehow be revived to meet it, that connection would be effected.

Smith was also a man who liked to look ahead: a month sometimes, a year perhaps, even a decade or more. Like Hill, he foresaw the death of the steam packet at a time when the river trade seemed to be at its height. Smith also saw the threat to the fur trade even when the fur trade seemed invulnerable. As early as 1860 he predicted that the Hudson's Bay Company could not go on forever sealing off the North West, and he realized that once the company's charter was modified or cancelled there would have to be a railway from Lake Superior to the Red River.

Thirteen years after that forecast was made, Smith contemplated the two streaks of rust out of St. Paul. The twin railway companies (one was known as the St. Paul and Pacific, the other as the First Division of the St. Paul and Pacific) were in a terrible legal and financial snarl. One was in receivership, the other was about to go into trusteeship. Most of the bonds were held out of the country by Dutch investors.

In the fall of 1873, on his way through St. Paul en route to Ottawa, Smith dropped in on "Commodore" Norman Kittson, the Hudson's Bay representative and the president of the steamboat line which, with the company's secret connivance, held a monopoly on the river. Smith asked Kittson to find out everything possible about the Dutch-held bonds. If the price was right, Smith thought, he might consider raising the money to help complete the line.

Kittson mentioned the matter to his other silent partner, Jim Hill, who had been grappling with the puzzle of the bankrupt railway, wondering where the money would come from when the time was ripe to buy it. Now he had the answer. From that moment on, Hill became a monomaniac on the subject of the St. Paul and Pacific.

When Donald Smith passed back through St. Paul, Hill and Kittson were able to tell him that most of the bonds, totalling almost eighteen million dollars face value, were now held by Dutch investors who had formed themselves into a committee of bondholders.

The strategy was clear: buy the bonds as cheaply as possible, form a new company, force a fore-

Norman Kittson of Sorel, Quebec, was the most famous of the bootleg fur traders who battled the Hudson's Bay Company and later joined it. By 1858 he was mayor of St. Paul, by 1879 a multimillionaire, thanks to Jim Hill.

Jim Hill's freight office on the Mississippi levee at the time he was planning to take over a bankrupt railway. He amused his fellows by predicting that locomotives would one day replace steam packets.

closure, buy the bankrupt railroad, complete it to the border, cash in on the resultant land subsidy, and reap the profits. But there were many obstacles. It was no use buying the railroad without being certain of getting the land grant. The Minnesota legislature, however, had passed a law making the land grant non-transferable to any new company after foreclosure. A good deal of lobbying – and perhaps more than lobbying – would be needed to get that law revoked. There was also a variety of lawsuits pending against the railway lines. Then there was the stock. Most of it was held by a speculator named Edwin Litchfield who was himself trying to get control of the railway through court action. The depression was at its height, money was hard to come by, and plagues of grasshoppers were ravaging the land. For the moment nothing could be done. Smith, Hill, and Kittson bided their time for two full years but Hill was

not inactive, for he was studying the railroad down to the last cross tie. Within two years, it was said, he knew more about it than the men involved in running it. Two things he certainly knew that few others knew: it was worth far more than it appeared to be; and it could be made to show a profit.

The law was finally changed on March 6, 1876. With this obstacle removed, Hill left for Ottawa on March 17 to meet Smith. It was now or never. Litchfield was trying to reach a compromise with the Dutch bondholders which would give him effective control and prevent foreclosure. Hill's whole scheme rested on the certainty of foreclosure. Whoever owned the bonds could foreclose if mortgage payments were in default. Then the railroad would go on the block and the new bondholders could buy it for a song. If the price for the bonds was favourable, Smith told Hill, the money could probably be raised.

It was now Hill's task to figure out the price at which the Dutch were prepared to sell. In January, 1877, he pretended he was ready to deal. Actually his plan was to write a letter to the Dutch committee that would sound like an offer so that he might get some idea of the actual price. The Dutch rejected the offer, as Hill knew they would; but their reply indicated the kind of deal they would accept. The time had finally come to stop dreaming dreams and playing games. The time had come to put some money on the line. The time had come to broach the subject to George Stephen, the president of the Bank of Montreal, one of the keenest financial minds in Canada and a first cousin of Donald A. Smith.

Enter George Stephen

EVER SINCE 1874, Donald Smith had been boring his cousin with talk about the St. Paul railway. George Stephen listened politely but, like most Montreal businessmen, he had a confused and inaccurate picture of the country west of the lakes. But, though he thought the railway scheme "an impossible thing for us to accomplish," he agreed to meet Hill and Smith early in 1877 to discuss the matter. Hill, armed with facts and figures, papers and documents, gesturing with that insistent finger, never letting up for an instant in his infectious enthusiasm, changed Stephen's attitude from one of "languid attention" to whole-hearted interest; and Stephen's interests were never idle ones.

Stephen is a shadowy figure in Canadian history. Yet, apart from the politicians, he, more than any other single man, was responsible for the shape and direction of the new Canada that sprang up west of Toronto after 1881. Outwardly reserved, publicly reticent, and privately unassuming, he was inwardly subjected to the tugs and pressures of a mercurial psyche, reckless in its enthusiasms, magnificent in its audacities, faithful in its loyalties, consuming in its antipathies, and single-minded to

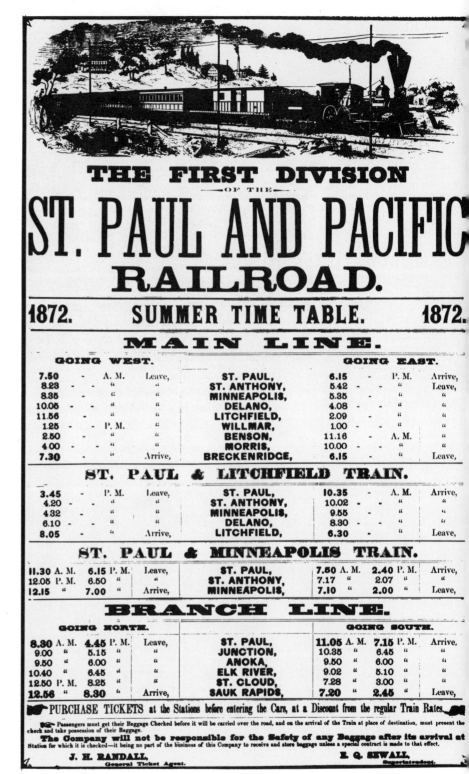

the point of intolerance. He was used to the blunt directives of the business world and was maddened by the circumlocutions of the political. Unlike Macdonald, to whom he poured out his inner soul in an astonishing series of personal letters, he indulged himself in the luxury of maintaining his animosities. As far as Stephen was concerned, you were either for him or against him. There was rarely a middle ground.

He could operate with a gambler's daring when the occasion demanded it, and in Smith and Hill he found men like himself – shrewd in business, willing to take long risks, and, perhaps above all, wedded to the idea that a man was placed on earth to work, day and night if need be.

As a draper, Stephen's idea of a spare-time activity had been to make a study of banking, and this led him eventually to the top of the financial pyramid. His only real form of relaxation was salmon fishing, a passion which he indulged at his summer retreat of Causapscal on the Matapedia River in the Gaspé. That almost certainly went back to his school days in Banffshire, where he came under the influence of a brilliant mathematician, John Macpherson. Top students were rewarded with an invitation to go salmon fishing. Stephen was certainly a top student; Macpherson was to recall that in thirty years of teaching, Stephen was one of the three best mathematicians he had known. The salmon-fishing expeditions must have been frequent.

A mathematician must think logically and tidily and reason creatively. Stephen had that kind of mind. He easily grasped Hill's Niagara of statistics and sorted them into a pattern. His gambler's instincts tugged at him insistently. If the coup could be pulled off it would be a masterstroke comparable to the exploits of a Gould, a Fisk, or a Morgan. If it failed, it would beggar them all.

George Stephen shunned the limelight, refused to own a telephone because he said it was only used to spread gossip, and, before his death, burned his personal papers.

115

Officials of the St. Paul and Pacific Railroad with their crinolined and well-bustled spouses pose in front of one of the few working locomotives available to the road. The line was first chartered in the mid-1850's at a time when no fewer than 27 railroad companies came into existence in the United States. Most went bankrupt. By 1873, when this photograph was made, the St. Paul line had been milked dry and chopped up into two companies by financial robber barons who used that device to milk it further. One company was again bankrupt and the other was in trusteeship. Nobody thought the railroad was worth its axle grease – except for James J. Hill.

He could not resist the adventure. He sat down and began to figure, with Hill and Smith, the price at which the bonds should be purchased. They worked it out at a little more than four million dollars. If the Dutch bondholders agreed, Stephen said, he thought he could raise the money in London that fall. He still had to see the railway for himself, but from that day on George Stephen was totally captivated, to the exclusion of everything else.

The new associates had a great deal of delicate negotiating to do, however. Before Stephen could leave for Europe, they would have to make a firm deal with the bondholders. Then, to forestall a legal battle, an attempt must also be made to corner Litchfield's stock. After that Stephen would have to raise the money. By September, Hill had made a detailed inventory of the railroad's assets and liabilities. His supple mind had grasped a point that had eluded everyone else: though the net earnings of the First Division Company seemed to have dropped, they had in reality nearly doubled because almost two hundred thousand dollars had been charged to operating expenses instead of to construction and equipment. This meant that the railroad was doing much better than the books showed.

Hill knew something more: although he figured that it would cost some five and a half million dollars to buy the bonds and complete the line, he was able, by close reckoning, to estimate the total value of the railway and its properties at almost twenty millions. In short, if the bondholders accepted the offer, he and his associates would get the railway for about a quarter of its real value.

By mid-September, the Dutch, manipulated by Hill's shrewd bargaining, were ready to deal. If Stephen could raise the money, the partners could buy themselves almost eighteen million dollars' worth of bonds for slightly more than four millions. It was a fantastic bargain.

The four partners agreed to share the risks and the profits equally, each taking a one-fifth share in the enterprise. The remaining one-fifth went to Stephen to use at his discretion in raising a loan. At the end of September he set off for England, full of optimism.

But in London, the bankers were gun shy. The panic of 1873 had made American railway securities a bad risk, and among all the bad risks, the St. Paul and Pacific was held to be the worst. Stephen was not able to raise a shilling.

In Montreal, on Stephen's return, four bitterly disappointed men met on Christmas Day, in no mood for Yuletide merriment. Stephen, however, had no intention of giving up. In that precise mind, an unconventional plan was taking shape which, if accepted, would be far better than the original. Stephen decided to take the negotiations into his own hands and deal directly with the Dutch committee's New York agent.

Early in January, Stephen met for the first time John S. Kennedy, the New York banker who represented the Dutch interests in the United States. Kennedy was yet another self-made Scot and the two swiftly became friends. Stephen's plan was as bold as it was simple. He offered to buy the bonds on credit, depositing a mere one hundred thousand dollars on account and paying the balance *after* foreclosure. The payment could be made either in cash or in the new bonds of the reorganized company. The Dutch were encouraged to accept the bonds by the offer of a bonus of $250 in preferred stock for every thousand-dollar bond they took. The partners, in turn, agreed to finish the railway and put it into working order.

They were, in short, proposing to get control of eighteen million dollars' worth of bonds for a cash outlay of only one hundred thousand dollars. By this time the Dutch had worked themselves into a frame of mind to deal at any price. Under Kennedy's prodding they accepted. The purchase was concluded on February 24, 1878, and the partners took control of the railway on March 13.

Though they had possession of the bonds, they were by no means out of the woods. A whole series of complicated problems now faced them, any one of which could wreck the enterprise.

First, more money had to be raised. The line owed $280,000 which had to be paid immediately. Then there was the one-hundred-thousand-dollar deposit to the bondholders. The stock, if it could be purchased from Litchfield, would cost around half a million dollars. Finally, the railroad must be finished swiftly if the land grant was to be earned.

There was only one place to get this kind of financing – the Bank of Montreal. Stephen was president and Smith was a director, and they were now proposing to borrow money personally from an institution under their care. It did not look well, but there was no help for it.

Stephen wrote to Hill that he and Kittson must pledge everything they owned in order to get a line of credit from the bank. He and Smith had already handed over "every transferable security of every kind we have got." It was all or nothing.

Stephen's next move was to go straight to Ottawa and negotiate with Mackenzie for a ten-year lease of the Pembina Branch so that the St. Paul road would have a connection to Winnipeg at the border. This, too, was fraught with uncertainty. Smith's name was already being mentioned as a major shareholder in the company and it was impossible for him in Parliament to maintain the fiction that he was disinterested.

Almost simultaneously a new problem arose. The Minnesota legislature set a series of deadlines for the construction of the railway. Two sections had to be completed by the end of the year, otherwise everything would be forfeited.

There were other problems. The partners must haggle with Litchfield for his stock and simultaneously fight off the Northern Pacific, which was threatening to build its own line to the border. If either Litchfield or the rival railway knew how badly off they were, the game would be over.

The financing of the railway was left to Stephen while Hill moved in to build the line. He had two months in which to lay track from Melrose to Sauk Centre and he had to find rails, ties, rolling stock, and labourers in a hurry. By the time all this was assembled, Hill realized that he would have to lay at least a mile of track a day to make the deadline. He took charge himself, fighting mosquitoes, sunstroke, rattlesnakes, and dysentery, firing bosses on the spot if they could not maintain the mileage.

The Northern Pacific was threatening to build a parallel line to the Canadian border, but Hill was convinced his rivals were bluffing; it was his tactic to convince them that *he* was not. Hill declared he would start at once to survey a line all the way to the Yellowstone River and would ask Congress for half of the land grant that had been promised the Northern Pacific as far west as the Rockies. The rival railway knuckled under.

He met his first construction deadline with just twenty-four hours to spare and secured the vital land grant. He did not slacken his pace, for he had to finish the second stretch before December 1, 1878. He made his deadline well ahead of time and kept going, for he wanted to get the full railway operating as swiftly as possible. On November 11, he had the satisfaction of seeing his first through locomotive arrive at Emerson, Manitoba, from St. Paul.

Stephen meanwhile was having his own problems with the recalcitrant Litchfield. As long as he held the stock he could hamper the foreclosure proceedings and prevent the reorganization of the railroad company. The partners launched a legal suit against Litchfield to recover money that had been furnished to complete the main line and that he had converted to his own use; but the financier remained stubborn. In mid-January Stephen personally went to New York and managed to secure all the stock for a half-million dollars. There could no longer be conflicts between stockholders and bondholders since they were one and the same.

The partners borrowed their half million from the Bank of Montreal and moved for foreclosure. It was granted in March, 1879. In May, they formed a new company, the St. Paul, Minneapolis and Manitoba Railroad Company. In June, the new firm bought the bankrupt railway for less than seven million dollars – not in cash but in receiver's debentures and bonds. They floated a sixteen-million-dollar bond issue at once, some of which was used to pay back the Dutch. Then they sold the greater part of the land grant for $13,068,887. Already they had realized an incredible profit.

Hill wanted to create fifteen million dollars' worth of stock.

"Aren't you afraid that the capitalization will startle the public?" Smith ventured. "Isn't there some danger that we will be charged with watering the stock?"

"Well," Hill replied, "we have let the whole lake in already."

Three years after the stock was issued, each partner had made on paper a clear capital gain of more than eight millions. At that point – 1882 – they issued another two million dollars' worth of

R. B. Angus, in just 12 years, soared from $600-a-year clerk to general manager of the Bank of Montreal. Then Stephen seduced him into the St. Paul adventure – and the CPR.

stock to themselves and then, in 1883, they issued to themselves ten million dollars' worth of six per cent bonds for one million dollars – an additional profit of nine millions.

From the beginning, the railroad was fabulously successful. The grasshoppers vanished. The soil began to yield bumper crops. In 1880, the net earnings of the railroad exceeded the interest on the bonded debt by sixty per cent – an increase of one million dollars in a single year. The "Manitoba" road, as it came to be called, formed the nucleus of Jim Hill's Great Northern, the only transcontinental line in the United States that never went bankrupt or passed a dividend. Within two years its four promoters went from the brink of disaster to a position of almost unlimited wealth.

They had also become controversial figures in Canada. The deal with the Bank of Montreal was looked at askance by press, public, and shareholders, who asked pointed questions about the propriety of directors appropriating bank funds for a private venture. The criticisms increased when R. B. Angus resigned as the bank's general manager to take a job as manager of the new railway.

Meanwhile, Stephen and his colleagues were being attacked on another front. The new company, which operated the only trains from St. Paul to the Red River, had also taken over the Kittson Line and thus had a monopoly of all traffic to Winnipeg. That aroused the full ire of the Conservative press, to whom the name Donald Smith was still profanity.

Such was the climate in which the CPR Syndicate was eventually formed. All the controversy served to illuminate one fact: there was now available a remarkable group of successful men who had experience in both railway building and high finance. In the summer of 1880, the Macdonald government was looking for just such a group. It was John Henry Pope, the blunt minister of agriculture, who had first drawn his prime minister's attention to the St. Paul associates.

"Catch them," he said, "before they invest their profits."

"Capitalists of undoubted means"

FROM THE MOMENT that George Stephen's success became public property, he was transformed, whether he knew it or not, into a leading candidate to build the great railway. Long before Macdonald took power, Mackenzie had been seeking just such a man – a successful Canadian financier, in league with other Canadians of means, with practical experience in financing and constructing a profitable road. After Mackenzie's fall, Macdonald took up the vain search. Then, just when it seemed impossible to find such a man, an entire group of them suddenly popped out of nowhere, loaded with credentials.

In the fall of 1879, Macdonald, Tupper, and Tilley had set out for England to seek an Imperial guarantee to help build the road. It was a fruitless excursion. One English financier laughed aloud when he first heard of Macdonald's plan to raise a loan to build a railway across the half-frozen continent. Years later he related to Donald Smith his impressions at the time: " 'Good Heavens,' I thought, 'somebody will have to hold these Canadians back, or they will go plunging themselves into hopeless bankruptcy before they come of age.' I felt I would as soon invest in a Yankee 'wild-cat' mine."

By 1880, George Walkem, back again in power in British Columbia, was bluntly threatening secession. It was clear that the Canadian government would have to finance the railway on its own – and swiftly – if it was to keep the nation whole. The contract for the Yale-Kamloops section had to be let hurriedly as a sop to the British Columbians, and by the spring of 1880, to everyone's relief, Andrew Onderdonk was on the spot preparing to blast his way through the canyons of the Fraser.

But the Government determined to move slowly on the prairies. Its plan was to build a cheap railway; only two hundred miles would be placed under contract, and the construction would be as flimsy as possible. The steel would creep across the plains, year by year, a few miles ahead of advancing settlement. This was anticlimax after all the brave talk of a two-thousand-mile transcontinental line built to Union Pacific standards, and it did not sit well with Charles Tupper, who had learned of the incredible success of Stephen's group. In a memo of June 15 to the Privy Council he made reference to it. He recommended that "authority be given to negotiate with capitalists of undoubted means and who shall be required to give the most ample guarantee for the construction and operation of the line on such terms as will secure at the same time the rapid settlement of the public lands and the construction of the work." There was no doubt about who the capitalists of undoubted means were.

But even as the Cabinet met to consider the terms it was prepared to offer – a twenty-million-dollar subsidy and thirty million acres of prairie land – it was obvious that the atmosphere was changing and that other capitalists were sending feelers to Ottawa. The depression was at an end; the harvest had been a bumper one; the climate for railway building suddenly seemed better. There was word that the principals behind Andrew Onderdonk were interested. So was Thomas Brassey's firm, in England. And up from New York came a British peer, Lord Dunmore, a front man for Puleston, Brown and Company, a British financial house.

There was another offer before the government that June. It came in the name of Duncan McIntyre, who was engaged in building the Canada Central Railway from Ottawa to Lake Nipissing. It was no secret that his principals were Stephen and the other members of the St. Paul group. The arrangement was a marriage of convenience: McIntyre's line stopped where the CPR was to begin; the alliance could mean that the through route from Ottawa to the Pacific Ocean would be controlled by a single company.

The Stephen-McIntyre offer was a tempting one, especially as it was the only one that came from Canada, but it asked more than the Cabinet was prepared to grant: a subsidy of twenty-six and

THE ANNUAL BLOW-OUT!

Sir A. T. Galt. What! you here personally; am I not, then, capable of transacting the business of the Dominion as High Commissioner?
Sir John — The business? Oh, certainly, but we couldn't have our annual junketing by *proxy*, you know!

STARTLING AFFAIR IN LONDON!

A PROMISING YOUNG WOMAN OFFERED FOR SALE TO THE HIGHEST BIDDER.

Opposition newspapers spoofed the ministerial trips to London. Macdonald, Pope, and Tupper were seen as freeloaders on a junket. And the idea that the Canadian North West was being auctioned off cheaply was widely promulgated.

THE CANADIAN GANGES

Or, The Contemplated Sacrifice

The cry of "monopoly" was beginning to be heard as early as July, 1880, when this cartoon appeared. Macdonald's railway scheme was seen by the Liberals as a gigantic land grab to enrich friendly insiders. At this point he had not yet found a company to build the line.

THE CANADIAN GANGES;

OR, THE CONTEMPLATED SACRIFICE.

121

a half millions and a land grant of thirty-five million acres. The Syndicate would not bargain. Macdonald determined again to seek help from overseas. He, Tupper, and John Henry Pope sailed for England on July 10. The Prime Minister intended to see both Puleston, Brown and Company and Sir Henry Tyler, president of the Grand Trunk. As for McIntyre, he was sailing on the same ship and, as the mail steamer touched at Rimouski, a letter arrived for Macdonald from George Stephen, from his fishing camp. In it, Stephen managed very subtly to damn all other aspirants to the contract while obliquely selling his own group. He pointed out the difficulties of a large bonded indebtedness in which "the real responsibility is transferred from the Company to the people who may be induced to buy the bonds . . . while the projectors pocket a big profit at the start. . . ." He suggested that any English financial organization would indulge in this kind of manipulation at great risk to Canada.

His own plan, Stephen remarked, would have been to limit the borrowing to the smallest point. He would expect his profit to come from the growth of the country after the railroad was built. He had no intention of going to England; he would be outbid there. No English or American organization could do the job as well or as cheaply.

It was a letter dictated from a position of strength and confidence, written when Stephen was salmon fishing with Angus. In it, Stephen played Macdonald like an angler. He had thrust the bait towards him: the Minnesota experience, the desire to take risks, the special knowledge of Canadian conditions, the unquestioned ability of his group to do the job. Then, in a final paragraph, he pulled back slightly but left the bait dangling: "Although I am off the notion of the thing now, should anything occur on the other side to induce you to think that taking all things into consideration, our proposal is better upon the whole for the country than any offer you get in England, I might, on hearing from you, renew it and possibly in doing so reduce the land grant to some extent. . . ."

It was a hard letter for Macdonald to resist; moreover, the other candidates were dropping away. In August, the Onderdonk group passed: the Fraser Canyon was occupying all their efforts. In London, Macdonald and Tupper approached Sir Henry Tyler, the president of the Grand Trunk. Tupper reported his reaction: "If you'll cut off the portion of the railway from Thunder Bay to Nipissing I'll take up the project; but unless you do that, my shareholders will simply throw the prospectus into the wastepaper basket." There it was again: the terrible geography of North America conspiring against the efforts of the struggling nation to consolidate. Tupper replied that Canada could not consent to be for six months without any communication with Manitoba, the North West, and British Columbia except by a long detour through a foreign land. But the Grand Trunk's philosophy did not encompass a transcontinental nation; in the eyes of its absentee owners Canada was not much more than a way point on the route that led from the Atlantic to Chicago.

The interest from Puleston, Brown and Company, from the Onderdonk syndicate, and from the Brassey firm all came to nothing. That left Duncan McIntyre, who was also in London. Macdonald and McIntyre began a series of discussions; Sir John Rose, Canada's unofficial ambassador in London (he represented one of the smaller British financial houses), was present and George Stephen, in Canada, was at the end of the cable line. By September 4, the provisional agreement was made: twenty-five million dollars and twenty-five million acres it was to be. McIntyre returned to Canada at the end of the month and so did the Prime Minister, to whom Stephen immediately wrote. He had seen "the important document," he said, and he hoped there would be no difficulty in coming to terms on all points.

He and his colleagues had taken on a job that no one else in the United States, Britain, Europe, or Canada had been persuaded to tackle. It was a huge responsibility, and already in Montreal finan-

A friendly cartoon showed Sir John handling the Syndicate as Sindbad handled the Old Man of the Sea.

MONTREAL.—SIR JOHN A. MACDONALD EXPLAINING THE OUTLINES OF THE PACIFIC RAILWAY CONTRACT, AT THE HOCHELAGA STATION.

Wrote the Daily Witness: "Rarely have political and financial circles been so agitated over any public event."

cial circles there were murmurings that this time the reckless Stephen had bitten off more than he could chew.

"... my *friends* and my *enemies* agree," he wrote, "in affecting to think [that it] will be the ruin of us all."

And it almost was.

Success!

THERE WAS ENORMOUS EXCITEMENT when it was learned that Macdonald would be arriving at Hochelaga Station, Montreal, on the afternoon of September 27 with news of the railway contract. By late afternoon people of all classes were streaming towards the station. And when Macdonald appeared on the rear platform of his special car, every neck strained forward. The Government, Macdonald indicated, had secured financing for the great railway. He could not spell out the details, for these must first be presented to the Governor General. From this short speech in Montreal and interviews with friendly reporters, no one could have divined that the railway was to be built by a predominantly Canadian group. Macdonald made a good deal of the German element in the Syndicate, which was actually very small. It was considered politically important, however, to get token money from Germany, which would, it was hoped, divert the tide of immigration to Canada. The Prime Minister mentioned no names but in an interview talked about "a Syndicate composed of eminent capitalists from Frankfurt, Paris, London, New York and Canada."

COME TO DINNER!

Gordon B.—"Yes, but we *demand* to know what yon Hash is made of, before we go in!"

THE CANADIAN SPHYNX.

Since McIntyre had returned home on the same boat, his connection with the new syndicate was generally accepted. The United States element was played down to a point where the Conservative Winnipeg *Times* even denied its existence. But Macdonald was able to reassure the cheering crowd at the station on several points: the new syndicate would finish the line in ten years, it would not build the easy portions first or save the hard ones for the last, and, finally, the road would not cost as much as Sir Hugh Allan had offered to build it for in 1872. Moreover, it would not cost the taxpayers a cent: the sale of western land would pay for it all.

Almost as soon as the train puffed out of the station the great debate over the Syndicate, as it was now called, began. By October, the composition of the new group had leaked out even though the actual contract was not signed and the specific details had still to be worked out. The members were George Stephen and Duncan McIntyre of Montreal; John S. Kennedy of New York; James J. Hill and Richard B. Angus of St. Paul; Sir John Rose's old firm of Morton, Rose and Company, London; and the German-French financial syndi-

cate of Kohn, Reinach and Company. There was one name conspicuous by its absence – that of Donald A. Smith. He was, of course, to be a major shareholder, but since his name was an obscenity to the entire Conservative Party there was no way in which he could be publicly connected with the enterprise.

It had been a bad year for Smith. Following his successful re-election to the constituency of Selkirk in 1878, a petition was filed charging that the seat had been secured through bribery. Smith ran again in a by-election in September, 1880, but his connection with the St. Paul and Manitoba railway told against him and he was defeated. That marked his retirement from politics.

The result was scarcely known when Smith suffered a second blow to his ego: the knowledge that he could not be publicly associated with the greatest of all national enterprises. Nonetheless, his presence as a silent partner was assumed by both press and public and a great to-do resulted.

The usually imperturbable Smith dropped his mask briefly and gave Stephen a rare, private glimpse of his ambitions. Stephen wrote to Macdonald that

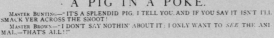

"A PIG IN A POKE."

MASTER BUNTIN:—"IT'S A SPLENDID PIG, I TELL YOU, AND IF YOU SAY IT ISN'T I'LL SMACK YER ACROSS THE SNOOT!
MASTER BROWN:—"I DON'T SAY NOTHIN' ABOUT IT; I ONLY WANT TO *SEE* THE ANI MAL.—THAT'S ALL!"

WAITING FOR THE CAT!

Smith was "excited almost to a craze and so troublesome that I do not care if he does withdraw though his money and co-operation would be useful, so would his knowledge and influence in the North West." Smith did not want to withdraw his money but he did want recognition, and so the fuss continued.

The inability to deal swiftly and conclusively with matters he considered to be purely business had already begun to torment Stephen in this, his first venture into the periphery of politics. The wretched contract seemed to be taking weeks to complete, and after it was signed Parliament would have to consider it before any company could be formed and the actual work of construction could be begun. He began to fire off letters to Macdonald urging speed. He was almost breathless with impatience, but nothing moved as quickly as he hoped. He had expected to embark for London at the end of October to meet Tupper. He had to postpone his sailing date.

Among other things, the status of the Pembina Branch had to be ironed out. Stephen wanted a monopoly and in mid-October he made it clear that he

was prepared to cancel the entire contract if he did not get it. The Pembina Branch would have to subsidize the lonely line that ran through the Precambrian desertland. Macdonald was reluctant for he saw the political disadvantages, but he was caught between two unyielding points of view. He must have an all-Canadian railway; to get it he would have to give in to the importunate Stephen who feared "strangulation in the hands of our Chicago rivals hanging over our heads."

Stephen had never talked so toughly before and only Macdonald knew, perhaps, how hard a bargain he was driving. For this was the basis of the "Monopoly Clause" in the CPR contract, which would turn the West against the railway and against the East and lay the basis for almost a decade of bitterness before it was voluntarily revoked. The impotence of the Manitobans in the matter of building their own railway lines became, in that province, a *cause célèbre* which was to lead to a long-term disaffection towards Ottawa and towards the railway itself. Macdonald could see that clause returning to haunt him – returning to haunt the nation. But there was nothing he could do.

125

The Great Debate

THE CONTRACT was finally signed on October 21 and the battle lines were drawn for the greatest parliamentary struggle since the Pacific Scandal. This was the most important Canadian document since the British North America Act and one of the most important of all time, for it was the instrument by which the nation broke out of the prison of the St. Lawrence lowlands. It represented a continuation of the traditional partnership between the private and the public sectors, which would continue to be a fact of Canadian life whenever transportation and communication were involved. The geography of the nation dictated that the government be in the transportation business – either fully or in a kind of working partnership with private industry.

Apart from the all-important subsidies of twenty-five million dollars and twenty-five million acres of land, the chief provisions of the CPR contract, drawn up by the same J. J. C. Abbott who had once been Sir Hugh Allan's solicitor, were these:

The government would turn over to the company, upon completion, all the lines built with public money.

The government would waive duty on the import of all railway materials, from steel rails to telegraph cable.

The free land would be taken in alternate sections of 640 acres each from a strip of land forty-eight miles wide running along the right of way between Winnipeg and the Rockies, but the company could reject any land "not fairly fit for settlement." The company could issue up to twenty-five million dollars' worth of land grant bonds, secured against this acreage. It must deposit one-fifth of the bonds with the government as security, but it could if it wished sell the rest of the bonds, as the land was earned by construction, in the proportion of one dollar per acre.

The land would be exempt from taxation for a twenty-year period or until sold. Stations, grounds, workshops, buildings, yards, etc., would be exempt forever and the land for these would also be provided free.

For twenty years no other line could be constructed south of the CPR to run within fifteen miles of the United States border.

The company, in return, promised to complete the road within ten years and forever after to operate it "efficiently." That adverb was significant since it relieved the CPR of future responsibility for unprofitable aspects of its operations – passenger service, for example.

The Ottawa *Free Press* figured out that the Syndicate was being handed a gift amounting to a cash equivalent of $261,500,000. Stephen's private estimate was considerably lower, but he neglected to count such items as freedom from taxation, duty-free imports, and free land for company property. He figured the value of the 710 miles of completed government line at thirty-two millions and the cost of the work to be completed by the company at forty-five millions. The Syndicate had thirty millions in hand, including the cash subsidy, and could raise fifteen millions from its own resources. But this was a wildly optimistic piece of reckoning, as future events were to prove.

The press attacked on several fronts. Even such loyal western papers as the Winnipeg *Times* found it hard to stomach the monopoly clause, especially in the light of the experience with the Kittson Line's exorbitant rates. The eastern Opposition press hit hard at the monopoly clause and also the proposition regarding duty-free construction materials; after all, Macdonald's victory had been secured by the promise of increased protection. Nor did the press believe the Syndicate would actually commence building the Lake Superior section. But more than anything else, the papers harped upon the American influence in "the St. Paul Syndicate," as its opponents called it.

These misgivings only reflected the doubts and, in some cases, the shock of Macdonald's own followers. Some said the contract would be the ruin of

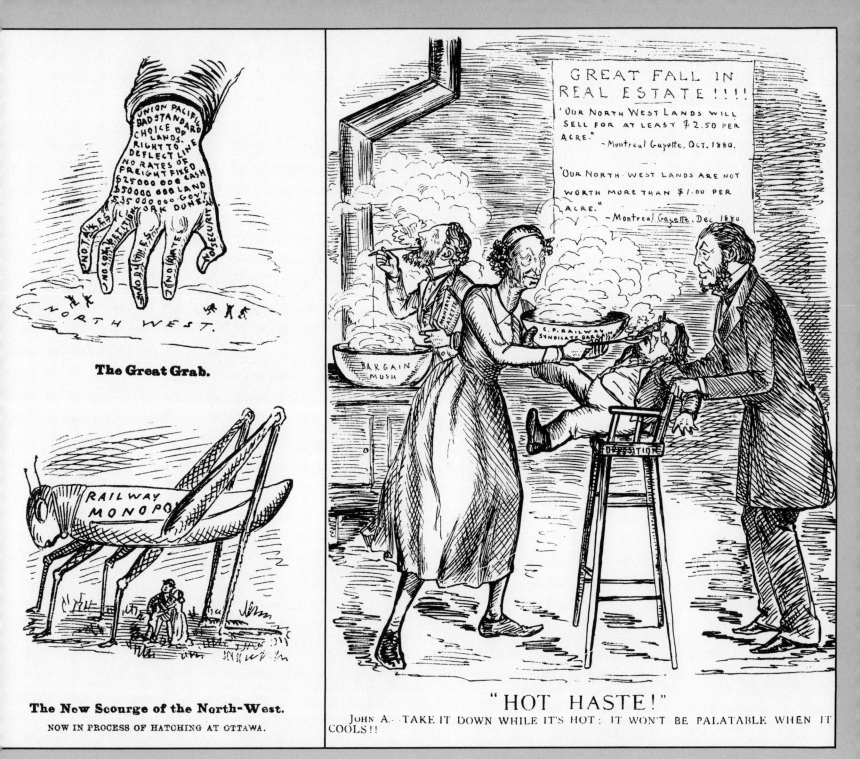

After the details of the railway contract were laid before Parliament, the Grit press was in full cry, renewing its charges of Monopoly and Land Grab. In the cartoon above, Tupper holds a wriggling Blake as Macdonald forces him to swallow the Syndicate bargain. At the stove is the editor of the Tory Montreal Gazette.

the country; the obligations were so great that the credit of Canada would be destroyed. Others saw in the contract the ruin of the party; an alarmed nation would turn against the Tories. Already some papers were coining slogans like "the Pacific Swindle" and "the Pacific Disgrace." It was an indication that the great Canadian debate, which had been going on since 1871, was about to reach its immediate climax. Was the country prepared to stand behind this first great national undertaking? How much did the nation care whether it was united by these costly bands of steel? Was the price too high? Was the bargain a fair one? Could the country afford it? Was it just another piece of railway jobbery (as the Grits suspected) or a great nation-building device (as the Tories proclaimed)? Could the opponents of the great railway prolong the debate long enough to rally public opinion, as they had in 1873, and force the Government to climb down? Would Macdonald's own supporters stand behind him or would they again fall away like dying leaves? The battle lines were drawn. As the opening session approached, Macdonald was reasonably confident of victory. But, unlike the impetuous and optimistic Stephen, he knew the fight would be long and consuming.

He had called the session to open on December 9, 1880 – two months in advance in order to dispose of the contract before the construction season began. The Prime Minister was ill and so was Mackenzie, the latter an unhappy ghost in the bulky shadow of Edward Blake, who had, in effect, overthrown him as Liberal leader. Blake was outraged by the contract, which he considered a national scandal, and he meant to oust the Government on the strength of it, as he had seven years before. He was convinced that he held in his hands a political issue as explosive as the Pacific Scandal. What he lacked in parliamentary power he felt he could make up in rising public wrath over such a massive giveaway to private capitalists.

The Opposition tactic was to talk forever, to speak at every stage of the debate, to propose amendments at all points, to divide the House at every opportunity, and to portray themselves as the saviours of the country. They would paper the nation with tracts, engulf it with oratory, rouse it with mass meetings, and expose Macdonald's attempt to ride rough-shod over Parliament with his steamroller majority. Blake believed that history would repeat itself, that he could force an election and carry the issue of the contract to the country. If that happened, he had no doubt that he would win.

The debate, which began in early December and ran until the end of January, was one of the longest in all the history of the Canadian parliament. During that period, more than one million words were uttered in the House of Commons on the subject of the Canadian Pacific Railway contract – more words by far than there are in both the Old and the New Testaments. Though the proceedings were not immune from personal invective, there was a very real sense of occasion. Tupper called it "the most important question that has ever engaged the attention of this Parliament" and speaker after speaker on both sides echoed these words. They realized, all of them, that once the contract was committed, the small, cramped Canada they knew could never again be the same. Some felt the nation would be beggared and ruined, others that it would blossom forth as a new entity. All understood that a turning point had been reached.

Meanwhile, the misgivings among Macdonald's followers had to be met head-on. This became Tupper's task. The party caucused in the railway committee room on Saturday, December 11. Tupper let them talk, and they talked all day. Then, with a forceful speech he brought them round. His most telling argument was political: the construction of the railway would give the party such *éclat* throughout the nation that they would be rendered invincible in the next election. They gave him, finally, a unanimous vote of confidence.

The debate began on December 14 and by the twenty-first the Opposition was itching for a Christmas recess. It needed as much time as possible to

Seasonal references to the contract debate enlivened Grip's pages during the Yuletide recess. The CPR Syndicate was portrayed receiving a treeful of gifts from an accommodating Tory government.

The following week, Bengough returned to the theme. As usual, Macdonald and Tupper are the objects of his gibes, with the contentious details of the contract clearly spelled out.

THE SYNDICATE CHRISTMAS TREE,
OR, THE TIME FOR GIVING THINGS AWAY.

THE CHARITY SEASON.
ON AN ERRAND OF "GENEROSITY!"

take the case to the people through public meetings and to mount petitions. But Macdonald did not intend to give them any more time than necessary. The House did not adjourn until December 23. It was due to resume on January 5. That left Blake with less than two weeks in which to rouse the nation. The Conservatives caucused again as the House adjourned. Macdonald's following had grown alarmingly shaky. A new attempt was made to persuade the Prime Minister to modify the contract terms. Again it was Tupper who, in a three-hour speech to the dissenters, held them, for the moment, in line.

Meanwhile, the Opposition was in full cry across the country. Blake's speech in Parliament was printed as a pamphlet and the Liberals were smothering the nation with it. The Conservatives replied with a similar blizzard of tracts reprinting Tupper's speech. Christmas or not, every Liberal member was under orders to call a series of public meetings, to attack the Syndicate and the contract, and to force through a series of resolutions to be forwarded to Ottawa. Petitions were to be circulated on the same theme so that hundreds of thousands of signatures would fall like a storm upon the capital.

The speaker most in demand was Edward Blake. Tupper offered to attend Blake's meetings if Blake would grant him half the time for speaking, an offer which Blake declined. Tupper then detailed a man to attend every Blake meeting to announce that he, Tupper, would reply to Blake, point by point, the following night, and the dramatic spectacle occurred of Blake racing from city to city, in one politician's words, "pursued by the Honourable Minister of Railways as though he were an avenging fury."

It made for exciting holiday fare in an era devoid of electronic entertainment and both Blake's and Tupper's meetings were jammed. But it was becoming apparent that the great wave of public opprobrium that Blake had expected was largely non-existent. Though there were many misgivings, the people manifestly wanted the railway question settled. They had been hearing about it for almost

129

a decade. In 1871 it had been a new and frightening idea. Ten years later they had come to accept it as a probability.

Nor were they put off by the cries of scandal. If there was scandal, the people wanted proof, and there was no proof. The Syndicate might be controversial but anyone could see that it was possessed of the kind of boldness that, after a decade of vacillation, could only be refreshing. A total of 266 petitions finally arrived at Ottawa. They contained 29,913 signatures, scarcely the avalanche that Blake and his followers had envisioned. Moreover, a suspicious number seemed to be in the same handwriting. "Generally speaking," the *Bystander* reported, "the attempts of the Opposition leaders to fire the heart of the people were not very successful. . . ."

But Blake had no intention of giving up. He had almost a month left to fight and one more major card to play.

Blake versus Macdonald again

EARLY IN JANUARY, as the session began, there was a kind of insistent buzzing that something big was being planned: the Syndicate, the contract, and the Government were about to be challenged in a dramatic fashion.

Macdonald had a reasonably clear idea of what his adversaries were contemplating, but he was more concerned with the troubles he faced from his own supporters. From Halifax came word that several leading Tories were expressing doubts about the Government's policy. The Premier of Quebec was in town trying to sell the votes of his federal followers in exchange for a fancy price for the Quebec-owned railway. Macdonald had to put him off with evasions. The Manitoba members intimated that they could not support the bill unless it were modified; Macdonald did not yield. He was sixty-seven years old and very ill; the Opposition

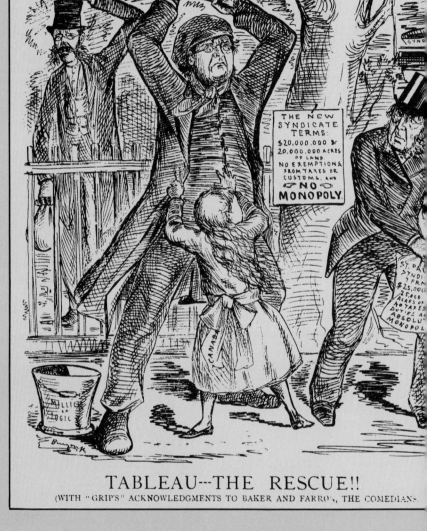

TABLEAU---THE RESCUE!!
(WITH "GRIP'S" ACKNOWLEDGMENTS TO BAKER AND FARRON, THE COMEDIANS.

When the new syndicate was announced by the Liberal Party, Grip made use of a popular vaudeville turn to cast Edward Blake in the role of hero protecting Canada from a villainous Charles Tupper. The cartoon appeared three days after the details were announced but before Tupper laid them before the house.

ETWEEN THE D—— AND THE DEEP SEA!

*The following week Tupper is portrayed as the Devil himself,
bent on destroying the Conservative Party by rejecting
the "infinitely better terms." But Tupper had already told the
Tory caucus that by passing the controversial contract
the party would ensure itself of another generation of power.*

papers were slyly insinuating that he was drunk again, while some of his friends feared that he had cancer. But ill or not, he intended to stand firm. There would be no compromise. When the vote came he meant to regard it as a vote of confidence. Let his supporters betray him at their peril! If the bill failed to pass, he intended to resign.

On January 12, the ailing Mackenzie, who had been absent from his seat for all of that session, made his first speech as the bill was read for the first time. He referred to "public reports that eminent men on both sides of politics are, at this moment, preparing offers to the Government of a much more favourable character than those that are now before it." This was the Opposition's final tactic – to mount a rival syndicate, which would offer the Government a much better proposition divested of all the objectionable clauses in the original contract and at a cheaper price. On the face of it the gambit was irresistible.

Even as Mackenzie spoke, the new syndicate was meeting in Toronto to draw up a tender to be sent post-haste to Ottawa. The chairman and president was Sir William Howland, a former lieutenant-governor of Ontario and a prominent Liberal. The new syndicate was prepared to ask for only twenty-two million acres of land and twenty-two million dollars in cash. They rejected the monopoly clause and wanted no exemptions from the tariff on railway materials. Nor would they ask for exemptions from taxation on either land or railway property. On the matter of the construction of the line they were equally obliging. They would be willing to postpone the building of both the Lake Superior and the mountain sections and would cheerfully release the government from the liability of building the difficult Fraser River section. They would also be willing to construct a line to Sault Ste Marie to connect with the U.S. railhead in return for a bonus of twelve thousand dollars a mile.

Such was the Opposition's ploy – to paint the new syndicate as totally non-partisan and totally

131

businesslike, and to convince the country that all the unpalatable clauses in the contract were unnecessary.

Macdonald, weak though he was, knew what he must do. The talk about the new syndicate was having its effect. It had raised the morale of the Opposition and it had caused new murmurings among his own followers in both House and Senate. Until now he had taken only a minor part in the debate, leaving the infighting to Tupper. He saw that he must kill the new syndicate – slay it so thoroughly that no man would ever dare to mention it again. He must lay bare its weaknesses, expose the dangers that it posed to the country, and then assassinate it with ridicule.

He rose on Monday, January 17, as soon as Tupper laid the new tender before the House. Blake, he knew, would follow the next day, with one of those earnest orations for which he was so well known and for which he was preparing himself with his usual meticulous labour. There was a strange feeling of repertory about it all: the same chamber and the same adversaries of 1873, the same charges of scandal, corruption, and dictatorship, the same feeling of age and infirmity, and the same subject – the railway. In a sense he was back where he had started, fighting for the contract as he had fought eight years before. But it was not quite the same; this time Macdonald had no apologies to make.

He had to be helped to his feet, but his words carried all the force of a pile driver: the road *would* be constructed. "Notwithstanding all the wiles of the Opposition and the flimsy arrangement which it has concocted, the road is going to be built and proceeded with vigorously, continuously, systematically and successfully" – the adverbs fell like hammer blows – "until completion and the fate of Canada will then, as a Dominion, be sealed."

Now the time had come for him to scupper that "flimsy arrangement," the new proposal. Seven of the signatories to the document, Macdonald pointed out, were disappointed or defeated Liberal candidates in former elections. "No man, be he ever so simple, who is fit to be elected, can read else on these papers than that it is a political trick. . . ."

He had to pause for a moment. "I am speaking at some disadvantage," he said, "because I am not well. I will make myself heard."

He gathered his strength and continued: the joker in the pack was the optional clause in the proposed contract which suggested that the new syndicate had no real intention of building anything but the easiest section of the railroad. The first clause, Macdonald showed, did away with the Superior section, the second provided for a rail line to Sault Ste Marie and the United States, the third provided for the government to abandon the British Columbia section, and the fourth gave up building anything west of the Rockies. The scheme, then, was nothing more than "an impudent offer to build the prairie section and to do it by means of political friends." Connecting with the Yankee railways at the Sault would be "to the utter ruin of the great policy under which the Dominion of Canada has been created, the utter ruin of our hopes of being a great nation. . . .

"They would be relieved from running any portion of the road that would not pay. Canada might whistle for these connections . . . but the people would . . . see that the colonies would gradually be severed from each other; and we should become a bundle of sticks, as we were before, without a binding cord, and then we should fall, helpless, powerless and aimless, into the hands of the neighbouring republic."

He fought next for the monopoly clause; and here all his passionate distrust of the American colossus came to the fore. The Rhine, he said, had a miserable, wretched end, "being lost in the sands of the approaches to the sea; and such would be the fate of the Canadian Pacific Railway if we allowed it to be bled by subsidiary lines, feeding foreign wealth and increasing foreign revenue by carrying off our trade until, before we arrived at the terminal points of Ontario and of Montreal, it would be so depleted that it would almost die of inanition."

THE SYNDICATE GIANT.

FEE, FUM, FI, FO,
I SMELL THE BLOOD OF ONTARIO.

BE HE ALIVE OR BE HE DEAD
I'LL GRIND HIS BONES TO MAKE MY BREAD.

To portray the Syndicate, Bengough invented a hydra-headed giant wearing an enormous tam-o'-shanter. The faces, left to right, are those of Angus, Stephen, and Duncan McIntyre.

What chances, Macdonald asked, would an infant country of four million have against the whole of the United States' capitalists? "The road would become shrunken, shrunken, shrunken, until it fell an easy prey to this ring. We cannot afford to run such a risk."

He was almost finished, but he wanted to nail down in the clearest possible language his vision of the railway and his vision of the nation. He wanted, he said, an arrangement "which will satisfy all the loyal, legitimate aspirations, which will give us a great and united, a rich and improving, developing Canada, instead of making us tributary to American bondage, to American tolls, to American freights, to all the little tricks and big tricks that American railways are addicted to for the purpose of destroying our road."

He had spoken for two hours and a half and he had made his point. The *Canadian Illustrated News*, which was less partisan than the daily press, reported that his criticism of the new syndicate "was so searching that he practically killed it, even in the eyes of the Opposition members themselves."

The following day the Commons got down to business again. Blake had been waiting for this moment. On this afternoon of January 18, he was prepared to deliver another five-hour speech, crammed with facts and figures to prove why the contract was a disaster and why, indeed, the whole concept of the Canadian Pacific Railway was, as in his view it had always been, insane.

On almost every point Blake was convincing. The idea of the railway *was* insane, if you thought in terms of an undivided continent; it *was* perfect madness to try to punch it through that sea of mountains and across those rocky Precambrian wastes. Immigration would not come as swiftly as the Government implied, and events were to prove Blake right on that point. The land sales would not pay for the railway. It would be easier and cheaper for everybody to go west by way of the United States, at least in the foreseeable future. Logic, then, was on Blake's side.

The key to Macdonald's argument was emotion: the only way Canada could hold onto British Columbia – and, thus, the land in between – was to build the railway; that was the point he continued to hammer home. British Columbia would not wait, or at least that was what the British Columbians were saying. Meanwhile, the reorganized Northern Pacific was creeping west again; with no parallel line on the other side of the border, this great artery would drain off all the commerce of British North America.

Blake's speech was a model of logical argument. On a previous memorable occasion he had used earnestness accompanied by pitiless fact to bring Macdonald down. In this contest between logic and passion, would logic win again? Blake was a man of ideals with a strong political philosophy, but he had little imagination. Macdonald, on the other hand – a practical politician, whose only real philosophy was expediency – was endowed with a lively imagination. That, really, was where Blake foundered in the matter of the railway. He could not see the new Canada as Macdonald could see it, for Canada in the seventies was an imaginative dream more than a nation. Blake lacked both the imagination and the daring (he thought of it as recklessness) to lead in the development of that dream. If Macdonald's political gamble had failed, then Blake might have been hailed as a Cassandra and have gone on to become the leader of his country – the very epitome of a sober, sensible, frugal Canadian prime minister. But that was not to be.

The dawn of the new Canada

THE EXHAUSTING DRAMA was drawing to its close but it was not quite over. It was not until January 25 that word spread that Parliament was to see the end of the longest debate in history. Macdonald meant to force a vote even if he had to keep the House in session all night.

"TAKING THE BULL BY THE HORNS,"
OR THE "NOBLE ATTITUDE" OF THE OPPOSITION.

Much was made of the Government's enormous majority which allowed it to bulldoze its opponents, but the country at large clearly wanted the railway built, in spite of some misgivings over certain contract clauses.

THE OPPOSITION KNIFE-ACT.

PROFESSOR BLAKE.—I WILL KEEP *THIS* KNIFE TO FINISH HIM WITH IN '83.

By the time this cartoon appeared, the CPR bill had passed its first reading. Blake's twenty-four amendments failed to ruffle Macdonald; they were little more than political gambits. The Liberals' only hope was that the Tory railway policy would cause the party's defeat in the next election. That explains Macdonald's later reluctance to countenance any further aid to the company, whose executives were invariably portrayed as canny, grasping Scotsmen.

Finally, in the small hours of the morning, the time came for a division on the first amendment to the resolution offered by the Opposition leader. The amendment was typical of Blake, being the longest ever offered in Parliament to that moment. It covered three and a half pages of Hansard's small type and raised fifty-three distinct objections to the proposed legislation.

This was the moment of truth. Macdonald had told his wavering supporters in the bluntest terms that if the bill was lost the Government would resign immediately and they would be forced to go to the country with all the opprobrium of a parliamentary defeat hanging over them. The threat was enough: the first amendment was defeated by a vote of 140 to 54. The House adjourned that morning just before six.

It was not yet over. The Opposition had twenty-three more amendments and it proposed to move them all. The galleries were thin the following day;

all the old habitués were asleep. The House reconvened at three and sat until eleven that night. Five more amendments were defeated.

The long nights and the gruelling verbal skirmishes were taking their toll. Macdonald, Mackenzie, Tupper, and Pope were all seriously ill. Amor de Cosmos was ill. Keeler of Northumberland East was ill. Bannerman of South Renfrew was ill. Others, the press reported, were breaking down under the strain. And still Macdonald drove them on. On January 26, he decided that, though there be a thousand amendments, the first reading of the bill should be voted on before the sitting ended.

He kept his word. The house sat from three until six, recessed for dinner, and then remained in session for twelve hours without a break while amendment after amendment was offered and voted down. A kind of gay lunacy settled over the House of Commons. The bitterness drained away, and as each amendment was offered it was greeted with cheers by both sides. The speeches were mercifully short but even these were interrupted by whistles and desk-pounding. Paper pellets were flung about and caps placed over the heads of slumbering members. As night gave way to morning, a choir was organized and the members began plaintively to sing "Home, Sweet Home."

Finally, the last amendment was voted down and the main divisions on the two resolutions – the first on the land and the second on the cash subsidy – were carried. In Tupper's absence, Macdonald introduced the bill founded on these resolutions respecting the Canadian Pacific Railway. Not until it was read for the first time did he allow the weary House to adjourn. By then it was eight in the morning.

There were two more readings to go through before the bill could become law. The first of these was a clause by clause consideration of the full text and this was bound to take time. Even the Governor General's fancy-dress ice carnival on January 31 could not lure Macdonald from his duties in the House. At 12.30 that night, while Lord Lorne and his costumed guests were skating under the glare of two locomotive headlights beneath flag-draped arches, festoons of evergreens, and Chinese lanterns – "an overhanging panorama of grotesque and fanciful figures" – the bill at last passed its second reading.

The following day, February 1, just before midnight, the bill was given its final reading. The formality of Senate assent was still needed, but it was now as good as law and the Canadian Pacific Railway Company was a reality.

Finally, it was over. It had been ten years, almost to the month, since the subject of a railway to the Pacific had first been broached to the House of Commons. For all concerned it had been a desperate, frustrating, and often humiliating decade; yet it had also been exhilarating. Macdonald was ill with fatigue, stomach trouble, and nervous tension, but he was triumphant. The railway, which had hurled him into the abyss of despond, had now hoisted him to the pinnacle of victory. It had consumed many of the men who were closely allied with it. Mackenzie was a political has-been. Blake was in retreat. Sir Hugh Allan had never lived down the events of the Pacific Scandal. Fleming had been driven back to England. Moberly had quit his profession. Marcus Smith hung grimly on but in a minor post. Joseph Whitehead was out of business. In every instance, the railway had changed and twisted their futures.

Far out beyond the Red River, the prairie land lay desolate under its blanket of shifting snow, still bereft of settlers. In just twelve months, as Macdonald knew, all that must change. Before the present parliament was dissolved, cities yet unnamed would have their birth out on those windswept plains, passes yet uncharted would ring to the sound of axe and sledge. Within one year an army of twelve thousand men would be marshalled to invade the North West. Other armies would follow: ten thousand along the Fraser, twelve thousand attacking the mountain crevices, fifteen thousand blackening the face of the Shield. Nothing would ever be the same again. The tight little Canada of Confederation was already obsolete; the new Canada of the railway was about to be born. There was not a single man, woman, or child in the nation who would not in some way be affected, often drastically, by the tortured decision made in Ottawa that night.

The future would not be easy and all the cries of dismay that had echoed down the corridors of the seventies would return to haunt the eighties. The granite shield of Canada had to be cracked open to let the railway through. The mountain barrier must be breasted and broken. There would be grief a plenty in the years to come – frustration, pain, hard decisions and, as always, bitter opposition.

But the great adventure was launched. Tomorrow would take care of itself, as it always did. At last the dream was about to become a reality. The triumph lay just a few short years ahead.

In April, the Canadian Illustrated News *ran this cartoon of school breaking up, "with faithful portraits of the good boys who got the prizes." With Macdonald, left to right: Tilley, Langevin, Stephen, McIntyre. Background (left): Cartwright, Laurier, Blake, and Mackenzie. Lord Lorne, the Governor General, presides.*

From a cracked glass plate, made in 1882, a platoon of Van Horne's mighty army is immortalized as the grade begins its record sweep across the plains.

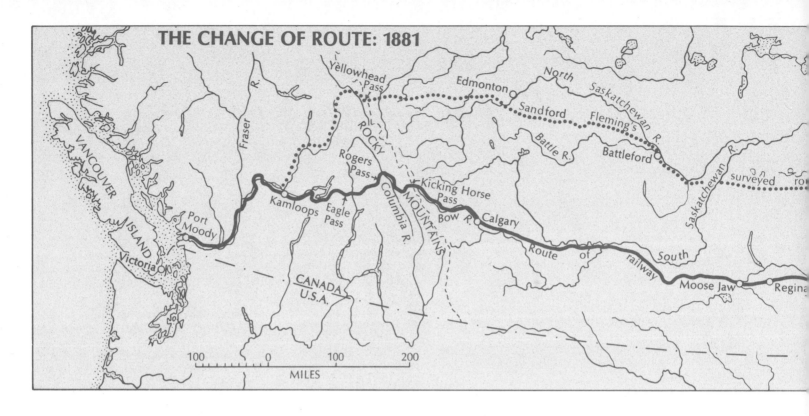

The following labels appear on the map: Yellowhead Pass, Edmonton, North Saskatchewan R., Sandford Fleming's, Fraser R., ROCKY MOUNTAINS, Battle R., Battleford, surveyed ro, Rogers Pass, Kicking Horse Pass, Columbia R., Kamloops, Eagle Pass, Bow R., Calgary, Saskatchewan R., Port Moody, VANCOUVER ISLAND, Victoria, CANADA U.S.A., Route of railway, South, Moose Jaw, Regina

100   0   100   200
MILES

The steel moves west

WHEN THE GREAT DEBATE came to an end, Ottawa settled into a kind of doldrums. The glittering social season burned itself out, the session limped to its close, and the capital reverted to the status of a backwoods lumber village. When the young governor general, Lord Lorne, arrived to prorogue Parliament on March 21, there was scarcely anybody left in the House.

In contrast to the lassitude of the capital, Winnipeg, a thousand miles to the northwest, was in a turmoil. Within a fortnight of its formation, the Canadian Pacific Railway Company had established a headquarters there. Fourteen new locomotives were on their way – all samples from various makers in the United States, sent up on trial for the company's inspection. Contracts had already been let for half a million railroad ties, six thousand telegraph poles, and fifty thousand feet of pilings. Mountains of timber were heaped in the yards waiting to be moved to the end of track. The great triple-decker construction cars were rolling westward and workmen were pouring into the city by the hundreds from Montreal and Minneapolis. Five hundred teams of horses had been hired to move construction supplies. A trickle of new settlers was already seeping through town.

The railway builders estimated that they had close to two thousand miles of trunk-line to construct. It could be divided into three sections:

In the East, some six hundred and fifty miles between Callander on Lake Nipissing and Fort William at the head of Lake Superior, all heavy construction across the ridges of the Precambrian Shield.

On the prairies, some nine hundred miles from Winnipeg across the rolling grasslands to the Rocky Mountains.

In the West, some four hundred and fifty miles of difficult mountain construction.

In addition, the railway company was to be given, as a gift, some seven hundred miles of line being built as a public work: the 65-mile Pembina

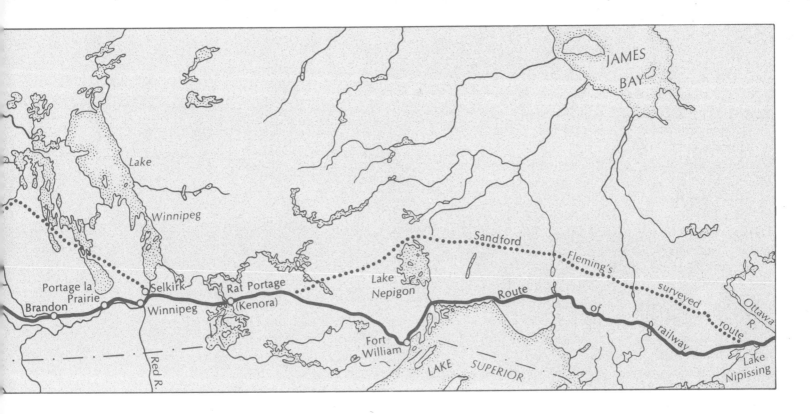

Branch from Winnipeg to the Minnesota border, already completed; the line between Fort William and Selkirk – 433 miles long – still under construction; and the 215-mile stretch that led from Savona's Ferry on Kamloops Lake through the Fraser Canyon to Port Moody on Pacific tidewater.

The hustle in Winnipeg, that spring of 1881, was in sharp contrast to the vacillations of the previous year. Though the government had let contracts for two hundred miles beginning in 1879, only about seventy miles had actually been laid to Portage la Prairie. This section of the line, which the CPR purchased from the government, was virtually useless; the company determined to rebuild it entirely and relocate most of it. A different mood had settled upon railway construction in Canada. For the first time in the long, tangled history of the Canadian Pacific, the rails were being laid under the supervision of the same men who would eventually operate the road; it would not profit them to cut corners.

On May 2, 1881, the company was ready to begin. At Portage la Prairie the navvies waited at the end of track, like soldiers poised on the start line, until the company's chief engineer, General Thomas Lafayette Rosser, ceremonially turned the first sod. Then the horses, the men, and the machines moved forward and began to fashion the great brown serpent that would creep steadily west, day after day, towards its rendezvous with the mountains.

Meanwhile in St. Paul, Minnesota, a handful of men was altering the shape and condition of the North West. Their decision affected the lives of tens of thousands of Canadians and ensured the establishment close to the border of cities that otherwise might not have existed for another generation, if ever. It affected aspects of Canadian life as varied as the tourist trade and the wheat economy. In addition, it gave the railway company something very close to absolute control over the destinies of scores of embryo communities along the right of way.

The new route was determined by three members of the four-man executive committee of the CPR – George Stephen, Jim Hill, and Richard Angus.

141

Only Duncan McIntyre was absent, that day in St. Paul. The catalyst was John Macoun, the same botanist who had accompanied Fleming and Grant on their trek from ocean to ocean a decade before.

Macoun had come to St. Paul at Hill's behest because he was familiar with the southern prairie. As a result of that original trip he had become enamoured of the North West. In 1879 and again in 1880, the Canadian government sent him on further explorations and by then he had become convinced that the southern plains were not the desert that almost everybody thought them to be.

In spreading this doctrine Macoun was flying in the face of previous scientific reports by Palliser and Hind. His estimates of arable prairie soil were far in excess of anyone else's and helped confirm John A. Macdonald's conviction that profits from the sale of prairie land could underwrite the cost of the railway subsidy – a telling point with Parliament as well as public.

How could one explorer have seen the plains as a lush paradise while another saw them as a desert? How was it that Macoun found thick grasses and sedges where Palliser reported cracked dry ground? The answer lies in the unpredictability of the weather in what came to be called Palliser's Triangle. Palliser saw the land under normal to dry conditions; Macoun visited it during the wettest decade in more than a century. If the former was too pessimistic, the latter was too enthusiastic.

Macoun was brought to St. Paul to convince the Syndicate that a more southerly route to the Rockies was practicable. It did not take the voluble naturalist long to effect that conversion. The three old friends together with the CPR's new chief engineer, General Rosser, a one-time Confederate officer, sat around a table littered with maps of the Canadian North West while a torrent of words poured from Macoun's lips. After he was finished, a brief discussion followed. Then Hill, according to the botanist's own account, slammed his hands on the table.

"Gentlemen," he said, "we will cross the prairie

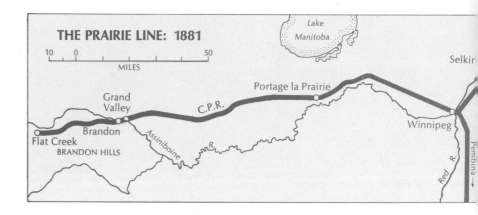

and go by the Bow Pass [Kicking Horse], if we can get that way." With that statement, the work of ten years was abandoned and the immediate future of the North West altered.

Few single decisions by a private corporation have had such widespread repercussions. As a result, the most spectacular mountain scenery in North America was opened up: Banff, Lake Louise, Glacier, and Yoho parks were all by-products of Jim Hill's table-pounding. But so were the costly locomotives that had to be harnessed to haul the trains over the Great Divide, and so were the miles of snowsheds in the Selkirks and the costly diversions of the spiral and Connaught tunnels. From the company's point of view, it remains to this day a toss-up whether or not the change of route was really an economically sensible decision. Who can say how important the mountain scenery was to a once-profitable passenger trade? Who can estimate whether or not the profits on new townsites (for the road would now pass through virgin territory) and the advantages of a shorter line cancelled out the increased construction costs and additional carrying charges over the mountain peaks?

From the point of view of the nation, a better guess can be hazarded. It is probable that the switch to the southern route was one factor in delaying the settlement of the North West for twenty years and thus partially frustrating John A. Macdonald's

General Rosser, the CPR's chief engineer, had refused to surrender with Lee at Appomattox, preferring to charge the federal lines with two divisions of cavalry. A local paper called him "one of the most pushing men on the American continent."

dream of filling up the empty plains. The settlers tended to take up land as close as possible to the railway; often enough they were driven off it by drought conditions.

The wet cycle, which had such an effect on Macoun in 1879 and 1880, continued through 1881 and 1882. Then, in 1883 – the peak year for immigration – the dry cycle returned. By 1886 the land was so dry in many places that cracks a foot wide opened up in the parched soil. Immigration figures in the North West began to decline after a record year in 1883. In 1884 homestead entries were halved. Thousands abandoned the embryo farms they had so eagerly taken up. By 1896, half of all contracts entered into with the railway by the various colonization companies had been cancelled; a total of 1,284,652 acres reverted to the CPR.

With the acceptance of more adaptable farming methods, the prairie country became, after the turn of the century, the granary of the world; Regina, which might not have existed had the northerly route been chosen, was found to be in the very heart of the richest grain-growing soil on the continent. In those portions of Palliser's Triangle where cereals would not grow, a healthy ranching economy developed. But the cycle of drought continued. The undue optimism of the seventies and early eighties was replaced in the decade from 1884 to 1894 by an extreme pessimism. So many farms were abandoned that the Canadian government began to entertain doubts about the future of the West. Once again, John Macoun was dispatched to the southern prairies to report on the seriousness of conditions and once again, just as he arrived on the scene, the rains came and Macoun was able to predict the end of the drought. The vast wave of immigration that filled up the prairies in the following years appeared to vindicate him. It was not until the desperate years of the 1930's, when the rains ceased once more and the grasshoppers and the cutworms and the hot, dry winds returned, that there took place a rueful reassessment of his strange role in the shaping of the nation.

The first of the CPR towns

GENERAL ROSSER's newly surveyed route led out of Portage la Prairie towards Grand Valley on the Assiniboine and then through the Brandon Hills to Flat Creek (later known as Oak Lake). It was here, near the crossing of the Assiniboine, that Brandon, the first of the CPR towns, sprang up. The method of its selection by the General provided an object lesson for the company in the value of establishing its own communities instead of building on existing ones.

Rosser was a Virginia gentleman of the old school – tall, handsome, swarthy, and popular. A West Point chum of General Custer, he had fought opposite him as a guerilla officer during the Civil War. In 1881, as chief engineer of the CPR, he brought the same dash and impulsiveness to the establishment of townsites.

A fortnight before the first sod was turned, rumours of a great new city west of Winnipeg began to fly. Everyone knew that the railway would require a divisional point about one hundred and thirty miles west of Winnipeg. That fitted almost to a mile the location of the little settlement of Grand Valley, clustered on the banks of the Assiniboine at the exact spot where the railway was to cross the river. Tents and shacks began to spring up in the vicinity as the surveyors drove in their stakes. Land speculators poured in. The excitement increased day by day as a general store and a "hotel" of canvas spread over wooden frames sprang up. Dugald McVicar, the pioneer resident, whose wife was the local postmistress, started making improvements to his home. His brother John announced that he would also extend the size of his house. It was on the McVicar property that the new city would presumably be situated. Certainly the McVicars expected to get rich from the Grand Valley boom.

Rosser Avenue, Brandon, in 1881. The "lots for sale" sign hints at the real estate boom which was then in full swing. One Nova Scotian made two hundred thousand dollars on land sales. General Rosser himself, in a quick turnover, made a profit of ten thousand.

In April, General Rosser paid a visit to John McVicar and made him an offer for his property as a future townsite for the CPR's divisional point. The accounts of exactly what took place are conflicting, but one thing is clear: McVicar, prodded by speculators, held out for double the amount offered. Whereupon Rosser is said to have retorted: "I'll be damned if a town of any kind is ever built here." The railway simply moved the site of its station two miles farther west. This would be the pattern in all future dealings when private individuals tried to hold up the company for speculative profits.

The new site, on the south bank of the river in the Brandon hills, cost the CPR a fraction of the Grand Valley price, and its choice marked the end of Grand Valley as a viable community and the beginning of the town of Brandon. What was not realized at the time was that Rosser and his immediate superior, Alpheus B. Stickney, the general superintendent of the western division of the CPR, were themselves speculating in real estate, using the inside knowledge that their positions provided them.

The main street of Brandon was named after General Rosser, who decreed that the lots should be small, since more money could be made from the land in that way. Once the location of the new town was known, people began to appear and tents to blossom all along the high bank of the Assiniboine. After the realtors, the first businessman on the scene, not unnaturally, was a lumber merchant: Charles Whitehead, the son of Joseph Whitehead, the railway contractor. Whitehead, whose descendants would own the Brandon *Sun*, purchased the first parcel of land sold by the CPR.

On Whitehead's heels, in late May, came a doctor, a grocer, and a hotelman. The grocery store was the one that had been erected the previous month at Grand Valley, but when it became clear that the original settlement was dying, the proprietors moved it in sections by barge to the new townsite. The McVicar brothers were stubbornly trying to sell lots on the old site in the wistful hope that the CPR might locate a station on their land, but their neighbours were less sanguine.

By June, two more stores and a billiard hall had been moved to Brandon. The first post office was nothing more than a soap box with a slit in it placed outside the tent of L. M. Fortier and his new bride. The first restaurant was a plank laid across two barrels on the trail that was to become Pacific Avenue. The first church service was held out of doors in a driving rainstorm in June by the Reverend Thomas Lawson, a Methodist. The local harness-maker held an umbrella over the minister's head while the congregation, composed entirely of young men, sang lustily, oblivious of the downpour.

In that golden summer of 1881, the pattern of the new Canada started to take hesitant shape along the line of the railway. Brandon was the beginning – the first of the scores of raw communities that would erupt from the naked prairie. Its birth pangs would be repeated over and over again as the rails moved west. There was a kind of electric feeling in the atmosphere – a sense of being in on the start of a great adventure – which those who arrived in Brandon that summer would never forget. In future years, when recollections of later events became blurred, they would still retain unclouded the memory of those first months when the sharp spring air was pungent with the incense of fresh lumber and ringing with the clamour of construction; when lasting friendships were forged among the soiled tents on the river bank; when every man was young and strong and in love with life; and when the distant prairie, unmarked by shovel or plough, was still a mysterious realm waiting to be claimed. Some forty years later, J. A. Smart, who had stood out in the rain during that first church service, wrote about those days "when the world, full of opportunity and hope," lay before him. "No small town in Canada or elsewhere," he wrote, "could possibly have contained a happier army of young men than did Brandon in its earliest years."

For the newcomer the opportunities were almost unlimited. Of the first seven lawyers who arrived, four became ministers of the Crown, and one the Leader of the Opposition in the Manitoba legislature. The first organist in Thomas Lawson's new frame church became mayor four times running. Douglas Cameron, from grading the bumps out of Sixth Street, rose to be Lieutenant-Governor of his province. And a jovial young Irish ploughboy from Kirkfield, Ontario, named Pat Burns, who broke sod on J. W. Sifton's farm at six dollars an acre, went on to become the meat-packing king of the Canadian West. Sifton's own sons, Arthur and Clifford, became, respectively, Premier of Alberta and Minister of the Interior in the federal government.

By October 11, when the first official passenger train pulled into the new station, a boom of epic proportions was in full swing. The coming of the railway was already transforming the West and the changes were spectacular enough to set the continent buzzing.

As for Grand Valley, which might have been the new metropolis, it lapsed into decay. A visitor in 1882 described the community as "a living corpse." Some years later, Charles Aeneas Shaw, one of Rosser's surveyors who had tried to persuade John McVicar to sell, happened upon him ploughing in the vicinity with a team of mules. The farmer ran out onto the road. "Oh, Mr. Shaw, I was a damn fool. If I had only taken your advice, I would have been well off now!"

To future speculators in townsites, the fate of the little community on the Assiniboine was an object lesson in how not to deal with the great railway.

The "paid ink-slingers"

SIR HENRY WHATLEY TYLER was the kind of man who enjoyed riding conspicuously on the cow-catchers of locomotives. He had been, variously, a captain in the Royal Engineers, a British railway inspector, and a Member of Parliament. Since 1876

he had been president of the Grand Trunk Railway of Canada, an enterprise that was directed from England. With the help of his shrewd general manager Joseph Hickson, Tyler had pushed his railway into Chicago, consolidated several lines in New England, and made the Grand Trunk one of the great railway systems of North America. But was it a Canadian system? Its ownership and its direction were largely British. Its main purpose seemed to be to link the American midwest with the U.S. Atlantic coast, using Canada only as a convenient route between Chicago and Portland. Its directors clearly did not grasp the significance of the Canadian North West.

In the midsummer of 1881, Tyler woke up to the fact that the Canadian Pacific was to be a major competitor. The first CPR shareholders' meeting, held in London on May 31, had approved the amalgamation of the new company with Duncan McIntyre's government-subsidized Canada Central – a

move that brought the CPR into Ottawa. On July 20, the CPR moved to extend its operations further into Grand Trunk Territory. Stephen and McIntyre were elected directors of the Ontario and Quebec Railway, a company that held a charter to build from Montreal to Toronto. It shortly became apparent that the CPR intended to swallow this line. The CPR, through Stephen, also had an interest in the Credit Valley Railway, which connected Toronto with Georgian Bay. In addition it had announced a branch line to Sault Ste Marie to connect with another line on the United States side being taken over by Jim Hill. The new company was not yet six months old and already it was posing a serious threat to the older railway.

Thus was the scene set for a battle between the two roads – a battle that was to run unchecked for the whole of the construction period. The Grand Trunk's strategy was to discredit the CPR in public while crippling it financially behind the scenes. In his campaign of attrition, Tyler had some powerful allies. Two great British financial houses, Baring Brothers and Glyn, Mills, were on his side (they had originally financed the Grand Trunk) and so were a large number of newspapers, many of which profited from Grand Trunk advertising.

A large section of the British press, led by *The Times* of London, had convinced would-be immigrants that Australia was a better prospect than the forbidding Canadian plains. The Governor General, Lord Lorne, determined to remedy this impression by a personal tour of the railway's route to the Rockies with four British journalists, including a man from *The Times*, invited along. The coverage was good and the newspaper ceased to thunder against Canada; but the gibes from other British journals continued. The most memorable, entitled "The Canadian Dominion Bubble," was published in *Truth* on September 1, 1881. The author said flatly that the floating of a Canadian government bond issue in England and ten million dollars' worth of CPR land grant bonds in New York and Montreal was a fraud.

The Marquis of Lorne

A SKETCHBOOK OF LORD LORNE'S WESTERN ODYSSEY.

The young new governor general was incensed at the way the British press treated the Canadian North West. On a memorable cross-Canada trek he took along four journalists including an artist, Sydney Hall, whose pencil sketches are reproduced here.

Lorne's party travelled all the way to the foothills by wagon and "ambulance" (above). Here, Hall sketches Fort Calgary, a settlement of false fronts and log cabins.

Nothing impressed the British journalists more than a Blackfoot powwow, presided over by the great Crowfoot, whose exploits were legend. Lorne promised the chief a buggy and a piano. When these were not immediately forthcoming, the Indians attacked a party of CPR surveyors in late October and, in lieu of the promised gifts, robbed them of their food and clothing.

Sydney Hall made this sketch on August 8, 1881, at End of Track. Note the Mounties in white helmets.

OVERLEAF:

A rare photograph of the Governor General's party crossing the Canadian Shield by canoe and portage, en route to the North West.

149

"The Canadian Pacific Railway will run, if it is ever finished, through a country frost bound for seven or eight months in the year, and will connect with the eastern part of the Dominion a province which embraces about as forbidding a country as any on the face of the earth."

As for British Columbia, it was "a barren, cold, mountain country that is not worth keeping." It would never have been inhabited at all had it not been for the mining boom: "Ever since that fever died down the place has been going from bad to worse. Fifty railroads would not galvanize it into prosperity." The CPR was "never likely to pay a red cent of interest on the money that may be sunk into it."

This broadside and others that followed had their effect on the British money market. They were accompanied that fall by the first of the anti-CPR pamphlets, written by the Grand Trunk's "paid ink-slingers," as Stephen called them. Stephen saw himself beset on all sides by formidable forces intent on crushing the CPR. In Manitoba two private railways were being built towards the United States border. The Northern Pacific had bought control of one and was ready to buy control of the other, believing, in Stephen's words that "they can force a connection at the boundary and so strangle the Canadian Pacific; which they are determined to do if they can."

Many of Macdonald's followers, especially those in Manitoba, were eager to subvert the spirit of the contract which protected the railway through its monopoly clause. Because of the British North America Act the clause did not prevent the provinces from chartering lines to the border in competition with the transcontinental railway. This was Stephen's fear and all that fall of 1881 he kept up a continual pressure on the Prime Minister to disallow by federal decree any provincially chartered lines that came within fifteen miles of the border. Repeatly he pointed out that a "Yankee line" into Manitoba would make it impossible to operate or even to build the Lake Superior section of the CPR.

151

There is no doubt that Macdonald intended to back Stephen up, but there is also no doubt that the monopoly clause was already causing him grave uneasiness. To ride roughshod over the legitimate desire of Manitoba settlers for more railways to service their communities was to alienate politically an entire province.

Stephen, who had once thought the idea of building the line north of Lake Superior "great folly," was becoming an enthusiastic champion of an all-Canadian route. In August, 1881, he confessed to the Prime Minister that "all misgivings I had last year . . . have disappeared with a better knowledge of the position of the whole country. . . . I am sure you will be glad to hear this from me because I do not think but for your *own* tenacity on that point, would the line North of the Lake *ever* have been built, events have shown you were right and all the rest wrong."

Some of this was flattery and some of it was close to being blackmail. Stephen had been aware, from the outset, of Macdonald's obsession with an all-Canadian railway. He used his knowledge to good advantage – to bargain toughly for the insertion of the monopoly clause in the contract. The Prime Minister was made to understand that he could not have one thing without the other. If the CPR was to pay through the nose for an unprofitable line through an uninhabitable wilderness, it must receive compensation. The contract gave it a monopoly of all traffic out of Winnipeg into the United States and it made the most of it.

Again Stephen and his colleagues had rejected Sandford Fleming's surveys. The Fleming line took the easiest route, well to the north of Lake Nepigon, but Stephen wanted to adopt a new location that would hug the granite ribbed shores of Superior. "The line north of Nipigon would be easy of construction and operation too, but it *never* can support settlers, there is absolutely no *land*, nothing but bare rocks and pools of water." Moreover, by building close to the lake the contractors could be supplied by water transport. Stephen argued that because of this, construction time would be cut, perhaps in half.

Jim Hill, of course, had no intention of blasting a railroad out of the black scarps that frowned down on the slate waters of the great lake. Like Villard of the Northern Pacific, Hill saw Canadian freight being diverted south of the lake and up through the underbelly of Manitoba. One of his chief reasons for joining the CPR Syndicate was that his St. Paul road would get all the construction traffic for the line being built west of Winnipeg. The line across the Shield, he was convinced, "would be of no use to anybody and would be the source of heavy loss to whoever operated it."

In the fall of 1881, Hill picked the best railwayman he could find to look over the Precambrian country to the north and west of Lake Superior. According to William Pearce of the Dominion land department, Hill's plan was to have the visitor damn the all-Canadian route as impractical. He chose for this task William Cornelius Van Horne, the dynamic young general manager of the Chicago, Milwaukee and St. Paul Railroad. Though no one yet realized it, his influence on the future of the young nation was to be enormous.

The new man was actually being considered for the post of general manager of the CPR. Stickney had managed to build only one hundred and thirty miles of railway that season; moreover, he was under a cloud because of his land speculations. Hill advised Stephen to replace him.

"You need a man of great mental and physical power to carry this line through," Hill said. "Van Horne can do it." He added a word of caution: "But he will take all the authority he gets and more, so define how much you want him to have."

On October 7, Hill brought Van Horne into Winnipeg to look over the CPR's prairie construction and also the government line being built out of Fort William. Winnipeg was a city of contrasts – buildings springing up everywhere; "the streets full of garbage, egg shells, rinds of lemons and other forms of refuse cast out in broad daylight"; stray

The only public portrait of William Cornelius Van Horne at the time he became general manager of the CPR. His features grew more Teutonic in later years as his beard whitened and his eyes turned pouchy. A true Renaissance man, he was the most engaging and versatile immigrant that Canada ever attracted. His secret: "I eat all I can; I drink all I can; and I don't give a damn for anybody." In ancient Rome he would have been a general, in the Middle Ages, a prince of the church, in the sixteenth century, the ruler of a dukedom. In the Victorian Age in North America, he was fated to be a railway magnate; they were, after all, the most powerful people in the land.

horses prowling around the suburbs where they "mangle shade trees, stamp around at nights and make a nuisance of themselves generally"; tents blossoming so thickly along the Assiniboine that the police tried to burn them out; workmen and settlers jamming the broad, muddy avenues.

Hill and Van Horne stayed overnight and then went west through Brandon to the end of track and then east again along the still unfinished line to Thunder Bay. It must have been a stimulating journey, for both men were insatiably curious. Van Horne, however, was the broader in his interests. Hill usually made his curiosity work for him in a business sense; transportation, fuel, forwarding attracted him. But Van Horne indulged his varied fancies for the sheer love of it. He was, among other things, an amateur geologist, a first rate gardener, a caricaturist, a conjuror, a mind reader, a violinist, a practical joker, a gourmet, and a marathon poker player.

All his appetites appeared to be gargantuan. He ate prodigiously and was known as a man who fed his workmen generously. He liked his cognac, his whiskey, and his fine French vintages, but he did not tolerate drunkenness in himself or others. Inebriates were fired out of hand. So were slackers, dunces, cravens, cowards, slowpokes, and labour organizers. Van Horne did not suffer laziness, stupidity, inefficiency, or revolt.

He was probably appalled by what he found between Winnipeg and Thunder Bay. Later Van Horne was to describe a section of the desert east of Fort William as "200 miles of engineering impossibilities." It may be that, at this juncture, he shared Hill's belief that it would be madness to try to push a railroad across the Shield. Did he actually damn the Lake Superior route? William Pearce, the land commissioner, believed that he did. "I have no doubt he carried out what he was asked to do," he wrote in a memoir years later. But Van Horne at the time was not a committed officer of the company, nor had he fallen under Stephen's spell.

Events, however, were moving rapidly. The pressure was on him to take over the Canadian railway. It was an enormous risk. His prospects south of the border were as bright as those of any rising young railway executive in the country. He could have had the pick of half a dozen sinecures, yet he chose the CPR. Certainly the salary that Hill was dangling before him was attractive, but it was not really the money that turned William Cornelius Van Horne into a Canadian. The Canadian Pacific Railway Company was launched on a breath-taking gamble. The steel was creeping across the prairie like an arrow pointed at the successive bulwarks of the Rockies and the Selkirks. At that moment, no one knew exactly how the rails were to penetrate those two mountain series or, indeed, if they could get through the Selkirks at all. The railway's future depended on that eccentric little wisp of a surveyor, Major Rogers, who all that summer had been clambering over the naked peaks looking for a notch in the rampart. Few Canadian engineers believed he would find what he was seeking, but Van Horne, the poker player, had talked to Rogers. The gamble, the challenge, the adventure, the desire "to make things grow and put new places on the map" were too much for a man of his temperament to resist.

Van Horne's appointment was confirmed on November 1. He began work on January 2, 1882, in the CPR offices in the new Bank of Montreal building in Winnipeg. By that time the astonishing real estate boom, which swept across all of western Canada from the Red River to Fort Edmonton and electrified most of the continent, was at its height. The smell of money was in the air. For the past several months, ever since the founding of Brandon, the people of Manitoba had seemed to be going stark, raving mad over real estate. When Van Horne arrived the insanity had reached a kind of crescendo. It would continue unabated until the snows melted and it was snuffed out by the angry floods of spring.

The new broom

VAN HORNE arrived in Winnipeg with a considerable reputation among railwaymen. He was known as "an idol-smashing heathen" who had no respect for the rigid dogmas of a tradition-ridden business. It was said that he could make eight hundred freight cars do the work of a thousand by his ingenious methods of loading. In Chicago he had astonished his contemporaries by the amount of trackage he had managed to work into a limited area in the yards. He had a reputation for doctoring sick railroads until they were made to pay. He was also known as a fighter: he had fought the grasshoppers, he had fought the labour unions, he had fought the encroachment of other railroads, and always he had won.

He seemed to know a terrifying amount about railroading. He knew all about yards and repair shops, he understood the mysteries of accounting, he could work out a complicated system of scheduling in his head, he could comprehend the chatter of the fastest telegraph key, and he could operate any locomotive built. He had even redesigned, with considerable grace and taste, that ugliest example of nineteenth-century American architecture, the railroad station.

There are a great many adjectives that apply to Van Horne: buoyant, capable, ingenious, temperamental, blunt, forceful, boyish, self-reliant, imaginative, hard-working, ruthless, puckish, courageous. But the word that best sums him up, and the one that his contemporaries used more than once, is "positive." He exuded confidence. J. H. E. Secretan, who worked for him as a surveyor, recorded that "the word 'cannot' did not exist in his dictionary." Was he ever bedevilled by doubts of his own or haunted by fears of private failure? If he was he hid his emotions well behind the grave mask of his face and those unrevealing eyes of penetrating blue.

He believed in coming to the point swiftly, with an economy of words. It was the same with railway lines. One of Van Horne's first tasks was to ensure that the CPR would reach Pacific tidewater by the shortest possible route. He had not yet met George Stephen, but he had encountered Major A. B. Rogers, "the Railway Pathfinder," whom Hill had sent off to the mountains early in 1881. After a summer of exploration in the mountains, Rogers (though he harboured some secret doubts) had decided to announce that the Kicking Horse Pass in the Rockies was feasible. In the second week in January, 1882, he and Van Horne went to Montreal to meet Stephen, McIntyre, and Angus to discuss the matter.

This resulted in two major decisions, the first of which was communicated to the press by Van Horne himself, with characteristic bluntness.

"We have changed the point," he said, "at which the road will enter the Rockies." Although, as the *Globe* pointed out, only the Dominion government could "change the point," it had in fact been changed almost without that authority.

The second decision confirmed the change of route between Lake Nipissing, the official start of the railway, and Fort William, to allow the line to hug the shore of Lake Superior. In addition, a branch line contemplated from Lake Nipissing to Sault Ste Marie would be greatly shortened, placing the Sault virtually on the main line. This announcement underlined the company's intention of proceeding with the Lake Superior section. Jim Hill had not contemplated that. Had his own scheme been adopted, it is conceivable that the CPR might have become part of the railway empire that the ambitious Hill was constructing – a Canadian feeder line for the Great Northern, which was to grow out of the original St. Paul railway.

But Van Horne had become that year the most trenchant advocate the Lake Superior line had. His railway sense rebelled against a connection with another railroad. He wanted a through line, independent of local traffic; and there is little doubt

At Eagle Lake, far out on the untrammelled prairie, a camp of CPR
*surveyors laying out the line of route between Brandon and the Rockies tries
to keep ahead of the track-laying teams, just over the horizon to the east.*

that he saw more clearly than the others the consequences to the CPR of linking up with Hill's road. When Hill heard of Van Horne's opposition to his plan he burst out that he would get even with him "if I have to go to hell for it and shovel coal."

No doubt Hill ruefully recalled his advice to Stephen that Van Horne would take all the authority he could. The new general manager was a man of towering ambition whose love of power had its roots in his youth. At the age of eighteen, he had breathlessly watched the arrival of the general superintendent of the Michigan Central coming forward to meet his assistants. When the "mighty man," as Van Horne called him, moved away, the youth walked around the official car and gazed on it with awe. He found himself wondering if he might not some day attain the same rank and travel about in a private car of his own. "The glories of it, the pride of it, the salary pertaining to it, all that moved me deeply," he told his grandson many years later, "and I made up my mind then and there that I would reach it." He did, in just ten years; at the age of twenty-eight he became the youngest railway superintendent in the world. Now, with a new railway in his grasp, he had no intention of sharing his power with any man.

He could get along quite easily with George Stephen, for Stephen was a financier, not a railroad man. But there was a quality of enthusiasm about him that Stephen must have admired, for Stephen had it too. When Stephen threw himself into a project he went all the way; so did Van Horne. Once he became general manager of the CPR, he was a Canadian railwayman through and through. The difference was that Van Horne, unlike Stephen, seemed able to switch from one pursuit to another and make himself master of all of them. He was convinced that "an object can usually be attained through persistence and steadiness of aim" and in all his activities – from track-laying to poker – he held fast to that credo.

Van Horne had been in office only one month and was still in Montreal when he fired General Rosser, who was using inside knowledge of future railway locations to speculate in real estate. Van Horne came across a letter in which the General had revealed to a railway contractor the exact location of the terminus of the CPR's Pembina Mountain branch. This was valuable and privileged information. On February 1, Van Horne wired to Rosser that he had seen the letter and on account of his "unwarranted and unauthorized action on this and other matters" he was notifying him that his services were no longer required.

Rosser's dismissal was followed shortly afterward by that of his entire engineering staff. On March 13, a fire destroyed the new Bank of Montreal building, in which the CPR had its Winnipeg offices. During the transfer of some of the engineering department's documents it was discovered that several were missing, including plans of the contemplated route of the railway west. Van Horne told Rosser's replacement, Samuel B. Reed (an old Illinois crony), to find the leak, and if he could not, to fire the whole staff on the spot. At the same time, Reed laid an information against his predecessor, charging that Rosser had fraudulently obtained the profiles of the line extending all the way to Calgary.

Ultimately, the CPR dropped the case. That might have been the end of matters had Rosser not accidentally encountered Van Horne on a hot July evening in the Manitoba Club. Van Horne was no man to back away from any encounter – as a child in Joliet he had taken on every boy in school. Winnipeg almost witnessed its only Western-style gunfight. Rosser and Van Horne both drew pistols, and a serious battle was averted only when, in the spirited account of the Winnipeg *Sun*, "the better counsels of cooler heads prevailed, and the belligerents were separated before their passions were cooled in gore."

Thomas Shaughnessy, dapper but aloof, was once described as a man "almost bloodless in his devotion to material ends." He was also an expert at stalling off creditors.

Five hundred miles of track

When Van Horne met the CPR directors in Montreal, he was able to convince them he could lay five hundred miles of track during the 1882 season. Stephen had already told Macdonald that the company was planning to finish the railway in half the ten-year period allowed by the contract. It was, indeed, essential that the through line get into operation as swiftly as possible; the CPR would stand or fall on its transcontinental trade – cargoes such as silk, for example, that demanded speedy dispatch. The Canadian road was far shorter than any United States transcontinental route, but it could not turn a dollar of profit on its through line until the last spike was driven.

Van Horne's announcement was greeted with considerable scepticism, but he gave no hint that he was embarked on anything remarkable. Back in Winnipeg in mid-February, 1882, he told J. H. E. Secretan, the surveyor, that he wanted "the shortest commercial line" between Winnipeg and the Pacific coast, and he added that he would lay five hundred miles of track that summer. Secretan ventured a modicum of doubt, whereupon Van Horne declared that nothing was impossible; all he wanted his engineers to do was to show him the road; if Secretan could not do that, then he would have his scalp.

The new general manager's reputation as a Yankee go-getter had another side to it. It was generally held, and not without considerable evidence, that he was favouring Americans over Canadians when new employees were hired for the railway. This was especially true in the key jobs, but it was not in Van Horne's nature to take notice of such criticism. In the summer of 1882 he was doing his best to lure another American into the fold, a Milwaukee Irishman named Thomas Shaughnessy who had once been on his staff in the United States. Van Horne needed Shaughnessy to act as quartermaster-general for the vast army that was gathering on the plains.

The contract to build the prairie section of the railway was probably the largest of its kind ever undertaken. The prize was awarded in February to the partnership of General R. B. Langdon of Minneapolis and D. C. Shepard of St. Paul. The firm undertook to build six hundred and seventy-five miles of railroad from Flat Creek to Fort Calgary. This was a formidable task – just fifteen miles short of the entire length of the Central Pacific.

On the day after the contract was signed, Langdon and Shepard advertised for three thousand men and four thousand horses. They faced a staggering job. Between Flat Creek and Fort Calgary the partners would have to move ten million cubic yards of earth. They would have to haul every stick of timber, every rail, fishplate, and spike, all the pilings used for bridgework, and all the food and provisions for 7,600 men and 1,700 teams of horses across the naked prairie for hundreds of miles. To feed the horses alone it would be necessary to distribute four thousand bushels of oats every day along one hundred and fifty miles of track. It was no wonder that Van Horne's boast about building five hundred miles in a single season was openly derided.

Winnipeg was transformed that spring of 1882 into a gigantic supply depot. Stone began to pour in from every available quarry, railroad ties from Lake of the Woods, lumber from Minnesota, and rails from England and from the Krupp works in Germany. Since the St. Lawrence would still be frozen well into the construction season, Van Horne had the steel shipped to New York and New Orleans and dispatched to Manitoba by way of St. Paul. Whole trainloads of material destined for the Canadian North West were constantly passing through American cities where hundreds of checkers reported on them daily so that the exact moment of their arrival could be plotted. As fast as the supplies arrived they were hauled away to the end of track. No newly completed line of steel had ever known such activity in the first year of its construction.

Record floods that isolated Winnipeg and drowned the line halted this activity in April, causing formidable log-jams. By the time the water subsided, scores of would-be homesteaders were disheartened and ready to quit the North West. Trunks were piled along the grade like cordwood, as high as men could throw them, but many of the owners were already trying to sell their outfits and leave. In late May an unexpected blizzard struck, destroying scores of tents and causing great suffering. Fuel was at such a premium that men resorted to stealing lumber, stick by stick. The first passenger train to leave Brandon for Winnipeg after the flood pulled three coaches loaded to the doors with men and women leaving the North West, never to return.

At last the waters subsided, the blizzards ended, and the sun came out to warm the frigid plains. The prairie evenings grew mellower and soon the sweet incense of the wolf willow drifted in from the ponds and sloughs to mingle with the more familiar odours of salt pork, tamarack ties, wood smoke, and human sweat. The early spring blossoms – wild pansies, strawberries, and purple pasqueflowers – began to poke their tiny faces between the brittle grasses. Then, as a flush of new green spread over the land, the ox carts started west again until they were strung out by the hundreds ahead of the advancing line of steel.

As soon as the waters ebbed, a mountain of supplies descended upon Winnipeg. With the freight came people. By June, three thousand immigrants were under canvas in Winnipeg, all buoyed up by the expectation of an entirely new life on the Canadian prairies.

The high water had thrown Van Horne's schedule off balance. The *Globe* ignored the weather and laid the blame at the feet of the general manager. On June 23 it reported that "Van Horne's men have not laid one solitary rail upon the grading done under his regime." The paper dug up "a well known track-layer who has been in the business out west for 20 years" who claimed it was impossible to lay

five hundred miles of track that season, and that there was "more construction in Stickney's little finger than in Van Horne's body."

Few people, in fact, believed the CPR could achieve its season's goal or anything close to it after the delays. Van Horne, however, was immovable. The general manager made it clear that he would cancel the contract if Langdon and Shepard did not live up to their obligations. "We shall show a record at track-laying which has never been surpassed on this continent," Shepard replied.

There followed a whirlwind of construction that was, in the words of the *Quarterly Review*, "absolutely without parallel in railway annals." The grade, winding snakelike across the plains, moved so swiftly that Secretan and his surveyors were hard put to stay ahead. Sometimes, indeed, they were awakened at night by the rumble of giant scrapers being dragged past their tents.

The prairie section of the CPR was built telescopically from a single base. Winnipeg was the anchor point: from there the steel would stretch for a thousand miles into the mountains; there would be no supply line for the railway builders other than the rails themselves. Van Horne's army worked that summer with a military precision that astonished all who witnessed it. "Clockwork" was the term used over and over again to describe the track-laying technique.

The pulse of the operation was at "End of Track," that unique community that never stayed in one place for more than a few hours at a time. Its nerve centre was the line of boarding cars – eight or nine of them, each three storeys high – that housed the track crews. These formed part of a long train of office cars, cooking cars, freight cars, shops on wheels, and, on occasion, the private car of the general manager himself. Van Horne was continually to be found at End of Track, spinning yarns with the workmen, sketching buffalo skulls, organizing foot races and target-shooting at night, and bumping over the prairie in a buckboard inspecting the grade. Every day some sixty-five

Boarding cars at End of Track on the prairie in 1882. The two top storeys served as a bunkhouse; the first floor was a mess hall.

A construction train steams up to End of Track and dumps half a mile of railroad ties onto the frozen prairie. These ties have been hauled a thousand miles from the Lake of the Woods country. A score of teams is waiting to distribute them along the line.

carloads of railroad supplies were dumped at End of Track. Most of these supplies had been carried an average of a thousand miles before reaching their destination.

The organization was meticulous, down to the last railway spike. Each morning two construction trains set out from the supply yards, far in the rear, each loaded with the exact number of rails, ties, spikes, fishplates, and telegraph poles required for half a mile of railway. One train was held in reserve on a siding about six miles to the rear; the other moved directly to the front where the track-laying gang of three hundred men and seventy horses was waiting.

The tracklayers worked like a drill team. The ties were unloaded first, to be picked up by the waiting wagons – thirty ties to a wagon – hauled forward and dropped on both sides of the graded embankment for exactly half a mile. As the ties were thrown out, two men with marked rods laid them across the grade, exactly two feet apart. Behind the teams came a hand-truck loaded with rails, fishplates, and spikes. Six men marched on each side of it, and when they reached the far end of the last pair of newly laid rails, each crew seized a rail among them and threw it into exact position. Two more men gauged these two rails for alignment. Four more followed with spikes, placing one in each of the four ends of the rails. Four others screwed in the fishplates and another four followed with crowbars to raise the ties while the spikes were being hammered in. All worked in a kind of rhythm, each man directly opposite his partner on each separate rail. More men followed with hammers and spikes to make the rails secure, but by this time the hand-truck had already moved forward, passing over the newly laid rails before the job was complete.

As each construction train dumped its half-mile of supplies at End of Track, it moved back to the nearest siding to be replaced by the reserve train. There was no time lost. As the track unfolded, the boarding cars were nudged ahead constantly by the

construction train locomotive so that no energy would be wasted by the navvies in reaching their moving mess halls and dormitories. Right behind the track-laying gang came the telegraph teams, working so efficiently that one hour after the day's track was laid, End of Track was in telegraphic communication with the outside world.

The operation was strung out for hundreds of miles across the open prairie. Up ahead were the survey camps, followed by the grading gangs and the bridge-makers. Far to the rear were other thousands – saddlers and carpenters, cooks and tailors, shoemakers, blacksmiths, doctors, and provisioners. Supply trains moved out of Winnipeg on schedule, unloading thousands of tons of goods at yards established every hundred miles. Here the material was sorted daily into train lots and dispatched to the front. When the steel moved past the hundred-mile point the yards moved, too. An entire community of office workers, sorters, dispatchers, trainmen, labourers, and often their families as well, could be transported a hundred miles in a single night without the loss of an hour's work, because the houses were all portable and could be fitted easily onto flatcars.

Far out on the barren plains, miles to the west of End of Track, were the bridging teams, grading units, and surveyors, all driven forward by the knowledge that the tracklayers were pressing hard behind them. The head contractor had a flying wing of his own men standing by, prepared to complete immediately any work that seemed unlikely to be ready in time for the "ironing" of the track.

The grading was accomplished by immense scrapers pulled by teams of horses. Their task was to build an embankment for the railway four feet above the prairie and to ditch it for twenty yards on either side. At that height the rails would be protected from the blizzards of winter and costly delays from snow blockage would be avoided.

The bridgers worked in two gangs, one by day and one by night. Every sliver of bridging had to be brought from Rat Portage, one hundred and forty

"The iron now is going down just as fast as it can be pulled from the cars," the St. Paul contractor, D.C. Shepard, announced in the summer of 1882. Here, at End of Track, navvies heave off newly arrived rails.

In this more sophisticated method of track-laying, the rails are winched off the flatcar and hoisted onto the ties. Up ahead men with markers exactly adjust intervening spaces.

miles east of Winnipeg, or from Minnesota; for this reason the bridge-builders were seldom more than ten miles ahead of the advancing steel. The timbers were unloaded as close to End of Track as possible and generally at night so as not to interfere with other work. "Sometimes," one eyewitness reported, "not a stick of timber nor any preparation for work could be seen one day, the next would show two or three spans of a nicely finished bridge. Twenty-four hours afterwards the rails would be laid, and trains working. . . ."

"The history of the world offers no such evidence of push as the work of this year has done," R. B. Conkey, Langdon and Shepard's general manager, declared at Winnipeg in August. "Sherman's march to the sea was nothing to it. When the road is completed there will be nothing in history to compare with it."

The nation was electrified by the speed with which the railroad was being forced across the plains. One man on the scene noted that it seemed to move as fast as the ox carts of the settlers who were following along beside the tracks.

The North West of Canada, once so haunting and so mysterious, was being transformed by the onslaught of the rails. One railway employee wrote that the progress of construction was so swift that antelope and other game that migrated north were cut off on their return that fall by the lines of rails and telegraph posts, "and terrified by the sight . . . gathered in hundreds on the north side, afraid to cross it." It was probably the last summer in which herds of buffalo and antelope freely roamed the prairie.

Father Albert Lacombe, back among his beloved Blackfoot nation, watched the approach of the rails with resignation:

"I would look in silence at the road coming on – like a band of wild geese in the sky – cutting its way through the prairies; opening up the great country we thought would be ours for years. Like a vision I could see it driving my poor Indians before it, and spreading out behind it the farms,

the towns and cities. . . . No one who has not lived in the west since the Old-Times can realize what is due to that road – that c.p.r. It was Magic – like the mirage on the prairies, changing the face of the whole country."

Onward the track moved, cutting the plains in two. It moved through a land of geese, snipe, and wild ducks, fragrant in the soft evenings with the scent of willow and balsam. It cut across acres of yellow daisies, tiger lilies, purple sage, and brier rose. It bisected pastures of tall buffalo grass and skirted green hay meadows, which in the spring were shallow ponds. As it travelled westward it pushed through a country of memories and old bones – furrowed trails fashioned decades before by thousands of bison, vast fields of withered herbage, dead lakes rimmed with telltale crusts of alkali. Day by day it crept towards the horizon where, against the sunset, flocks of wildfowl, disturbed by the invaders, could be seen in silhouette; or where, sometimes, a single Indian, galloping in the distance, became no more than a speck crawling along the rim of the prairie. This had been the Great Lone Land, unfenced and unbridged, which the early explorers had described as if it were on the dark side of the moon. The line of steel made Butler's phrase obsolete, for the land would never again be lonely. All that summer it reverberated with the clang of sledge and anvil, the snorting of horses and mules, the hoarse puffing of the great engines, the bellowing of the section bosses, the curses of thousands of sweating men, and the universal song of the railroad navvies: "Drill, ye tarriers, drill."

History was being made, but few had time to note that fact. Beecham Trotter, who worked with the telegraph gang, was to write, a little sheepishly, that "few, if any of us were historically minded enough to think of the interest that might attach to a running diary of what was seen, and said, and done, from day to day." Nor did William Oliver (a future mayor of Lethbridge, Alberta) in his ox cart heading west consider the significance of what

he saw: "It never came to my mind in watching the building of the railway . . . that in the next fifty years it would play so important a part in the commerce of the country and in fact of the world. . . ."

At the same time the spectacle of the steel-laying gangs was "a sight never to be forgotten...." They were a mixed lot. Charles Alfred Peyton came upon a gang of Italians who "looked like guys who would cut your throat for a dime." A few miles farther on, however, he joined a team of young Englishmen, "a very nice bunch of lads." Alex Stavely Hill, a London barrister, encountered a man ploughing, "throwing almost as much strength from himself into his work as he was getting out of his horses." It developed that he was a former doctor. That night, the man who cooked his dinner in the boarding car turned out to be the same solicitor's clerk who had once visited him in London.

The general run of railroad navvies was far rougher. One eastern reporter found them "ill-bred and offensive in their manners, applying the most obscene epithets to every passerby, jostling with their heavy teams every traveller they meet upon the trail, and in all respects making themselves as disagreeable as they know how to be. In their personal habits they are much more uncleanly than the poorest and most degraded of Indians, and in all respects they fairly represent the class from which they were drawn, that is, the scum and offscourings of the filthiest slums of Chicago and other western cities."

As autumn approached, the pace of the railway quickened still more. At the end of August one track crew managed to lay four and a half miles of steel in a day. Next day they beat their own record and laid five miles. It was all horribly expensive, as a worried Stephen reported to Macdonald in September: ". . . the road . . . is costing us a great

Like an advancing army, starkly etched against the flat prairie sky, the spikers march forward with drill-team precision. In just fifteen months, these men moved 675 miles across the plains, and the trains were running all the way to Calgary.

deal more than the subsidy and a great deal more than we expected."

There were those who thought that Van Horne "seemed to spend money like a whole navy of drunken sailors." Actually he counted every dollar. In the interests of both speed and economy he allowed steep grades and tight curves. In places, the road was like a switchback; it remained that way until the end of the century.

The contractors did not reach Van Horne's goal of five hundred miles; the spring floods had frustrated his ambition. By the end of the season, however, they had laid four hundred and seventeen miles of completed railroad, built twenty-eight miles of siding, and graded another eighteen miles for the start of the following season. In addition, Van Horne had pushed the Southwestern branch line of the CPR in Manitoba a hundred miles.

As far as the general public was concerned, he

had wrought a miracle. Only the waspish *Globe* refused to be impressed: "The public has nothing to gain by this breakneck speed. . . . If . . . a southerly pass had been found across the Rocky Mountains, there might be some object in making haste across the plains. But from present appearances, the entire Prairie section will be crossed long before it is positively known whether or not there is a better crossing than the Yellowhead Pass. . . ."

There was a modicum of truth in the *Globe*'s carping. In the heart of the Rocky Mountains that summer, Major A. B. Rogers was still plagued with doubts about the feasibility of the Kicking Horse Pass as a railway route. Equally serious was the whole question of the barrier of the Selkirks. The plain truth was that Van Horne and his men had been driving steel all summer at record speed, straight at that double wall of mountains, without really being sure of how they were going to breach it.

Edgar Dewdney's new capital

The Honourable Edgar Dewdney, Lieutenant-Governor and Indian Commissioner of the North West Territories, was a handsome giant of a man. It was not difficult to spot him at a distance, for he stood "like Saul, head and shoulders above most men," and in the late spring of 1882 there were a good many who wanted to keep him in view: the Lieutenant-Governor had been charged with staking out the site for the new capital of the Territories. No more profitable parcel of real estate could be imagined.

Battleford had been the original capital, but Battleford was no longer on the railroad. For all of the winter of 1881-82, Winnipeg land speculators, knowing that the seat of government was about to be changed, had been dispatching platoons of men to squat on every promising location. It is fairly clear that General Rosser himself had his eye on land profits in the vicinity of the new capital; that was one reason why the preliminary survey of the line in Saskatchewan was altered. A likely town-site had been at the crossing of the Wascana or Pile o' Bones Creek. When the railway location was moved half a dozen miles to the south, across an absolutely treeless plain, the land sharks were left out in the cold.

Most Canadians familiar with the country felt that the only possible site for a capital city of the plains lay a few miles to the northeast near Fort Qu'Appelle in the wooded valley of the Qu'Appelle River, perhaps the loveliest spot on all that sere steppe. The railway, however, was designed to skirt the valley. The reason given was that the steep banks would make construction difficult and costly. An equally strong motive was undoubtedly the company's policy of bypassing established communities in the interests of greater land profits.

There was also the fact that Governor Dewdney

had an interest in the land surrounding Pile o' Bones crossing. He and several friends, most of them leading politicians and public officials, had secretly formed a land syndicate earlier that year, in which Dewdney had a one-eleventh interest; it owned four hundred and eighty acres at the very spot that Dewdney selected, on June 30, as the site of the future capital.

At Fort Qu'Appelle, when the news of Dewdney's action came, there was anger, frustration, disappointment, and frenzy. Most of the settlers hitched up their teams and moved themselves and all their worldly goods to the bank of Pile o' Bones Creek. Squatters began to pour towards the embryo city. By fall they held most of the available homestead land in the area. Genuine settlers, who were supposed to get homesteads for nothing, found themselves paying up to five hundred dollars for them.

The matter of the capital was settled on August 12. Lord Lorne, consulted about the name, left the matter to his wife, Princess Louise, who chose Regina in honour of her mother. The choice of name produced an instant adverse reaction but the choice of the site provoked even greater controversy. Some of this resulted from a Canadian Press Association visit to the townsite in August. The eastern reporters, used to the verdant Ontario countryside, were dismayed to find nothing more than a cluster of tattered tents, huddled together on a bald and apparently arid plain. The London *Advertiser* called it a "huge swindle." The Brandon *Sun* said it should have been named Golgotha because of its barren setting. The Toronto *World* declared that "no one has a good word for Regina."

Early visitors were astonished that such a bleak plain should have been preferred over the neighbouring valley. Even George Stephen was dubious. He would have preferred Moose Jaw. But Dewdney stuck to his stated conviction that he had chosen the best possible location. He publicly declared that the site had been selected because "it was surrounded by the best soil, it has the best drainage, and the best and greatest volume of water, of any

place between the Assiniboine and Swift Current Creek." He told Macdonald, quite accurately as it turned out, that the new capital was in the very heart of the best wheat district in the country.

In the light of Dewdney's personal interest in Regina real estate these statements were greeted with jeers. Inevitably there was a clash with the CPR. The railway was already hard pressed for funds. Its main asset was the land it owned on the sites of new towns, and it did not intend to share these real estate profits with outsiders.

In Regina and in several other important prairie towns, the government and the CPR pooled their land interests and arranged to share the profits equally. That summer the railway, in order to raise funds, agreed to sell five million acres of land to a British-Canadian syndicate, the Canada North-West Land Company. The land company would manage townsite sales in forty-seven major communities, and the railway would receive half the net profits. Thus, in Regina, one quarter of the land profits went to the railway, one quarter to the land company, and a half to the government. Since, in Stephen's phrase, the land company was "practically a branch of the Land Department of the C.P.R.," the railway controlled all of the Regina land save for that held by the Dewdney syndicate.

A struggle now ensued between the land company and the CPR on one side and the Dewdney syndicate on the other over the exact location of Regina's public buildings. The former wanted the nucleus of the new capital on the railway's land; Dewdney wanted it on his property. The struggle moved to Winnipeg, where the rival properties were touted in huge competing advertisements. The railway won. It sold some half-million dollars' worth of Regina real estate that winter; the rival sales were negligible.

A further struggle developed over the location of government buildings. Dewdney wanted them on the river, where, as he pointed out, the drainage was good (and also where they would be next door to his syndicate's land); his opponents wanted them

171

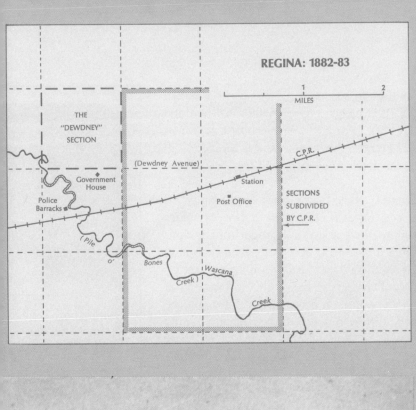

REGINA: 1882-83

THE "DEWDNEY" SECTION

Government House

Police Barracks

(Dewdney Avenue)

C.P.R.

Station

Post Office

SECTIONS SUBDIVIDED BY C.P.R.

(Pile O' Bones Creek) Wascana Creek

MILES 1 2

near the station where, they contended, the government as well as the railway would profit. In the compromise that followed Macdonald tried to placate everyone by scattering the various locations. As a result the queer community straggled for two and a half miles across the prairies, the various clusters of official buildings standing like islands in the prairie sea. In all the wheeling and dealing over land profits no public or corporate leader ever bothered to consider the interests of the settlers, who had an awkward town plan imposed upon them by men from eastern Canada, few of whom had any intention of making Regina their home.

It was typical of eastern indifference to local North West interests that when the first train arrived on August 23 with a carload of officials to christen the town, the residents themselves were given no part in the ceremony which took place in the general manager's private car. Van Horne, Donald Smith, Duncan McIntyre, and John McTavish of the CPR were all present along with the company solicitor, J. J. C. Abbott. (Stephen had come only as far as Winnipeg.) Both the Hudson's Bay Company and the Bank of Montreal were represented on the highest level. Judge Francis Johnson of Quebec, a former territorial official, proposed the toast to Mr. and Mrs. Dewdney and "Success to Regina, the Queen City of the Plains."

It makes, in retrospect, an ironic little scene: There are the eastern dignitaries in their dark coats, wing collars, and striped trousers, lounging on the

These photographs of Regina in the first year of its existence show the scattered nature of the town caused by the war between Dewdney and the CPR, each of whom had conflicting land interests. Vast gaps separated homes and public buildings. Nicholas Flood Davin's famous Leader *occupied a headquarters isolated from its neighbours. The noted journalist, visiting Regina in the fall of 1883, had, on a whim, accepted an offer of local businessmen to start a newspaper.*

173

rear platform of the private car with their well-bustled wives; and there are the first families of Regina in their shapeless clothing, peering curiously out from behind the protection of the canvas tent flaps. Among the onlookers that day were at least three future mayors and one future chief justice; in the years that followed they and their fellows would help to shape the destinies of Saskatchewan and perhaps to nurture the seeds of dissidence sown in those formative months. But none of this occurred to the gentlemen on the train, sipping their French champagne and squinting across the parched prairie, flat as a deal board, where the little tents stretched off in ragged clusters to the distant river.

The Grand Trunk declares war

FROM HIS VANTAGE POINT at Winnipeg, George Stephen must have contemplated the astonishing progress of the railway with mixed feelings. Certainly his strategy, and Van Horne's, was working; but the company itself was in a desperate cash position.

The strategy had been to get the prairie section of the CPR operating as swiftly as possible. In that way a great chunk of the subsidy, which was paid to the company on the completion of each twenty-mile section, could be gained. Equally important, the paying portion of the line could go into operation and begin to show a profit at once.

All that year the climate in the money markets of London and New York had been bad for Canadian Pacific bonds. Stephen made no effort to place CPR securities on the London market, though he hoped to intrigue British investors into ordering land grant bonds from Montreal and New York.

The market was so bad that when the CPR was driven to issue the remainder of its authorized stock in May, 1882, the best price it could get was twenty-five cents on the dollar. Stephen was loath to issue any more stock at all. First, he wanted to prove that the CPR was a paying proposition. But in 1882

he had to find $4,300,000 to buy up the western section of the Quebec government's railroad and its branch lines in order to give the CPR access to Montreal. To raise the money he was forced to sell four times as much stock as he had originally reckoned on.

The matter of the land subsidy was equally annoying. Every time the railroad moved twenty miles it was supposed to be given a proportionate number of acres. But even if every alternate section in the forty-eight-mile belt had been fit for settlement, it would have been impossible to locate all of the twenty-five million acres in that strip. By the end of 1882, Stephen realized, the company would have earned ten million acres of land; but there were only three million available along the completed right of way.

He was almost beside himself. In his letters he began to underline words for emphasis with great slashes of his pen: "It is most *essential* it should be settled *where* we are to get these lands," he wrote to Macdonald. The CPR's account at the Bank of Montreal was badly overdrawn. Without the land the railway had no hope of raising further cash. "Our pinch is *now*," he wrote in frustration at the end of November. Bit by bit the Canadian Pacific Railway got its land, but it was another twenty-two years before the last acre was finally set aside for the company.

Even the acreage the company received at the time did not produce the hoped-for revenue; the land grant bonds were not selling. Again, the only other possible source of ready cash was stock. In December, 1882, the company increased its authorized capital stock from twenty-five million dollars to one hundred million. Stephen, in New York, persuaded a number of leading American financial houses to form a syndicate to take a potential thirty millions over a nine-month period. To get cash Stephen was forced to sell the stock at slightly better than half price.

The Grand Trunk, meanwhile, was continuing to fight the railway on several new fronts. The

Joseph Hickson, general manager of the Grand Trunk, struck a characteristically Napoleonic pose for this portrait. A Northumberland man, involved with railways since boyhood, punctual as a conductor's

GTR's forceful general manager, Joseph Hickson, was no minor adversary. Married to a member of the Dow brewing family, he was a long-time crony and supporter of Sir John A. Macdonald. During his tenure of office, Hickson had been creating a route for the Grand Trunk through Ontario and into the American midwest, and he did not intend to stand idly by and watch a new railway destroy his creation.

In the election of 1882, Macdonald found himself caught between the Canadian Pacific and the Grand Trunk. He confidently expected that his railway policy would win him the election; but he needed Grand Trunk support, especially in Ontario where he faced a hard fight. The older railway's political muscle in that province was considerable. Among other things it told its employees exactly how they must vote.

The Prime Minister openly solicited Hickson's assistance, even naming specific candidates he wanted the Grand Trunk to back. Hickson, who put a private car at Macdonald's disposal during the campaign, was determined to exact a price for his support. On the very eve of the election he asked the Prime Minister to put a stop to the CPR's invasion of Grand Trunk territory. Macdonald wired vaguely: "Government not committed to any adverse line you may depend upon what I can possibly do personally to meet your views." With that fuzzy promise Hickson had to be content. But the Grand Trunk was moving into the Liberal camp.

Meanwhile, Hickson was attacking on a second front. The Grand Trunk's chief rival in southwestern Ontario was the Great Western, which operated a network of lines between Toronto, London, Hamilton, and Windsor. Hickson, by aggressive competitive tactics, forced an amalgamation in August, 1882. He now controlled every rail approach to the United States. If he linked up with the Northern Pacific at Duluth he would shortly be part of a transcontinental through line that could undercut the Canadian Pacific.

Hickson struck again in Quebec. The CPR now owned half of the Quebec, Montreal, Ottawa and Occidental Railway – the section between Montreal and Ottawa. Hickson, in a swift coup, bought the other half – the "North Shore Line" – to prevent the CPR from getting into Quebec City.

In London, a propaganda barrage aimed directly at the CPR continued. The Grand Trunk pamphlets harped on the foolhardiness of crossing the country north of Lake Superior. A letter in the *Money Market Review*, obviously planted, declared that "no more hopeless project than that line, or a more baseless speculation than its land grant . . . was ever started to enveigle the British public."

Perhaps if the public, which watched the battle of the two giants, had been privy to some of the general manager's private correspondence with his adversary, it might have viewed the contest with more cynicism. For in the matter of passenger and freight rates, business was still business and profits were still profits. Much of Van Horne's invective against Hickson in the years that followed was confined to charges that Grand Trunk personnel were breaking rate-fixing agreements, which the two companies, in spite of their public enmity, had secretly entered into in eastern Canada. Such rate cuts, in Van Horne's words, were "simply idiotic." He gave orders that any CPR agent who dropped rates below those established by the two companies should be subject to instant dismissal – and he wanted the same understanding from his rival.

In areas where direct revenue was not concerned, Van Horne continued to do battle with Hickson. When the Grand Trunk played down the CPR's route on its own folders, Van Horne instructed Alexander Begg, the company's general emigration agent, to strike back with a map of his own. He told Begg to show the GTR's Toronto-Montreal road as a faint line and to drop out their Toronto-Chicago line entirely. In the matter of cartography, the general manager was quite prepared to smite his rivals; but free enterprise in the nineteenth century did not extend to the costly competition of a rate war.

5

＝＝◦❈◦＝＝

The
West
Begins
to Come
Alive

＝＝◦❈◦＝＝

*A contemporary artist
made this lively pencil sketch
of Yale, British Columbia,
in its railway construction period.
On pay day, belligerent
Irishmen, Chinese coolies,
Indian girls, and drunks
paraded and often brawled
on the main street.
Some even went to church.*

Hell's Bells Rogers

ONE OF JIM HILL'S several executive strengths was an ability to settle upon the right man for the right job at the right moment. His choices, however, were not always obvious. Certainly his decision to employ a former Indian fighter to find a route through the Rockies and Selkirks must have seemed totally outrageous. Major A. B. Rogers had never seen a mountain – he was a prairie surveyor; yet here was Hill, sending him off to explore the most awesome peaks in British Columbia and expecting him to succeed where dozens of more experienced engineers had failed! Rogers was also one of the most heartily disliked men in his profession. He fed his workmen wretchedly, drove them mercilessly, and insulted them continually. His profanity had earned him the name of "Hell's Bells Rogers." Admittedly, he was honest – he pared corporate expenses with a fealty that almost amounted to fanaticism. He was also ambitious, not for money but for fame; and it was this quality that attracted Hill when he called him into his office in February, 1881, and proceeded to dangle before him a chance at immortality.

"Very few men ever learned to understand him," his friend Tom Wilson wrote of Rogers. Wilson, a packer and later a Rocky Mountain guide, was one of those few. Rogers, he said, "had a generous heart and a real affection for many. He cultivated a gruff manner to conceal the emotions that he seemed ashamed to let anyone sense – of that I am certain. His driving ambition was to have his name handed down in history; for that he faced unknown dangers and suffered privations."

James Jerome Hill understood those ambitions when he offered to put Rogers in charge of the mountain division of the CPR. Rogers's main task would be to locate the shortest route between Moose Jaw Bone Creek and Savona's Ferry on Kamloops Lake. That meant finding feasible passes through the southern Rockies and also through the mysterious Selkirks. There were several partially explored passes in the former, but no one had been able to find an opening in the Selkirk barrier. Hill made Rogers an offer he knew he could not refuse: if the Major could find that pass and save the railroad a possible hundred and fifty miles, he promised, the CPR would give him a cheque for five thousand dollars and name the pass after him.

Rogers did not care about the cash bonus. But to have one's name on the map! That was the goal of every surveyor. He accepted Hill's offer on the spot, and from that moment on, in Tom Wilson's words, "to have the key-pass of the Selkirks bear his name was the ambition he fought to realize."

Rogers's first move was to read everything that was available about the mountain country. An entry in Walter Moberly's journal of 1866 caught his eye:

"*Friday, July 13th* – Perry returned from his trip up the east fork of the Ille-cille-waut River. He did not reach the divide, but reported a low, wide valley as far as he went. His exploration has not settled the point whether it would be possible to get through the mountains by this valley but I fear not. He ought to have got on the divide, and his failure is a great disappointment to me. He reports a most difficult country to travel through, owing to fallen timber and underbrush of very thick growth. . . ."

Rogers determined to complete Perry's exploration. With his favourite nephew, Albert, he set off at the beginning of April for Kamloops. It took him twenty-two days to reach the town. When he arrived, he engaged ten "strapping young Indians" through a remarkable contract made with their leader, Chief Louie. Its terms rendered them up to Rogers as his virtual slaves, to work "without grumbling" until they were discharged. If any of them came back without a letter of good report, his

wages were to be forfeited and the chief agreed to lay one hundred lashes on his bare back.

The Major, who seemed to live entirely on beans and chewing tobacco (he believed too much food was bad for people), concluded, wrongly, that the expedition's slim commissariat could be augmented by game shot along the way and so set off with a minimum of supplies. He was to regret that parsimony.

The twelve members of the party left Kamloops on April 29. It took them fourteen days to cross the rounded peaks of the Gold Range. They proceeded down the Columbia by raft, with the unfortunate Indians swimming alongside, until, about May 21, they reached the mouth of the Illecillewaet. Here Rogers found himself standing on the exact spot from which Moberly's assistant, Perry, had plunged into the unknown, fifteen years before.

It must have been a memorable moment. The little group, clustered on the high bank of the Columbia, was dwarfed by the most spectacular mountain scenery on the continent. Behind them the rustling river cut an olive path through its broad evergreen valley. Above them towered the Selkirks, forming a vast island of forest, rock, ice, and snow three hundred miles long.

Now began a terrible ordeal. Each man balancing a hundred-pound pack on the back of his neck struggled upward, picking his way over mud-falls, scaling perpendicular rock points, wading through beaver swamps dense with underbrush and devil's clubs, whose nettles were almost inescapable. Albert Rogers later wrote that without the fear of his uncle's dreadful penalty, all the Indians would have fled. Rogers himself was to remark later that "many a time I wished myself dead."

In the gloomy box canyon of the Illecillewaet (later named for Albert Rogers) the snow was still several feet deep. Above them they could see the paths of the avalanches – the timber crushed to matchwood in swaths hundreds of feet wide. Sometimes, unable to move farther on one side of the river, they were forced to creep over immense snow

179

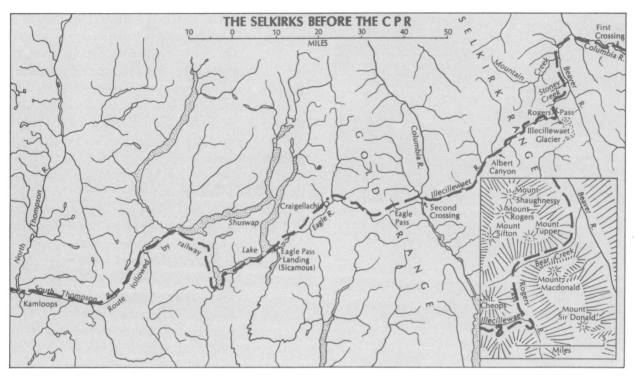

10 0 10 20 30 40 50
MILES

SELKIRK RANGE

GOLD RANGE

First Crossing

Columbia R.

Mountain Creek

Stoney Creek

Rogers Pass

Illecillewaet Glacier

Albert Canyon

Illecillewaet

Second Crossing

Beaver R.

Columbia R.

Craigellachie

Shuswap

Eagle R.

Eagle Pass

Eagle Pass Landing (Sicamous)

Route followed by railway

North Thompson

South Thompson R.

Kamloops

Lake

Mount Shaughnessy
Mount Rogers
Mount Sifton
Mount Tupper
Bear Creek
Mount Macdonald
Mt. Cheops
Illecillewaet
Rogers Pass
Mount Sir Donald
5
Miles

The great canyon of the Illecillewaet, shown here [as] it looked shortly after M[a] Rogers first explored it. Named Albert Canyon, after his nephew, it lay directly along the future route of the CPR, as the m[ap] on the left indicates. Whe[n] Rogers and his party reac[hed] this spot, the snow was st[ill] several feet deep and they were obliged to crawl gingerly over immense snow bridges suspended [a] hundred and fifty feet ab[ove] the frothing water course[.] High above them, feedin[g] the river, hung the vast Illecillewaet Glacier.

bridges high above the frothing watercourse. Occasionally they would catch glimpses of an incredible wedge-shaped glacier, hanging like a jewel from the mountain pinnacles. Before many years it would become one of the CPR's prime tourist attractions.

The Indians could no longer carry packs weighing a hundred pounds, the game proved to be non-existent, and the party was forced to go on short rations. They held cautiously to the lee of an obelisk-shaped peak, which would later be named Mount Sir Donald, after Donald A. Smith. At four o'clock one afternoon they came upon a level snowfield that seemed to be the summit. When the sun's rays vanished and the crust began to re-form they scurried across it. At the far end they heard the sound of gurgling water and to their satisfaction saw that it separated, some of it running westward, some to the east. They had reached the divide; was this the route the railway would take?

Mountains towered above them in every direction. A smear of timber extended half-way up one slope and they determined to make their ascent next day at this point. It was late when they reached the peak. They had neither wood for a fire nor boughs for beds. They were perched on a narrow ridge where a single false move could lead to their deaths. They crawled along the razorback until they encountered a little ledge in the shadow of a protective rock. Here they would have to wait until the crust on the snow formed again and the morning light allowed them to travel.

At dawn they crept back to the ridge and worked their way down to the south fork of the river. It seemed to Rogers that this fork paralleled the valley of the opposite side of the dividing range through which, he concluded, the waters of the Beaver River emptied into the Columbia on the eastern flanks of the mountain barrier. If that was true, then a pass of sorts existed.

170

A close-up view of the Illecillewaet Glacier, taken during the early stages of railroad construction. This vestige of the most recent ice age became one of the CPR's great tourist attractions, and Glacier House, erected only a short distance from its base on the railway line, was a favourite stopping point for travellers in the Selkirks. Since this photograph was made, however, the glacier has receded far up the mountain and Glacier House is shuttered forever. But there was a time when the view was so staggering that a lady from Seattle actually asked whether the ice sheet was real or if the CPR had installed it for advertising purposes. The glacier – or what is left of it – forms the core of Glacier National Park, one of several parks established as a result of the railway's change of route through the Selkirks.

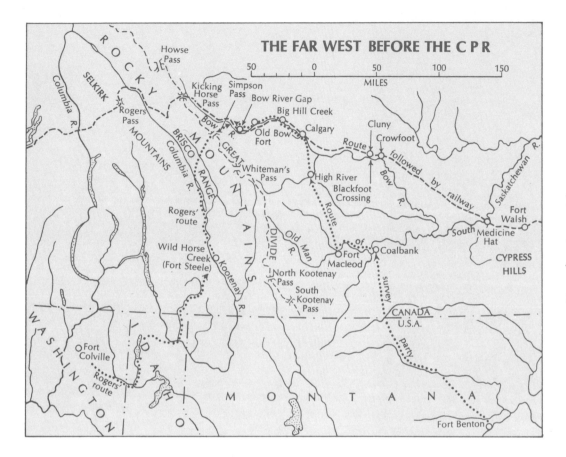

THE FAR WEST BEFORE THE CPR

This is the only photograph extant of Tom Wilson as a young man. When he left the mountains, after his first year with the surveyors, Wilson did not intend to return. When he did, the following summer, Rogers told him: "I knew you'd be back! You'll never leave these mountains again as long as you live. They've got you now." The Major was right. Wilson lived out his life in the mountains, enjoying a measure of fame in his later years as the best known of the Rocky Mountain packers as well as the discoverer of Lake Louise, Emerald Lake, and the Yoho Valley.

Unfortunately, he could not be sure. There were eighteen unexplored miles left, but by this time the party was almost out of food. Roger's notorious frugality had destroyed all chances of finding a pass that season. It would be at least another year before he could say for certain whether it existed at all. By that time the rails would be approaching the valley of the Bow, and he still had not explored the Kicking Horse Pass in the Rockies, which had scarcely been glimpsed since the day when James Hector first saw it in 1858.

Rogers sent all but two of his Indians back to Kamloops. The others guided him to Fort Colville in Washington Territory. There he hired a packtrain and made his way by a circuitous route back into the Kootenay country to the mining camp at Wild Horse Creek. He planned to join his main party of surveyors by crossing the Kootenay River, hiking over the Brisco Range, and then working his way down the Spray to the point where it joined the Bow, where they were waiting for him. It was wild country, unmarked by trails or guideposts, but it was the only route available.

He did not take his nephew with him. It was late June by this time and it was imperative that somebody explore the Kicking Horse Pass from its western approach. Rogers decided that Albert must take the packtrain to the mouth of the Kicking Horse River and from that point make his way to the summit of the continental divide. Only one white man had ever come that way before – James Hector; but he had descended from the summit.

Even the Indians shunned the Kicking Horse. Its terrible gorge was considered too difficult for horses. On his first trip into the Rockies, young Albert, aged twenty-one – "that little cuss" as the Major fondly called him – was being asked to attempt a feat that no human being had yet accomplished.

The Major finds his pass

MAJOR ROGERS and his men were advancing on the Rockies from three directions that spring of 1881. While Albert worked his way towards the Kicking Horse and his uncle guided his packhorses over the Brisco Range, the main body of surveyors was heading westward from St. Paul towards Fort Benton, Montana, the jumping-off point for the eastern slopes of the Canadian Rockies. Here they were joined by a 22-year-old stripling from Ontario who, after a brief stint with the Mounted Police, was positively lusting for adventure. His name was Tom Wilson and he was the youngest man to be hired by Roger's deputy, a stickler of a civil engineer named Hyndman, whose rules were so strict that they were promptly dubbed "Hyndman's Commandments." Three aroused the special ire of the men and almost caused a strike: *Not a tap of work was to be done on Sunday. Men caught swearing aloud were to be instantly discharged. Men caught eating, except at the regular camp meal, were to be fired on the spot.*

When the party, still smarting under these harsh strictures, reached its rendezvous at Bow River Gap in the Rockies, it was several days late and there was no sign of Rogers. Then about a week later – the date was July 15 – Tom Wilson was sitting on a narrow Indian trail west of the camp, smoking his pipe, when a mottled roan cayuse appeared around a curve carrying a man wearing an old white helmet and a brown canvas suit. Wilson realized at once that the tattered creature on the scarecrow horse must be the notorious Major.

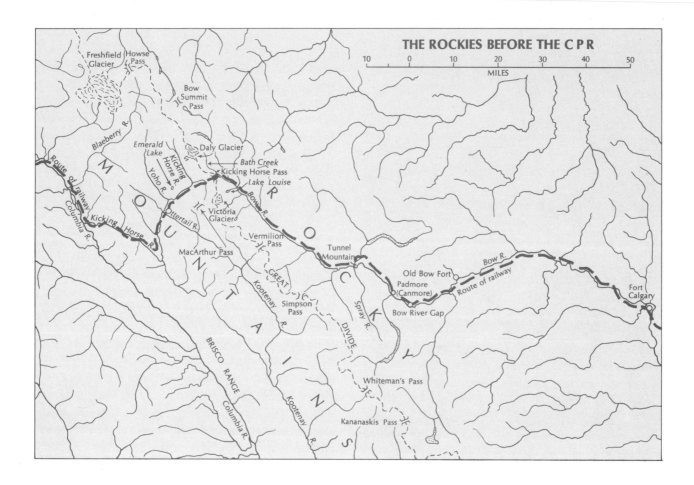

THE ROCKIES BEFORE THE C P R

"This Hyndman's camp?" Rogers asked in his jerky manner.

Wilson nodded and guided Rogers to Hyndman's tent. Hyndman stepped out, but there was no word of greeting from his chief.

"What's your altitude?" he shot at Hyndman. The engineer stammered that he did not know.

"Blue Jesus!* Been here several days and don't know the altitude yet. You ——!" There followed what Wilson described as "a wonderful exhibition of scientific cussing [which] busted wide all of Hyndman's 'Holy Commandments' and inspired delighted snickers and chuckles of admiration from the men who had quickly gathered around."

Three days later Rogers announced that he intended to set off on his own to do some exploring, but when he asked for a volunteer to accompany him, the request was greeted by silence. As Wilson put it, "Every man present had learned, in three days, to hate the Major with real hatred." But in spite of himself Wilson thought he might as well take a chance and follow Rogers.

The Major was clearly worried about the fate of his nephew. "Has that damned little cuss Al got here yet?" was his first question on riding into camp one afternoon after an exploration. It was some time before Wilson came to understand that Rogers's

---

*Tom Wilson's memoirs, written in the straight-laced thirties, reproduce the Major's favourite bit of profanity as "Blue——!" Since it is doubtful that he would have censored so mild a word as "blazes" (and equally doubtful that the Major himself would have lapsed into such a euphemism), I have filled in the blank with the most obvious expletive.

manner of speaking about his nephew was part of his armour – a shield to conceal his inner distress.

Two days of searching failed to locate the missing Albert. When Rogers and Wilson returned to the summit camp late one evening, after a long and vain exploration, they were met with silence. The Major tried to rout the men out to search at night, but they sensibly refused. "How the Major put in that night I do not know," Wilson confessed, "but I do know that at daybreak next morning he was on the warpath cursing about late risers." The members of the summit party were dispatched in all directions. Somewhere down below, on the tangled western slope of the Rockies, wrinkled by canyons and criss-crossed by deadfalls, was the missing youth – dead or alive, no one could say.

Down that slope Tom Wilson and a companion made their way until they reached the mouth of a glacial stream later to be called the Yoho. There they made camp. They had scarcely finished their meal when a shot cracked out in the distance. They sprang to their feet and began clambering down the stream bed, shouting as they went, until, rounding a curve, they came upon the missing man. Albert Rogers was starving and on the point of mental and physical exhaustion. His rations had long since been used up and for two days he had had nothing to eat but a small porcupine. He had picked it clean, right down to the quills.

The ascent back up the Kicking Horse, which the trio made the following day with Albert Rogers's two Indians, was so terrible that half a century later Wilson insisted that it could not be described. Nearing the summit, they fired a fusillade of revolver shots and a moment later the little major came tearing down the trail to meet them. He stopped, motionless, squinting intently at his nephew; and then Wilson was permitted, for a moment, to glimpse the human being concealed behind that callous armour of profanity.

"He plainly choked with emotion, then, as his face hardened again he took an extra-vicious tobacco-juice-shot at the nearest tree and almost snarled

. . . 'Well, you did get here, did you, you damn little cuss?' There followed a second juice eruption and then, as he swung on his heel, the Major shot back over his shoulder: 'You're alright, are you, you damn little cuss?' "

Al Rogers grinned. He understood his uncle. "He also knew that, during the rest of the walk to camp, the furious activity of his uncle's jaws and the double-speed juice shots aimed at the vegetation indicated our leader's almost uncontrollable emotions."

Wilson resumed his job as personal attendant to Major Rogers. A creature of whim, the Major had pinned his hopes on the Kicking Horse, with the Bow Summit as his second choice. Near the end of the season he played one hunch that was to cause him a good deal of mental anguish during the months that followed: he decided abruptly not to proceed further with the Howse Pass survey. Though he knew nothing about the pass, he had come to the sudden conclusion that it was not a feasible route and was not worth bothering with. As Wilson noted, "Always the Kicking Horse ruled his mind, and although at times he had doubts regarding it being the best route, yet those fears never lasted long." But his sudden decision caused him many misgivings the following summer, long after the Kicking Horse Pass had officially been chosen.

By the time Rogers reached Winnipeg, late in 1881, Van Horne's appointment had been announced. The new general manager took Rogers with him to Montreal in January, 1882, to convince the CPR directors that the Kicking Horse route was practicable with grades of 2.2 per cent and that there appeared to be a feasible pass through the Selkirks.

Rogers had not fully convinced himself, though his pronouncements exuded confidence. In truth, he had discovered half a pass only. To confirm his findings he would have to scale the eastern wall of the Selkirks and make sure that the gap he thought he saw from the Illecillewaet actually pierced the mountain barrier.

The mighty Columbia River all but encircles the great rampart of the Selkirks, which can be likened to an island of mountains, girdled by running water. From certain vantage points, such as this one, the great valley – misty blue in the summertime, chalk-white in the winter – has scarcely changed since Major Rogers first saw it. In 1881, Rogers approached the Selkirks from the west, not more than a rifle shot from the modern city of Revelstoke. The following summer he approached from the east – again from the valley of the Columbia, and directly across from the present town of Donald.

That May, he again attacked the Selkirks. No detailed account of that abortive journey remains but it was clearly an ordeal. Once again Rogers had failed to bring along enough supplies. Only the discovery of an old canoe, which brought them swiftly back to camp, prevented the entire party from starving to death. The pass had not been found.

On July 17 Rogers tried once more, setting off from the point where the Beaver flows into the Columbia. Here, before the railway builders helped destroy it, was some of the loveliest scenery to be found in the mountains. The timber was stupendous: the cedars were often ten feet or more in diameter; sometimes they rose two hundred feet above the matted forest floor. Through this unknown country Rogers and his party climbed for hours along a spectacular route that millions would one day traverse in comfort. The brush was so dense they could make little more than two miles a day. Rogers suffered severely from blackflies and mosquitoes. "Not one engineer in a hundred," his friend George Grant later remarked, "would have risked, again and again, health and life as he did."

Above them loomed glaciers fifty feet thick and mountains that would one day bear the names of famous Canadians – Shaughnessy, Sifton, Tupper, Macdonald – and of Rogers himself. The lower mountain slopes were scarred by the paths of snowslides, the trees snapped off dozens of feet from the base. These mountains looked familiar to Rogers, for he had seen them all the previous year from the opposite side. There, before them, was the very peak on which he had stood in the summer of 1881 and there the same broad meadow. He and his party had reached an altitude of forty-five hundred feet and were standing in a valley that seemed completely enclosed by mountains. Ragged black precipices stood guard at the entrance. To the north and west a smudge of timber rose up to blend with sloping meadows, the soft grasses flecked with wild flowers. Beyond these spangled pastures were glacial fields of glistening white, tilting upwards to curved ridges which, in turn, led the eye higher to frosted peaks. To the southwest more mountains stretched off into a haze of misty blue. Somewhere in the distance a brook gurgled above the sound of the rustling spruces. Here the waters flowed in opposite directions, spilling down both sides of the Selkirks. Now the Major knew he had found at last the long-sought passage through the barrier. In the face of considerable hardship – and some foolhardiness – he had done what his detractors had said was impossible. There was a way through the Selkirks after all, and its discovery would make him immortal. Almost from this moment, this smiling, mountain-ringed meadow would bear the name of Rogers Pass. The date was July 24, 1882, and Rogers, after searching vainly for an alternate pass, lost no time in retracing his steps so that he might let the world have the news of his discovery.

Tom Wilson, meanwhile, was engaged in packing supplies from Padmore in the foothills to the summit of the Kicking Horse in the Rockies. One day in August he heard the distant roar of avalanches and inquired about them. An Indian told him that these slides occurred on "snow mountain," which lay high above "the lake of the little fishes." The description intrigued Wilson and he asked the Indian to guide him to the lake. It was well worth the trip. The two men burst out upon a small emerald gem, framed by a backdrop of dark evergreens, a dazzling white glacier, and a curtain of blue mountains.

"As God is my judge, I never in all my explorations saw such a matchless scene," Wilson recalled. He sat down, pulled out his pipe and, as he smoked,

As seen from the Rogers Pass, the naked peaks of the Selkirks, wreathed in shifting mists, show the distinctive pyramidal shape that distinguishes them geologically from the more massive and cathedral-like Rockies or the old, rounded bulks of the Gold (or Monashee) Mountains. No wonder the early explorers named one of the Selkirks' peaks Cheops!

The Rogers Pass was adopted by the CPR only after considerable soul searching. The choice irked Canadian surveyors, who had once claimed no pass existed. Some tried to give credit for its discovery (wrongly) to Walter Moberly.

gazed for a long time on the mirror of blue-green water, soon to become one of the most famous tourist attractions on the continent. Wilson decided to name it Emerald Lake, and so it appeared on the first geological map. But even as the map was published the name was changed to Lake Louise in honour of the Governor General's lady.

True to Jim Hill's promise, the railway presented Rogers with a cheque for five thousand dollars. To the frustration of the CPR's accounting department, he refused to cash it.

"What! Cash that cheque?" Rogers cried. "I would not take a hundred thousand dollars for it. It is framed and hangs in my brother's house in Waterville, Minnesota, where my nephews and nieces can see it."

"I'm not here for money!" the Major added. It was an unnecessary comment – but one which must have given considerable satisfaction to James J. Hill, the man who originally made that puzzling decision to send a prairie surveyor into the unknown Selkirks.

Onderdonk's lambs

ALMOST EVERY LEADING FIGURE connected with the building of the great railway—with one notable exception—achieved the immortality of a place name. The map of western Canada is, indeed, a kind of coded history of the construction period. The stations along the way (some of them now abandoned) tell the story of the times: Langevin, Tilley, Chapleau and Cartier, Stephen and Donald, Langdon and Shepard, Secretan, Moberly, Schreiber, Crowfoot, Fleming, and Lacombe. Harry Abbott, the general superintendent, has a street named after him in Vancouver, along with Henry Cambie, the surveyor, and Lauchlan Hamilton, who laid out most of the CPR towns; Thomas Shaughnessy has an entire subdivision. Macoun, Sifton, and even Baron Pascoe du P. Grenfell, one of the more obscure – and reluctant – members of the original syndicate, are recognized in stations along the main line. Rosser and Dewdney are immortalized in the names of the main streets in the towns they founded. Most of the leading figures in the railway's story had mountain peaks named after them; Van Horne, indeed, had an entire range. But the connoisseur of place names will search in vain on mountain, village, park, avenue, subdivision, plaque, or swamp for any reference to the man who built the railway between Eagle Pass and Port Moody through some of the most difficult country in the world. There is not so much as an alleyway named for Andrew Onderdonk.

Perhaps he would have wanted it that way, for he was a remarkably reticent man. No biographer appeared before or after his death to chronicle his accomplishments, which included the San Francisco sea-wall, parts of the Trent Valley Canal, and the first subway tunnels under New York's East River. In the personal memoirs of the day he remains an aloof and shadowy figure, respected but

Andrew Onderdonk, the sophisticated contractor, dressed in muddy Yale exactly as he would have in his native New York. Described as "a very unassuming man," he had no observable eccentricities unless one counts the monumental reticence that made him a kingdom unto himself. His pretty wife, Delia, was "the most modestly dressed woman in Yale."

not really known. Rogers, Hill, and Van Horne were each referred to by their underlings as "the old man." Onderdonk was known to everybody by the more austere title of "A.O."

If Onderdonk presented a cool face to the world, it was partly because he did not need to prove himself. He came from an old New York family that had been in America for more than two centuries. And his sense of security was sustained by the knowledge that he had almost unlimited funds behind him. He was front man for a powerful syndicate whose chief ornament was the legendary San Francisco banker, Darius O. Mills. Charles Tupper, the Minister of Railways, had had his fill of underfinanced contractors and so was happy to facilitate Onderdonk's purchase of the four Fraser Canyon contracts. Some time later, when the government let the rest of the British Columbia line from Emory's Bar to Port Moody on the coast, Onderdonk was again awarded the contract, though again he was not the lowest bidder. Certainly in this instance, if not before, the government made use of some fancy sleight-of-hand to ensure that he was successful. Clearly, it wanted him to have the job, which was, admittedly, as difficult a one as had ever faced a contracting firm in the Dominion. As Henry Cambie wrote: "No such mountain work had ever been attempted in Canada before."

The CPR under the terms of its contract was to inherit the Onderdonk section of the railway. Onderdonk then, unlike Van Horne, was building a road that he would never have to manage. The distinction was to be the basis of a long and bitter dispute between the CPR and the government.

By the time the CPR turned its first prairie sod in May, 1881, Onderdonk's lambs, as they were called, had been at work for a year but had not laid a mile of track. There were four tunnels to be drilled within a mile and a half of the headquarters at Yale; it took eighteen months to blast them out of the rock of the canyon. That left twenty-three more tunnels to be drilled on the Onderdonk line. The

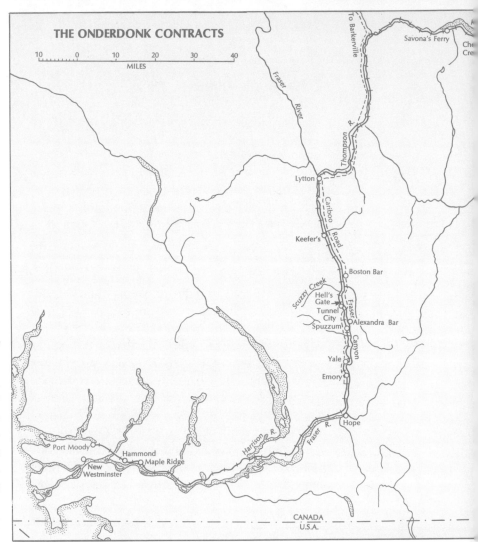

THE ONDERDONK CONTRACTS

FRASER CANON, SHOWING FOUR TUNNELS ABOVE SPUZZUM

WM. NOTMAN & SON, MONTREAL

Onderdonk faced the kind of terrain shown at left when he began work in the Fraser Canyon. Tunnel No. 7 and its half-finished gallery, fifteen miles above Yale, looked down on what was called "the slaughter pen."

Near Spuzzum in the Fraser Canyon, four tunnels and two trestles were visible. Mountains of compact granite striped with veins of quartz – the hardest rock in the world – rose eight thousand feet on both sides of the river.

blasting was painfully slow; even when big compressed air drills were used, it was not possible to move more than six feet a day. The flanks of the mountains were grooved by deep canyons; as a result, some six hundred trestles and bridges were required above Yale. To build them, Onderdonk would need to order forty million board feet of lumber.

At Hell's Gate on the Fraser, a traveller could stand and watch the agony of construction taking place directly across the foaming waters. Splintered trees toppled into the muddy gorge, huge rocks catapulted into the sky, vast chunks of mountainside slid into the river. Men could be seen suspended at dizzy heights against the rock walls, let down the cliffs on ladders secured by ropes to drill blasting holes into the rock face. To escape the resultant explosions they had to clamber back up as nimbly as possible. Engineers made their measurements and took their cross-sections suspended for hours and sometimes days "like Mahomet's coffin between heaven and earth." They worked in bare feet to ensure a better footing, but a break in the rope, a rock toppling from above, or a premature blast meant certain death.

Running along the same cliff face was the old corduroy road to the Cariboo mines, jammed with traffic – twelve-mule teams and ungainly prairie schooners pulled by sixteen oxen with six spares plodding behind. The road – itself an engineering miracle – was the only link between the coast and the interior of British Columbia. In some spots it was carried around the precipices on trestle-work, like the balcony of a house, so that passengers on the Cariboo stage were travelling directly over the boiling waters three hundred feet below.

This 1881 photograph of a section of track between Yale and Boston Bar shows the precarious position of the old Cariboo road. Note the gravel slide at the rear, where the road has been temporarily blocked. Rockfalls and constant blasting made travel hazardous.

Onderdonk was pledged to keep the road open; without it the economy of the Cariboo would be throttled. Besides, he needed it himself to bring supplies to his construction camps. Because the blasting and the building were going on above it, beneath it, or right beside it, great chunks of road sometimes slid into the Fraser. And when the railway itself required the right of way, construction had to be halted until a new section of road was built.

By June of 1882, when Van Horne launched his record-breaking push across the prairies, Onderdonk had driven scarcely twenty miles of steel. An explosives factory was turning out four thousand pounds of nitro-glycerine a day. Ten vessels containing six thousand Chinese coolies were on their way to swell his labour force. Expenses were mounting alarmingly and the freight rates on the old Cariboo corduroy road were strangling him. As a result he decided to attempt a task generally considered impossible: he proposed to build a steamer to negotiate the most treacherous section of the Fraser Canyon, known as Hell's Gate, at a point where the river hurled itself at ten knots over a ledge of black basalt.

The sturdy little craft built on the spot was called *Skuzzy* after a nearby mountain stream and was launched on May 4 by Mrs. Onderdonk. But it was easier to construct such a craft than it was to man it, especially as the river was in spring flow. At the last moment a skipper was found to attempt the feat. He set off on May 17, using every river trick he had learned to pit the *Skuzzy* against the furious waters. Time after time he was beaten back until, at length, he turned the boat about and returned in defeat.

To the astonishment of all, Onderdonk announced that another attempt would be made to force the boat through the canyon. That summer he went all the way to the upper Columbia to find three expert boatmen foolhardy enough to make the attempt. On September 7, he brought five flat-cars loaded with guests from Yale to witness the ordeal. They crowded the high bank of the Fraser, laying wagers on the outcome – the odds running as high as a hundred to one against the boat's getting through.

The crowds could not stay to witness the full struggle. After four days only a few miles of headway had been made. After ten it became apparent that the *Skuzzy* was losing the battle. At this point Andrew Onderdonk took command. He ordered ring-bolts driven into the rock walls of the canyon and he placed one hundred and fifty Chinese labourers at intervals along the banks passing heavy ropes through the bolts. These ropes were attached to the ship's capstan. Finally on September 28, with the aid of the engines, the steam winch, fifteen men on the capstan, and the mass of coolies tugging and straining along the bank, the boat finally got through, and a public holiday was declared in Yale. For the next year the *Skuzzy* worked the river between Lytton and Boston Bar, emerging splintered and battered after every journey.

All this time men were being mangled or killed by falling rock, by slides, by runaway horses, and above all by the incessant blasting. Often, huge rocks came hurtling out of the mouths of the tunnels like cannon-balls. One sank a boat, causing a man to drown. Another knocked down a bridge. The larger blasts touched off avalanches and mud slides. One of these slid down from such a height that it carried part of an oak forest and an entire Indian burying ground into the river, allowing the oaks to continue to grow "and the dead men's bones to rest without being in the least disturbed – fences, roots, images and all."

The battered Skuzzy, *following her successful negotiation of Hell's Gate, saw service between Lytton and Boston Bar before being shipped for further freighting to Kamloops Lake. She was a 250-ton craft, 127 feet long with a beam of 24 feet and with twenty bulkhead compartments to keep her buoyant.*

A slide in November, 1882, blocked the track so badly that it was mid-April before the debris could all be cleared away. A similar heap of debris was struck by a train with such impact that the locomotive became detached. It hurtled over a 250-foot embankment, did a full somersault, and landed upright at the river's edge. The fireman and engineer climbed out, unhurt.

There were other odd mishaps caused by the treacherous terrain. It was not even safe to get drunk. A veteran railroader who did staggered to the top of a bluff not far from the Big Tunnel one January day and toppled to his death. The danger was so great that it became difficult to get men who were willing to be suspended by ropes to drill powder holes in the chasm walls. The Indians were the most fearless; fortunately, they turned out to be first-class rock workers. But they also had a habit of quitting on payday.

Six months after Onderdonk began his contract the hospital at Yale had to be enlarged to take care of the accident victims. By August, 1881, the *Inland Sentinal*, which had been reporting deaths almost weekly, had become alarmed at the accident rate: "Life is held too cheap, generally, in this country, and it will evidently require severe punishment to teach parties that they cannot trifle with other people's lives even if they are careless of their own existence." Exactly one week after those words were written, two more men working in Number Seven Tunnel were killed by falling boulders.

Onderdonk used oxen to help clear sections of the British Columbia rain forest through which the rails made their way. Note that the ties here are not the roughly dressed half-logs that were used on the prairies but clearly come from planing mills which the contractor constructed to turn out bridge timber.

200

"The beardless children of China"

WHEN ANDREW ONDERDONK arrived in British Columbia there were only thirty-five thousand white citizens in the province. He would need to employ at least ten thousand men (actually many more, because of the turnover); from the very outset there was a kind of terror that he would solve his labour problem by importing and employing Chinese.

As soon as he arrived in Victoria in April, 1880, Onderdonk was met by a deputation from the Anti-Chinese association. He assured them that he would always give white labour the preference. When the white labour of the province was exhausted Onderdonk said he would, if necessity compelled him, fall back on the French Canadians of eastern Canada. Should that not be sufficient, he would with reluctance engage Indians and Chinese.

The first Chinese had come to British Columbia from California in 1858, attracted by the Fraser's gold. Anti-Chinese feeling had been rising steadily since that time. By 1878, when their employment in public works was banned, there were some three thousand Chinese in the province. All were prepared to work for lower wages than any white labourer, and that was the chief cause of the discontent. It was considered political suicide for a public figure to take any stand but one that was anti-Oriental.

The feeling elsewhere in Canada, though less intense, was generally against the Chinese. Almost all newspapers were editorially opposed to Oriental immigration. In Winnipeg, where Chinese were all but unknown, the *Times* published a fairly typical series of opinions about "the beardless and immoral children of China," as it called them; they possessed "no sense whatever of any principle of morality"; their brains were "vacant of all thoughts

THE HEATHEN CHINEE IN BRITISH COLUMBIA.
AMOR DE COSMOS, i.e.:—The Love of the World or the Lover of Mankind.
HEATHEN CHINEE: Why you sendee me offee?
A.D.C.:—Because you can't or won't assimilate with us.—HEATHEN CHINEE:—What is datee?
A.D.C.: You won't drink whiskey, and talk politics and vote like us.

This cartoon, published in 1879, is a comment on Amor de Cosmos, the founder of the British Colonist *and one-time premier of British Columbia, who was almost pathologically anti-Oriental. That year de Cosmos supported in the House of Commons a petition signed by 1,500 British Columbians asking that Chinese labour be banned in railway work. The* Colonist, *meanwhile, talked of "the Chinese ulcer eating into the prosperity of the country."*

This was Victoria's Chinatown as it looked from the harbour in the 1880's. Clearly it was a firetrap. Bitterness against the Orientals reached a peak just before the CPR construction when B.C. tried to impose a ten-dollar head tax on all Chinese. The Chinese workers struck and the whites were without laundry, vegetables, or servants. The law was thrown out but the ill-feeling remained.

which lift up and ennoble humanity"; and "it is an established fact that dealings with the Chinese are attended with evil results."

The Prime Minister himself agreed that the Chinese were "an alien race in every sense that would not and could not be expected to assimilate with our Arian population," but he was far too pragmatic to exclude Orientals from Canada until the railway was built. He put it bluntly to Parliament in 1882: "It is simply a question of alternatives: either you must have this labour or you can't have the railway."

Onderdonk was operating on a tight budget. He had been forced to accept four contracts at bids that were more than a million and a half dollars lower than his own tendered price. He had paid out an additional two hundred and fifteen thousand dollars to buy up the contracts. He was trying to get men to come all the way to British Columbia for lower wages than the Northern Pacific was offering – as little as $1.50 a day for labourers.

Chinese coolies, on the other hand, could be employed for one dollar a day. In addition, they did not require all the paraphernalia of a first-class camp. The coolie was prepared to move about in the wilderness, set up his own camp, and pack all his belongings, provisions, and camp equipment on his back. Michael Haney, who went to work for Onderdonk in 1883, discovered that it was possible to move two thousand Chinese a distance of twenty-five miles and have them at work all within twenty-four hours. The same task could not be performed with a similar number of white workmen in less than a week. It is small wonder, then, that almost from the outset Andrew Onderdonk began hiring Chinese in spite of a volley of protests. His first consignment came from the Northern Pacific Railroad in Oregon in 1880, the second from the Southern Pacific in California in 1881.

In the winter of 1881-82, Onderdonk chartered two sailing ships to bring an additional one thousand coolies each from Hong Kong. They arrived after a long, rough winter passage – "the men below decks slept in closed hatches with bad ventilation," Cambie recalled – but in good physical condition. Altogether in 1882, Onderdonk brought ten shiploads of Chinese, a total of about six thousand.

The coolies came from Kwang Tung province whose capital, Canton, was the only port in China through which foreign trade was permitted. The average wage there was seven cents a day; five years in North America could give any Chinese financial independence if he saved three hundred dollars. No wonder they clamoured to come!

They were not hired individually but in large groups through agents representing the Six Companies of Kwang Tung. Each Chinese promised a fee of 2½ per cent of his wages to the company, together with his passage money – about forty dollars. The company, in its turn, was pledged to look after each man's welfare in North America. From the point of view of the individual coolie, who could speak no English and who was totally uninformed about North American society, the Six Companies represented the only real method of getting to the promised land.

Michael Haney declared that in his entire experience of dealing with the Chinese, he could not recall one case of dishonesty. They lived up to their contracts, and if there was a dispute with a subcontractor, "it only needed the presence of a representative of the contractor to assure them that their grievances would be considered, to send them cheerfully to work again." But if they thought their rights were being trampled on, they ceased to be docile. George Munro, a construction boss, ruefully recalled his first payday when through an error in the payroll department, the Chinese workers received one cent less per hour than had been agreed upon. ". . . there was a little war declared right there. They stormed the Company's stores like madmen, and it didn't take the men at fault long to discover their mistake. The Chinamen were paid their cent and peace reigned once more."

Such incidents were not uncommon. The coolies were divided by the company that provided them

The Chinese were not skilled labourers and were not so used. Their main task was to ballast the line – to fill the gaps between the ties with wheelbarrow loads of gravel, so that the rails would not move when a train passed over them. "As a railway navvy," wrote J. A. Chapleau in his royal commission report, "the Chinaman has no superior."

A Chinese camp on the Onderdonk contract. Because they considered their stay in Canada temporary, the coolies made no effort to learn the language or change their mode of life. Many continued to wear the loose blouses and pigtails (here wound in a topknot) that they brought with them from Canton.

into gangs of thirty labourers plus a cook, an assistant cook, and a bookman, whose task it was to keep count of the payments to be made to each individual. In charge of each work gang was a white boss, who dealt directly with the bookman. Any foreman who did not get along well with his Oriental labourers could expect trouble. Once when a white boss refused to allow his coolies to build a fire along the grade to heat their big teapots, they all quit. On several occasions, white foremen were physically assaulted. One tried to fire two Chinese over the head of the gang's bookkeeper and precipitated a riot near Lytton. He and the white bridge superintendent, the timekeeper, and a teamster were attacked by the entire gang, which seriously mangled one man with a shovel. The following night a party of armed whites attacked the Chinese camp, burned their bunkhouses, and beat several coolies so severely that one died.

In such instances feeling ran high against the coolies. The Chief Justice of the province, Matthew Baillie Begbie, was horrified by "the terrible outrages against Chinamen" in the neighbourhood of Lytton. Begbie was aghast that in all cases "the perpetrators have escaped scot free." In one instance the ringleaders were positively identified by four of the surviving victims but were acquitted by the jury "upon evidence of an *alibi* which the prosecutors might well deem perjured."

Many inflammatory incidents occurred because of accidents along the line, for which the Chinese blamed the white foremen. On one occasion, about ten miles below Hope, a foreman named Miller failed to give his gang proper warning of a coming explosion; a piece of rock thrown up by the subsequent blast blew one coolie's head right off. His comrades took off after Miller, who plunged into the river to save himself. Several Chinese dived in after him while others on the bank pelted him with stones. Miller was saved by one of the tunnel contractors who rowed a boat through the hail of missiles and hauled him in, but not before one of the Chinese had got off two shots from a pistol. Miller

and his rescuer rowed desperately upstream, followed for two miles by an angry mob, before they made good their escape.

Deaths appeared to be more frequent among the Chinese labourers than in the white group, but the coolies were generally fatalistic about it. Haney, calling one day at a tent where a sick Chinese lay, asked the bookman: "Will he die to-day?" The bookman shook his head. "No, to-morrow, thlee o'clock." Haney claimed that at three, to the minute, the man expired.

The Chinese subsisted mainly on a diet of rice and stale ground salmon and, as a result, died by the score from scurvy. No real attempt was made to succour them. Two hundred who came over from China died during their first year in Canada. As in other deaths of Chinese there was no coroner's inquest and no medical attention supplied by either the government or the contractor.

The cold winters caused the coolies great hardship. Most found it impossible to work after mid-November. Cambie, one November 22, noted: "Chinamen who are still at work . . . appear to suffer dreadfully from cold. They work in overcoats and wrap their heads up in mufflers." In the winter of 1883-84, when Onderdonk's work force was diminished, the suffering was very great. When the contractors had no more need of them; the Chinese were discharged and left to scrabble for pickings in the worked-out bars of the Fraser or to exist in near destitution in the dying towns along the completed track.

Not all of the Chinese who came to Canada with the hope of securing financial independence achieved their dream. Although a Chinese labourer was paid about twenty-five dollars a month on the railway, it was difficult for him to save very much. He was not paid for the three months of winter when work was close to a standstill, and expenses for clothes, room rent, tools, fares, taxes, doctors, drugs, and other sundries left him with little more than forty dollars after a full year of toil on the railway. That only covered his debt to the steamboat company. The census figures of 1891 indicate that some five thousand coolies were unable to go back to Asia in the years following the completion of the Onderdonk contracts.

Because the Chinese left home expecting to return in a few years, they made no attempt to learn the language or alter their mode of life. Thus they were forever strangers in a foreign land, and their continued presence gave to British Columbia a legacy of racial tension that was to endure for the best part of a century.

The railway workers who remained left few descendants (since they brought no women with them) and few, if any, memories. Some, however, returned to Kwang Tung and then came back to Canada with their families to settle permanently in British Columbia. One of whom there is some slight record was a farmer from Toyshan named Pon Git Cheng. One of his sons became a houseboy for Benjamin Tingley Rogers, the Vancouver sugar magnate. And one of *his* sons, Dr. George Pon of Toronto, was in 1971 a vice-president of Atomic Energy of Canada. Dr. Pon was told something of his family background and was able to return to China to visit his grandfather's village in Toyshan. But he never discovered exactly what it was his grandfather did on the railway – how he was hired, where he worked, or what he felt about the strange, raw land which was to become his home. Such details were not set down and so are lost forever – lost and forgotten, like the crumbling bones that lie in unmarked graves beneath the rock and the rubble high above the Fraser's angry torrent.

Chinese cabins at Keefers station between Lytton and Boston Bar. All the coolies came from Kwang Tung, a province with a long reputation for disaffection (it subsequently produced most of the revolutionary leaders, including Sun Yat-sen). That helps explain why these navvies always stood up for their rights. It also explains why most Chinese food in Canada is Cantonese.

Michael Haney takes over

CHEAP ORIENTAL LABOUR undoubtedly saved Onderdonk from bankruptcy. Without the Chinese he could scarcely have completed his contracts. Between 1880 and 1884, at their lower rate of pay, the coolies saved him between three and five million dollars.

The Governor General believed that the presence of the Chinese was keeping costs down by at least twenty-five per cent, but even with this advantage Onderdonk's operation was a marginal one. By 1883 he was clearly in financial trouble. Marcus Smith, the government engineer who acted as Ottawa's watchdog on the line, reported that winter that "it was painfully apparent to myself and even to outsiders that the men were not working to advantage nor were they being well directed." Unless some drastic changes were made, he felt, Onderdonk could not pull through without heavy loss.

By March, 1883, Onderdonk was showing a book loss of two and a half million dollars on the work completed. In desperation he hired Michael Haney, who was given the management of the entire line from Port Moody to Kamloops. The crusty Marcus Smith was of two minds about Haney. "He seems to fully realize the gravity of your position and is anxious to improve it," he told Onderdonk, but he added, "I hope Mr. Haney has not caught the disease of the American mind to do something rapid or astounding." Haney, after all, was known as an impulsive Irishman, given to bold escapades; he did, however, know a good deal about saving money. He immediately tightened up discipline and speeded deliveries. He introduced his invention, the wing plough, which unloaded gravel from a line of open cars at bewildering speed. He developed a large nitro-glycerine factory at Yale, and when it blew up, breaking every window in town, he rebuilt it. He travelled the line on horseback, using relays of steeds so that he could inspect as much as a hundred miles of track a day. In this way all of the work in progress came under his personal inspection twice each month.

One of the chief reasons for the delays, Haney discovered, was the huge amount of bridging required. Timbers had to be shaped and cut at each bridging point, always at enormous cost. Haney streamlined the operation by building a mill capable of producing one hundred and fifty thousand board feet of lumber a day – every stick marked and numbered for its exact position on the bridge for which it was destined. By this method, the great trestles, prefabricated in advance, were sent forward ready for immediate erection.

In spite of Haney's cost-cutting, Onderdonk's financial problems continued. In the fall of 1883 he set off for Ottawa to lobby for a further subsidy for the unfinished line. In Victoria he ran into James Hartney, who had been cutting timber for him and who had not yet been paid. It says something for the state of Onderdonk's finances that the railway builder, who had a continent-wide reputation for prompt payment, kept putting Hartney off. He was preparing to leave for San Francisco with his family on a Sunday evening, but just before the ship sailed, Hartney served him with a writ. Thus was the Island community treated to the strange spectacle of the province's biggest employer of labour being pulled from his bunk at two in the morning, haled back to shore, and lodged in jail, where he languished for two hours before friends bailed him out.

A pile scow at work on a timber railroad trestle across Sicamous Arm of Shuswap Lake. This was on the section of the line that Andrew Onderdonk built, not for the government, but for the CPR. Onderdonk's later exploits included the construction of the world's first Ferris wheel and part of the Trent Canal in Ontario. He died at the age of 56 while building a subway tunnel under New York's East River. The cause of death was given as overwork.

Michael Haney's prefabricated assembly line was made to order for truss bridges like this one over Skuzzy Creek.
Two other bridges can be seen in the distance. On the far side, the Cariboo wagon road clings to the rim of China Bluff.

Yale's brief joy-ride

THE OPTIMISM of frontier communities along the line of the railway in the 1880's knew no bounds. When it became clear that the Pacific railway was finally to be built and the details of the Onderdonk contract were made public, the price of lots rose swiftly in Emory, the steamboat landing at the head of the navigable section of the Fraser. Emory, the real estate ads announced, "cannot fail to become one of the most important and prosperous Cities on the Pacific slope."

But Emory was not destined to be a city. It was soon apparent that the real centre of the Onderdonk operations would be at Yale. "Next summer will be a boom for Emory sure," the *Inland Sentinel* wrote wistfully in January, 1881. But in May the *Sentinel* itself moved its offices to Yale – a roaring, wide-open community which for the next three years was to be the railway centre of British Columbia. Then it, too, would fade as merchants, workers, and major institutions – once again including the *Sentinel* – packed up and moved to Kamloops.

Every shape of face and every kind of costume were observable along Yale's main street. The saloons were packed with gamblers playing faro, poker, chuck-a-luck, and dice. Three-card monte, the confidence man's game, was to be found everywhere. Against the incessant hammering of drills and the periodic crump of blasting powder, there was a cacophony of foreground noises – saw, mallet, and hammer, mouth organ, fiddle, and concertina, blending with the harsher music of rattling wheels. The air reeked with the mingled pungencies of fresh salmon, sawdust, black powder, and tobacco smoke. Yale, in short, was very like any raw frontier town in Wyoming, Montana, or Arizona save for one thing: all the saloons were shut tight on Sunday.

The Toronto *Mail* dispatched a man to examine the phenomenal community. He observed that "people don't walk in Yale, they rush. . . . From 'peep o' day' til long into the night the movement of men, horses and wagons along the one business street goes on scarcely with intermission. As we gaze at the hurrying throngs we wonder how on earth they all find beds or even space in which to lie down when they seek repose."

For all of the railway period, Yale was a strange and rather artificial community, cut off from the rest of the world. Almost everybody must have known in his heart that its existence was temporary, but no one voiced that feeling. The impermanence of the community was underlined by the shifting population and by the terrible fires that ravaged the business section. Seen from the steamer, the chief characteristic of the community was its newness. The buildings were always new; so were the fences, the sidewalks, and the people. Yale had no opportunity to grow old.

In its brief, three-year joy-ride, the town suffered two disastrous fires, both started by drunks. On July 27, 1880, a third of Yale was burned to the ground. It took a second fire in August of 1881, which reduced half the town to ashes in three hours, before there was any serious talk about gathering funds to buy a steam pumper.

After this Yale began to take on a more sober appearance. Concerts, recitals, lectures, and minstrel shows vied with the saloons for patronage. The Chinese opened their own Freemasons' Lodge, with an ornamental flagstaff as well as a joss-house. Grand balls were held, in which people danced all night – and even longer – to the music of scraping violins. "A ball out here means business," wrote Dr. Daniel Parker, Charles Tupper's travelling companion. "The last one . . . commenced at 12 o'clock on Monday morning and lasted continuously day and night until 12 o'clock the next Saturday."

On the great fête-days the community, bound by a growing feeling of cohesion, turned out *en masse*. The Queen's Birthday on May 24 was an

Yale in 1884. The mists of the Fraser Canyon hang heavy over the boom town whose days were already numbered when this photograph was taken. John Irving's steamboats would also be made obsolete by the railway.

occasion for a half-holiday for whites and Indians. Chinese New Year, celebrated by the coolies early in February, ran for an entire week. The biggest event of all was the Fourth of July, since Yale was very much an American town. Half the population of New Westminster chugged up the river for the occasion. Cannons roared; locomotives pulled flat-cars crammed with excursionists from neighbouring Emory; Indians climbed greased poles; "The Star-Spangled Banner" was enthusiastically rendered outside of the Onderdonk home. Couples danced on a special platform erected on the main street. There were horse races, canoe races, caber-tossing, and hurdles. By comparison, July 1, celebrating a Confederation that was less than a generation old, passed almost unnoticed. British Columbia was part British and part American; it would require the completion of the railway to make her part of the new dominion.

Far off beyond the mountains – beyond the rounded bulks of the Gold Range, beyond the pointed peaks of the mysterious Selkirks – the rails were inching west; but as far as Onderdonk's lambs were concerned, that land was almost as distant as China. Any letters, if such had been written, would have had to travel down the muddy Fraser by boat, on to Victoria and thence to San Francisco, across the United States to St. Paul, north into Winnipeg, and then west again until they reached End of Track. The distance involved was more than five thousand miles, and yet, in 1883, End of Track, in the foothills, was only about three hundred miles away.

Sagebrush and tumbleweed speckled the parched hills above Yale, a town of wooden sidewalks and false fronts. This pastoral scene belies eyewitness descriptions. Henry Cambie wrote that Yale became "a curiosity in the matter of vice flaunting itself . . . along the main streets." The Sentinel *boasted it had "more saloons to the acre than any place in the world."*

The Promised Land

By the spring of 1883, Canada was a country with half a transcontinental railroad. Between Port Moody and Ottawa, the track lay in pieces like a child's train set – long stretches of finished road separated by formidable gaps. The easiest part of the CPR was complete: a continuous line of steel ran west for 937 miles from Fort William at the head of Lake Superior to the tent community of Swift Current in the heart of Palliser's Triangle. To the west, between Swift Current and the half-completed Onderdonk section in British Columbia, was a gap of 750 miles on parts of which not even a surveyor had set foot. The section closest to civilization was graded, waiting for the rails to be laid. The remainder was a mélange of tote roads, forest slashings, skeletons of bridges, and engineers' stakes. An equally awesome gap of more than six hundred miles extended east from End of Track near Fort William to the terminus of the newly completed Canada Central Railway on Lake Nipissing. Again, this was little more than a network of mired roads chopped out of the stunted timber and, here and there, some partially blasted tunnels and rock cuts.

By the time the snows melted, almost the entire right of way for twenty-five hundred miles, from the rim of the Shield to tidewater, was abuzz with human activity. In the east, the timber cutters and rock men were ripping a right of way out of the Precambrian wilderness. In the far west, more thousands were invading the land of the Blackfoot tribes. Little steel shoots were sprouting south, west, and east of the main trunk-line in Manitoba. And wherever the steel went the settlers followed with their tents and their tools, their cattle and their kittens, their furniture and their fences.

A new settler unloads his worldly goods from a CPR baggage car and prepares to guide his oxen towards his unploughed homestead. The rush for land was unexpected and every institution from post office to railroad was caught out. The number of letters for the West quadrupled to 12,000 in just two years. The CPR, faced with a shortage of rolling stock, was forced to use its dwindling cash to buy up second-hand cars to take care of the invading army.

RIGHT: *Strathmore, Alberta, as it looked during its first week of existence – a town totally dependent upon the route of the railway. If another route had been chosen there would have been no Strathmore. The rush for land was sparked by the CPR's emigration agent in London, Alexander Begg, a man who mounted a campaign worthy of Barnum to boom the North West with pamphlets, advertisements, and magic lantern lectures.*

This classic picture, usually entitled "Our First Home," tells much better than words the story of settlement in the North West during the early railway construction period. The hut is constructed entirely of blocks of tough sod, chopped from the surrounding prairie. The bleached buffalo bones, which whitened the plains for hundreds of miles, have been carefully husbanded. The CPR *was buying them up and selling them in Minneapolis for seven dollars a ton.*

From the famine-ridden bog country of Ireland, the bleak crofts of the Scottish hills, and the smoky hives of industrial England, the immigrants were pouring in. They sat crowded together on the hard seats of the colonist cars – patient people, full of hope, blessed by good cheer. Of the 133,000 who arrived in Canada in 1883, two-thirds sped directly to the North West. No one, apparently, had expected such an onslaught.

As many as twenty-five hundred settlers left Winnipeg every week on trains with every car crammed – some people, indeed, clinging to the steps and all singing the song that became the theme of the pioneers: "One More River to Cross." The CPR by April was able to take them as far as the tent town of Moose Jaw, four hundred miles to the west.

The immigrants brought everything to the prairies from domestic pets to livestock. One enterprising arrival from Ontario, sensing the loneliness of the settler's life, brought in a crate full of cats. They were snapped up at three dollars apiece. An early pioneer, Esther Goldsmith, always remembered the wild scene at the Brandon station when a

Medicine Hat was not yet a year old when this photograph was taken. Like all prairie communities spawned by the CPR, thus one straddled the rail line. The most prominent building in town was the station itself, sitting in splendid isolation on its tax-free land, which the company received gratis as part of the contract. In addition, the railway owned all odd-numbered sections in the vicinity and the picture above indicates how potentially valuable they were.

birdcage was sucked from a woman's hand in the scramble for the train. Another recalled her first real view of the prairie driving eighty-five miles north from Broadview with a canary in a cage on her lap.

"Freedom?" wrote William Oliver sardonically. "There never was such a thing; every acre was won by hard toil and the sweat of man." The breaking up of the tough prairie sod was gruelling work. A man with a good team of oxen was lucky if he could till three-quarters of an acre in a day.

In the North West, as the rails pushed steadily towards the mountains, new communities began to take shape. "These towns along the line west of Brandon are all the same," the Fort Macleod *Gazette* reported. "See one, see all. There are some board houses, but most of them are board frames (rough) with a canvas roof." Both Moose Jaw, with its "bare, freckled and sunburnt buildings" and Medicine Hat, another canvas town in a coulee of that name, were in this category. The former, in spite of its youth, already had three newspapers by 1883. The latter boasted six hotels, though most were mere tents sheltering half a dozen bunks.

221

The stark, classic lines of a prairie railroad station as it looked in the summer of 1884, when the West was still raw and blanketed Indians lounged in the shade, makes a strangely evocative photograph. The picture came from the famous Notman studio in Montreal and was probably taken by William McFarlane Notman, who joined his father's firm in 1880. The CPR fitted up a private car as a darkroom so that Notman was able to travel at his ease all the way to End of Track in the mountains. Several other photographs in this book came from the Notman firm which, as early as 1871, was commissioned to photograph the western surveys. The younger Notman's work, as this picture demonstrates, had at least as high an aesthetic value as that of his father. The firm continued to make official photographic expeditions to the West, on the CPR's behalf, for many years after its completion.

223

This was Sam Steele's territory. The remarkable Mounted Policeman had been named acting adjutant of the Fort Qu'Appelle district the previous year and placed in command of detachments along the line of CPR construction. As the rails made their way from the coulees of Saskatchewan to the final spike at Craigellachie, Steele would always be on hand to keep the peace. In his capacity as police magistrate, he worked without rest under primitive conditions. In Regina, his courtroom had been a marquee, sixteen by fourteen feet. It was so cold that winter that the water froze in the bathtubs and the clerks had to keep their ink-bottles on the tops of stoves. Between Moose Jaw and Medicine Hat, Steele had no courtroom at all. At Swift Current he tried cases while seated on a Red River cart, with planks stretched across it for a bench and the evidence taken down on the flap of his dispatch bag. As he worked he counted the trains roaring by to End of Track, loaded with ties, rails, and spikes. He could tell by the number how many miles were being laid that day.

By July, the organization had been perfected to the point where ninety-seven miles of track were laid instead of the monthly average of fifty-eight. As Langdon and Shepard approached the end of their contract, the track-laying guides were seized by a kind of frenzy; on July 28, about two weeks out of Calgary, they set a record that has never been surpassed for manual labour on a railroad: 6.38 miles of finished railway were completed in a single day.

The whole country marvelled over the feat of building the railway across the prairies in just fifteen months – everybody, that is, except the people it was displacing. To the Indians, the railway symbolized the end of a golden age – an age in which the native peoples, liberated by the white man's horses and the white man's weapons, had galloped at will across their untrammelled domain, where the game seemed unlimited and the zest of the hunt gave life a tang and a purpose. This truly idyllic existence came to an end just as the railway was thrust through the ancient hunting grounds of the Blackfoot and the Cree. Within six years, the image of the Plains Indian underwent a total transformation. From being a proud and fearless nomad, rich in culture and tradition, he became a pathetic, half-starved creature, confined to the semi-prisons of the new reserves and totally dependent on government relief for his existence. Without the buffalo, which had supplied them with food, shelter, clothing, tools, and ornaments, the Indians were helpless. By 1880, after the three most terrible years they had ever known, the emaciated natives were forced to eat their dogs and their horses, to scrabble for gophers and mice, and even to consume the carcasses of animals found rotting on the prairie.

On top of this the Indians were faced with the sudden onslaught of a totally foreign agrarian culture. Because of the railway, the impact was almost instantaneous. It did not matter that the various treaties guaranteed that the natives would not be forced to adopt white ways. With the buffalo gone and the grasslands tilled and fenced, such promises were hollow.

The government's policy, born of expediency, was a two-stage one. The starving Indians would be fed temporarily at public expense for a period. Over a longer period, the Indian Department would settle them on reserves and try to turn a race of hunters into a community of peasants. The reserves would be situated on land best suited for agriculture, all north of the railway and far from the hunting grounds. Thus the CPR became the visible symbol of the Indians' tragedy.

Some of the chiefs accepted the coming of steel with a certain amount of fatalism; Poundmaker, for one, urged his Cree followers to prepare for it. In the spring of 1881, after a fruitless search for game on the prairie, he realized that the old nomadic life was ended. He gathered his followers and told them to work hard, sow grain, and take care of their cattle: "Next summer, or at latest next fall, the railway will be close to us, the whites will fill the country, and they will dictate to us as they

At first, the Indians were afraid to touch the CPR *cars. Chief Piapot insisted that train smoke was evil medicine. For him, the* CPR *was.*

please. It is useless to dream that we can frighten them; that time is past; our only resource is our work, our industry, and our farms. Send your children to school . . . if you want them to prosper and be happy."

It was sensible advice, given the inevitability of settlement, but not every chieftain took it, not even Poundmaker himself. His fellow Cree leader, Piapot, ran afoul of Secretan's survey crews in 1882, pulling up forty miles of the surveyors' stakes on the line west of Moose Jaw.

In May, Piapot ordered his followers to camp directly upon the railway's right of way. That led to one of those gaudy little incidents that helped to build the growing legend of the North West Mounted Police:

The two young men from the Maple Creek detachment ride up on their jet-black horses. There squats Piapot in front of his tepee, quietly smoking his pipe, directly in the line of the railroad. Around him the young braves wheel their horses, shouting war-cries and firing their rifles into the air, egged on by a whirling mob of shrieking squaws. The prairie, speckled with spring wildflowers, stretches off to the low horizon. From somewhere in the distance comes the ominous sound of hammers striking on steel.

The sergeant tells the chief that he must make way for the railway. The brown old man refuses to budge. The sergeant takes out his watch. "I will give you just fifteen minutes," he says. "If by the end of that time you haven't begun to comply with the order, we shall make you."

The braves jostle the policemen, trying to provoke them into a fight. The two young men in the pillbox hats and scarlet tunics quietly sit their horses. The minutes tick by. Birds wheel in the sky. The chief remains impassive. The young Crees gallop about. Finally, the sergeant speaks again. "Time's up!" he says and, throwing his reins to the constable, he springs from his steed, strides to the tepee, and kicks down the tentpoles. The painted

buffalo-skin collapses. Other tepees topple under the kicks of his polished boot. "Now git!" says the sergeant and, astonishingly, the Indians obey. Piapot has been stripped of his dignity.

This incident helped to bolster the tradition of the redcoats as fearless upholders of the law. Yet, in the light of the Indians' tragedy, it is inexpressibly sad; and the day was swiftly approaching when no Mounted Policeman would again dare to act in such a fashion. The Indians were growing bolder.

Not far from Calgary, the railway builders encountered the most remarkable Indian leader of all, the sagacious Crowfoot, chief of the Blackfoot nation, renowned for his many feats of bravery. Long before his fellows he saw what was coming. He pinned his hopes on the government and signed a treaty. Thus, when the tents of the construction workers went up on the borders of the Blackfoot reserve, there was anger and bitterness among Crowfoot's followers. The chief sent envoys to warn the foremen that no further construction work would be permitted and that seven hundred armed braves stood ready to attack.

At this point, Albert Lacombe stepped into the picture. The priest had known Crowfoot for years and the two men respected each other. During a smallpox epidemic in 1870 Lacombe so exhausted himself in succouring the victims that hundreds of Indians became Christians in tribute to his selflessness.

At the CPR's behest he set out to placate his old friend. He arrived at Crowfoot's camp bearing gifts, and at his suggestion the chief called a grand council where the priest, standing before the squatting braves, spoke:

"Now my mouth is open; you people listen to my words. If one of you can say that for the fifteen years I have lived among you, I have given you bad advice, let him rise and speak. . . ."

No one budged. It was a dangerous, electric situation. Lacombe kept on:

"Well, my friends, I have some advice to give you today. Let the white people pass through your lands and let them build their roads. They are not here to rob you of your lands. These white men obey their chiefs, and it is with the chiefs that the matter must be settled. I have already told these chiefs that you were not pleased with the way in which the work is being pushed through your lands. The Governor himself will come to meet you. He will listen to your griefs; he will propose a remedy. And if the compromise does not suit you, that will be the time to order the builders out of your reserve."

Lacombe sat down and Crowfoot stood up. "The advice of the Chief of Prayer is good. We shall do what he asks." The chief resigned himself to the inevitable. He did not believe in foolhardy gestures. Not long afterward, Dewdney arrived and agreed to give the Indians extra land in return for the railway's right of way.

In a curiously roundabout way, the presence of the Indians in the North West had aided the railway in its swift progress across the plains. Without them it is doubtful whether prohibition would have existed; without prohibition it would have been impossible to drive steel so efficiently. The entire North West Territories were dry by law. Long before the railway started, the liquor traffic west of Manitoba had been driven underground.

During all the railway construction period, the Mounted Police were locked in a battle of wits with the whiskey peddlers. Every device that human guile could invent was used to smuggle liquor into the North West and to keep it hidden from official eyes. Egg-shells were blown of their contents and alcohol substituted. Imitation Bibles, made of tin, were filled with intoxicants and peddled aboard CPR passenger cars; metal kegs of alcohol were concealed in the centre of barrels of kerosene; mincemeat soaked in brandy and peaches marinated in Scotch were also common. At Silver City, not far from Calgary, the police seized nineteen tins of corn, peas, and tomatoes which, on inspection, were revealed to contain alcohol, not vegetables – all shipped by an Ontario distiller.

The Cree chief, Piapot, photographed in a warlike stance in a photographer's studio. Though the Mounted Police were able to move him from the railway right of way, the tribes, driven to extremes by hunger, were growing bolder and more restive.

WAITING FOR THE SIGNAL.

On the treeless prairie where concealment was difficult, the ingenuity of the bootleggers met its greatest test. One favourite hiding place was the boiler of a disabled or wrecked locomotive laid up on a siding. Another was one of the many carcasses of pack horses that lay strewn along the route of the line. It was said that hundreds of these dead animals were used to conceal bottles of liquor. Known variously as Chain Lightning, Tangle Foot, Death on Wires, and Injin Killer, prairie booze was generally a fearsome concoction made by mixing a gallon of good liquor and nine gallons of water into which was sunk a quantity of blue-stone and oil of smoke and later, for colouring, a little black tea. The bootleggers' price was twenty-five cents a glass.

Perhaps the most ingenious of the whiskey peddlers on the prairie was a Mrs. Hobourg of Regina, who used to arrive back in town from a trip to the wet cities of Winnipeg and Brandon looking more than pregnant from a circular rubber bag she wore around her waist. Another of her devices was to dress up a keg of liquor to resemble one of her offspring asleep on the seat beside her or to disguise it as a pillow on which to rest her head while the police rummaged through her old-fashioned bag.

Prohibition or no, a good deal of liquor was

quor was
perly seen as a
luting force in a
neer nation
ere cheap rye
iskey rendered
ny a man
ensible and
mpetent. Few
the temerity to
ck prohibition in
North West.

THE CURSE OF CANADA.

IS THERE NO ARM TO SAVE?

SIR JOHN SURRENDERS HIS SWORD.

consumed along the CPR right of way during the construction period. Sam Steele, who resented the strict laws and the nuisance of enforcing them, went so far as to claim that "the prohibitory law made more drunkards than if there had been an open bar and free drinks at every street corner." That is scarcely credible. When Edwin Brooks, migrating from Quebec, reached Regina in August, 1883, he was able to write to his wife Nellie: "I can tell you they (the police) look after these whiskey dealers awfully sharp. One never sees a drunken man in this N.W.T. or if ever very seldom. . . ." The truth was that because of prohibition the CPR was able to keep its men on the job and, in spite of occasional sprees, to stabilize a work force whose training and precision made it possible to drive almost nine hundred miles of steel in fifteen months. When it was all over and the trains were running from Winnipeg to the base of the Rockies, the Moose Jaw *News* summed it up:

"The order and quiet which have prevailed during the construction of the Canadian Pacific, where thousands of men, proverbially not of the tractable kind, have been employed far in advance of civilization and settlement, have been unexampled in the history of any similar enterprise."

The founding of Calgary

LANGDON AND SHEPARD completed their contract in mid-August, 1883, when the rails reached Calgary. Until that moment, the old Hudson's Bay fort and its cluster of adjacent log buildings had been more closely linked with the United States than with Canada. To a newcomer from the East, such as William Murdoch, the harness-maker, who put up the first commercial sign on the site in May, the embryo town seemed like a distant planet. "I was dreaming about home almost all last night," Murdoch wrote in his diary on a bitter, windy June day. "How I long to see my wife, mother and little ones. My heart craves for them all today more than usual." Murdoch, who would become Calgary's first mayor, could not get so much as a sliver of dressed lumber, for there were no sawmills in the foothills. All that was available were rough planks, whipsawed vertically by hand. Fresh fruit was so rare that when half a box of apples arrived they were sold at fifty cents each (the equivalent of more than two dollars in modern terms); they were the first that had been seen in that part of the North West.

The railway was to change all that. It was even to change the location of the town, as it had in the cases of Brandon and Regina.

Until the railway arrived, Fort Calgary was situated on the east bank of the Elbow River near its confluence with the Bow. As usual, there were squatters living in rough shanties, hired by Winnipeg land speculators to occupy the most likely ground until the townsite was subdivided.

Calgary watched the railroad approach with a mixture of apprehension and anticipation. Where would the station be located? Under the terms of its contract, the CPR had title to the odd-numbered sections along the right of way. The fort and surrounding structures, together with all the squatters' shacks, were situated on an even-numbered section – Number Fourteen. But the adjacent section, Fif-

William Murdoch (right), a harness-maker and a future mayor, posed in front of his log shack in Calgary on September 3, 1883, less than a fortnight after the railway arrived.

teen, on the opposite bank of the Elbow, had been reserved by Order in Council as pasturage for the police horses. Surely then, everyone reasoned, the town would have to be put on the east bank, where the fort was located.

The tension began to mount. The bridge across the Bow was completed on August 10. Two days later a construction train puffed in. On August 15, a train carrying a temporary station arrived, and the community held its breath. Where would it stop? To everyone's dismay it shunted directly through the settlement, across the new bridge, and was established on Section Fifteen on the far side of the Elbow.

The east bank of the Elbow River in the fall of 1883. Because nobody was sure where the railway would put the station, no one wanted to build anything permanent; hence the tents. Though this area now forms part of Calgary, land sales here were doomed in the early days because the CPR *decreed that the business area would grow on the west bank (in the background).*

Nobody quite knew what to do. The ownership of Section Fifteen was in dispute. The town was growing rapidly on the east bank, but because everyone wanted to wait for the decision about the townsite, no one wanted to go to the expense of erecting anything permanent; and so for all of 1883 Calgary was a tent city.

On August 27, the leading directors of the CPR arrived aboard Van Horne's private car and invited Father Lacombe to be their guest at luncheon. On a motion by Angus, Lacombe was made president of the CPR for one hour. Taking the chair, the priest immediately voted himself two passes on the railroad for life and, in addition, free transportation of all freight and baggage necessary to the Oblate missions together with free use for himself for life of the CPR's telegraph system.

After honouring the priest, the distinguished visitors departed Calgary without leaving the settlers any wiser about a future over which they themselves had no control. The state of indecision continued all that fall, with half the community swearing that it would not budge an inch to accommodate the railway. "There are some people here who have a mind of their own and do not propose to follow the meanderings of the CPR," the Fort Macleod *Gazette* declared.

But the CPR itself and nobody else – editor,

banker, merchant, or real estate man – would make the decision as to where Calgary was to be; and in January, when the Order in Council regarding the NWMP pasturage was finally rescinded, the CPR spoke. The city would be on the west side of the Elbow River and not on its original location on the east side. To underline that point, the government, which stood to profit equally with the railway, moved the post office across the river to the west.

In vain the newly laid-out subdivision on the east side advertised that it was "the centre of Calgary City." As soon as the post office crossed the river, James Bannerman followed with his flour and feed store. All the solemn pledges about staying put and refusing to follow the meanderings of the railway were forgotten and a kind of wild scramble ensued as butcher shop, jeweller, churches, billiard parlour, and hotels packed up like gypsies and located on the favoured site. The *Herald* reported that buildings were suddenly springing up "as though some magical influence were being exerted" and that what had been barren prairie just three weeks before "is now rapidly growing into the shape of a respectable town."

Once again the railway, in truth a "magical influence," had dictated the lineaments of the new North West.

Stephen's disastrous gamble

WHEN GEORGE STEPHEN returned from the North West on October 1, 1883, the company's financial situation was even darker than before. Van Horne had spent the thirty million dollars raised the previous year. Hill had left the company and was selling out most of his stock – the decision to build an all-Canadian line north of Lake Superior was too much for him. Donald A. Smith replaced Hill as a director of the CPR. J. S. Kennedy's subsequent resignation from the CPR board – it was inevitable that the New York banker would follow Hill –

Calgary landmarks in the fall of 1883, about the time the first train arrived: ABOVE, *the original* CPR *station, brought in on wheels on August 15;* BELOW, *the Calgary* Herald's *tent headquarters. The publishers, Andrew M. Armour and Thomas B. Braden, are, respectively, second and fourth from the left. Braden is also seen above, third from left.*

ABOVE: *Calgary, as seen from the railway, circa 1884.*
Like every prairie city along the line of the CPR,
it was strung out lengthwise beside the track with
the station (left rear) as the business nucleus.

BELOW: *Stephen Avenue, Calgary's main stem in*
1883-84. By the fall, the town had advanced to
the point where the Herald *could urge that people*
adopt "as part of their creed that the moral
tone of our town should have in it the ring of purity."

made a bad impression in financial circles, since Kennedy's firm had made its reputation in railroad securities. Moreover, the country was entering a depression. CPR stock began to drop. By October 31, it was selling for less than half its original price of one hundred dollars a share.

That same fall, the North West, still reeling from the collapse of the real estate bubble, was struck a second blow. An early frost wiped out the wheat crop. In the United States, the Northern Pacific was teetering on the edge of insolvency. A "demoralization in railway stocks occurred" (to quote Charles Tupper); if the CPR were to throw any more of its outstanding common stock on the market it would be sacrificed.

Stephen decided upon a bold gamble. The CPR had forty-five million dollars' worth of authorized stock as yet unissued. No one would buy it, except at a fire-sale price. Stephen wanted to force the price up. To do that, he was prepared, with the government's help, to guarantee a five-per-cent dividend for the next ten years on *all* stock.

Stephen wanted the government to guarantee three per cent; the remainder, he felt, could be paid out of the company's resources. In effect, he was buying a government annuity. The price tag came to twenty-five millions. That sum was to be deposited with the government, which would be acting merely as trustee for the fund. If the gambit succeeded, Stephen could sell the rest of the company's stock at something close to par and get enough money – he needed about thirty millions – to finish the railway.

Macdonald liked the idea and the Cabinet passed it. The Prime Minister felt that the guarantee would boom the CPR's stock to seventy or more, but that rosy prediction did not come true. The stock shot up briefly to a little over sixty-three dollars, hovered there for a few days, and then began to drop back again. By the end of 1883 it was down to fifty-two.

Long before that point was reached, Stephen was forced to revise his plan. He would guarantee a dividend on only sixty-five millions. Since fifty-five millions were already issued, he had only ten million dollars available. He dared not put that up for sale at the reduced price but was able to use it as security for a loan of five millions in New York.

The gamble had been disastrous. To raise five million dollars, Stephen had put up nine millions in cash and pledged another seven millions in securities. The company was worse off than it had been before he took the plunge. The railway had scarcely a friend left in the international financial capitals. Stephen was close to despondency, for his reputation had suffered a bad blow.

With great reluctance, Macdonald decided that the government would have to find some way of forcing a new CPR loan down the throat of Parliament. As John Henry Pope had reminded him: "The day the Canadian Pacific busts the Conservative party busts the day after."

But Alexander Campbell was totally opposed to further help, and Leonard Tilley, the finance minister, was openly advocating that the government take over the railway. Macdonald desperately needed Tupper at his side. Sir Charles had been dispatched to London to replace Alexander Galt as High Commissioner. On December 1 Macdonald sent him a curt cable: "Pacific in trouble. You should be here." Tupper arrived post-haste and "found everybody in despair."

Stephen was frantic. "Something must be done at *once*," he told the Prime Minister, otherwise he must give up and let the government take over the railway. A bank crisis was not inconceivable. Stephen himself feared that if the heavy advances to the railroad, made without adequate security, became known to the public, there would be a run on the Bank of Montreal. The bank's chief executive officers were in a state of terror. Tupper privately told them that they must advance the railway the money it needed; the government would guarantee payment. In a close vote they agreed to extend the loan.

This short-term aid did not solve the railway's long-term problems. There could, in fact, be only

One of Major Rogers's survey parties laying out the route along the Kicking Horse canyon, circa 1881. This was difficult location work, since by contract the grade could not exceed 2.2 per cent. The original location crossed several boulder slides, passed under a vast glacier, and called for a 1,400-foot tunnel through solid rock. Van Horne scrapped this switchback route for a steeper 4.4 incline known as the Big Hill. The result was an operating nightmare until, a quarter century later, the famous spiral tunnels were drilled here.

one solution – a government loan. Stephen needed thirty million dollars to pay the CPR debts and complete the main line. In mid-January, he asked formally for a loan of $22,500,000 due in 1891, and a five-year postponement on the second instalment of more than seven millions that he had so recklessly promised in order to guarantee the dividend. This was an enormous sum; it represented almost a whole year's revenue of the federal government. To get it Stephen was forced to mortgage all the CPR's assets and promise to finish the line in five years instead of ten.

That was the medicine that Macdonald and Tupper must force their reluctant followers to swallow. It would not be easy. A platoon of powerful forces was arrayed against the railway: the Opposition under Edward Blake; half the newspapers in the country; the great international press associations – Reuters and AP – which seemed to be spokesmen for the Grand Trunk; the large financial houses; and a good many of Macdonald's own followers, including several Maritimers (who had no interest in a western railroad), most of the Quebec *bleus* (who wanted an equal share in any largesse the government intended to dispense), and the Manitobans, who represented a growing popular antagonism to the CPR.

On January 22, 1884, Stephen scribbled a note to Macdonald that he was going back to Montreal to try to "keep things moving...until relief arrives." There was a note of despair and resignation in this letter: " . . . you must not blame me if I fail. I do not, at the moment, see how we are going to get the money to keep the work going. . . . If I find we cannot go on I suppose the only thing to do will be to put in a Receiver. If that *has* to be done the quicker it is done the better."

It was the first time that the possibility of bankruptcy had been mentioned, and Stephen sounded almost comforted at the prospect: "I am getting so wearied and worn out with this business that almost any change will be a relief to me."

In Montreal, he learned the magnitude of the railroad's financial dilemma. Every cent coming in from the government subsidy had to go directly to the Bank of Montreal to cover its loan. Nothing could be diverted to pay wages or meet the bills for supplies that were piling up in Thomas Shaughnessy's office. He must have an advance of at least three and a half millions by February 8 to pay off the bank. "If this cannot be obtained," he told Tupper, "it is not a bit of use of my trying to carry on any longer."

But he had to carry on as he had been carrying on all the last year, putting off creditors, trimming costs, postponing expenses. In spite of further threats to Ottawa, cries of despair, and attacks of fatigue and nerves, he would continue to carry on. It was not in his nature to give up.

Macdonald to the rescue

THERE WAS TROUBLE north of Lake Superior, where John Egan had been forced to cut off the cost-of-living bonuses. Some thirty-five hundred men struck and the work on the line was suspended. In the end, most were forced to give in because at that season jobs were hard to get.

Van Horne, too, was pinching every possible penny. There scarcely seemed to be an expenditure in 1883 that did not come under his personal scrutiny, from the cost of the paymaster's revolvers to the hiring of a cab at Portage la Prairie. He could berate a man for sending a telegram "containing 35 words and costing this Coy about $2.00 and which could have just as well have been sent by mail," and he could also give orders for mammoth savings north of Superior, where construction had just got underway. When John Ross, his general superintendent there (no relation to the James Ross in charge of mountain work), asked for sixteen steamshovels, Van Horne turned him down. The company could not afford them.

Van Horne's idea was to get a workable line

In the fall of 1883, the graders sped out of Calgary up the easy incline of the Bow Valley towards the Rockies. Not far from Bow Gap, where the line entered the Kicking Horse Pass, the Canadians set another record by laying six hundred feet of steel in four minutes, forty-five seconds. But once the pass was entered, the work slowed down.

through – one that would stand up for at least six years – make it pay, and then begin improving it. Masonry could wait; all rock quarrying would have to cease. Wooden trestles could replace earthworks; the cuts could always be filled in later.

One thing was clear to the public: the CPR was in deep trouble. On February 17, a mass meeting was held in Quebec City to protest the Government's railway policy. On February 20, there were rumours of Cabinet resignations; the Quebeckers were locked in a heated caucus. Forty-two of them, it was whispered, had bolted the party. To keep them in line Macdonald was forced to promise a retroactive subsidy to Quebec on the somewhat dubious premise that the line between Montreal and Ottawa, now owned by the CPR, was a work of national importance. To a casual newspaper reader, it must have seemed that the debate was tearing the country apart.

The following Tuesday the *Globe*, which never let up, summed up the state of the nation in an editorial that was only too accurate:

"To what a sad condition Sir John Macdonald and his colleagues have reduced the country! Quebec, separating herself from the other Provinces, compels the Government to yield to her demands.

Manitoba talks secession, and is certainly discontented. The other Provinces, including Ontario, are dissatisfied, and the Indians – ill-treated, cheated and half-starved by the partisans whom Sir John tries to satisfy at their expense – threaten hostilities. Perhaps it is sufficient offset to all this that the Grand Old Schemer maintains his serenity, that Lieut. Governor Dewdney has received an increase of salary, that Sir C. Tupper is content, and that the c.p.r. Syndicate are satisfied." Only British Columbia, once "the spoilt child of Confederation," appeared to be at peace.

It was the first time, really, that Canadians had become aware of the new kind of nation they were tying together through the construction of the railway – an unwieldy pastiche of disparate communities, authored under varying circumstances, tugged this way and that by a variety of conflicting environmental and historical strains and all now stirred into a ferment by the changes wrought through the coming of steel.

Macdonald was forced to offer a familiar threat to keep the remainder of his irresolute followers in line: if they did not support him, Parliament would be dissolved and they would face the prospect of going to the country on the heels of a Government defeat in the House.

The political arguments in the House were wearing Stephen down. He wanted another extension on his Bank of Montreal loan but, in spite of Tupper's intercession, the bank refused. On February 27, 1884, the cpr president wrote another desperate note to the Prime Minister:

"McIntyre goes down to N.Y. tonight to raise by way of a loan for a few days $300,000 which we think will keep us out of the sheriff's hands till Tuesday or Wednesday. I hope he will manage this, though he may not be able. In that case I do not know what we shall do. . . ."

The following day, the cpr relief bill passed the House. How soon could Macdonald get it through the Senate? Again Stephen implored the Prime Minister to move swiftly. It would have to be made

law by Wednesday, when McIntyre's short-term loan (negotiated successfully in New York) fell due; on Wednesday, dramatically, it was done. At the very last moment the company had been saved from ruin. That final denouement was reminiscent of one of the cheap yellow-backed thrillers that Macdonald liked to read to clear his mind from the cares of the day.

Those cares were very real ones. The Prime Minister was in his seventieth year and was complaining more and more of being tired every night. When he had driven the original cpr contract through Parliament in 1881 he had believed his main worries to be at an end, at least as far as the railroad was concerned. Stephen, he thought, would take the responsibility off his back. But the railroad, which was wearing Stephen down, too, was pressing upon Macdonald's stooped shoulders like a great weight, as it had a dozen years before in the days of Sir Hugh Allan. Once more the papers were hinting that he would retire – he was suffering again from an old nervous disease, inflammation of the stomach; but he could not retire while the railway remained unfinished. "It is only because I want to be *in* at the completion of the cpr that I remain where I am," he had told Stephen the previous November. "I may say I groan for rest."

By the summer of 1884, Macdonald was worried that Stephen himself might give in. "I would leave the Govt. tomorrow," he admitted to Tupper in July, "if it were not that I really think George Stephen would throw up the sponge if I did. He was so worried & sleepless that his wife became alarmed." The Prime Minister insisted that Stephen go off to the seaside for a vacation. A few days later, he himself came down to visit him, and for three days the two men on whom so much depended basked in the sun and talked about the railroad and the future of the country. Macdonald thought Stephen had "chirped up a good deal" as a result of his rest. He would need to, to survive the trials that lay ahead.

The track reached this point when winter set in late in 1883. This is Laggan (*now Lake Louise station*) *near the summit of the Kicking Horse Pass. For most of 1884, the construction headquarters of the* CPR's *mountain division remained at this spot. The camp, "raucous with the pandemonium of squeaking fiddles," had its quota of blind pigs and gambling-joints. Only a skeleton crew remained here during the winter, but 12,000 men arrived in 1884.*

239

6

The Last Rock-bound Barriers

*The decision to allow the line to
hug the shores of Lake Superior forced
the railway builders to blast their
way through the diamond-hard rock of
the Precambrian Shield, whose ribs
extended sheer to the water's edge.
This scene, photographed at Jackfish
in the summer of 1884, shows why
some contracts were let out for only
a single mile of railway.*

McKay's Harbour (Rossport) in 1884. The wisdom of moving the line close to the lake is seen here. Supplies were dumped at hundred-mile intervals and rough roads were blasted between each delivery point. Three hundred dog teams worked all winter keeping the navvies supplied.

242

The armoured shores of Superior

THE PRICE OF BUILDING the line north of Lake Superior was appalling. By the summer of 1884, John Ross had close to fifteen thousand men working between Lake Nipissing and Thunder Bay, which meant that every month the company had to send a pay car out along the line with $1,100,000 in wages. One single, memorable mile of track was laid through solid rock at a cost of seven hundred thousand dollars. To save money and time, Van Horne had three dynamite factories built in the Caldwell-Jackfish area, each capable of turning out a ton a day. The bill for explosives came to seven and a half million dollars. The awesome quantities of food consumed by the workmen flabbergasted old-time traders. In winter it required three hundred dog teams, working incessantly, to keep the railroad supplied.

The line hugged the armoured shores of Lake Superior, where construction was heavy but supply relatively easy. Van Horne had imported two big lake boats built in Scotland to do duty between Algoma Mills and Thunder Bay. In this way freight could be shipped by water from Montreal to Port Arthur and by rail from Port Arthur to Winnipeg – a distance of 1,320 miles – in sixty-six hours. This was the start of the Canadian Pacific Steamship service under Henry Beatty, whose son was to become president of the CPR at a time when it was able to advertise itself as "The World's Greatest Travel System."

To Stephen, watching every penny in Montreal, the whole operation must have been disturbing. This was the section that almost everybody, Stephen included, had once said should not be built. This was the section that had caused Hill's disaffection – and Kennedy's. Now it was devouring the millions that the company had managed to pry loose from Ottawa.

There was no thought of stopping for winter.

Track must be laid in all seasons, in snow five feet deep and in temperatures that dropped to fifty degrees below zero. Sometimes the drifts were so high that in the absence of an embankment it was impossible to locate the centre line of the roadbed, and the rails had to be laid directly on the snow. In some places, when spring came it was found they were not on the grade at all.

All sorts of short cuts were attempted. There was one rock cutting east of White River on which the contractors were well behind. A delay of a month seemed inevitable until it was decided to lay the track directly on top of the escarpment, to one side of the half-finished cut. The first locomotive that attempted to reach the top slipped back. The rails were sanded and the track smoothed out until finally a single car was pulled over safely. When the engine crews grew used to the hazard they were able to cross it easily with two cars. By the time the cut was finished, track had moved on thirty miles.

In the interests of greater speed, Van Horne imported a track-laying machine. This was really a train loaded with rails, ties, and track fastenings. Shallow, open-top chutes, with rollers spaced along the bottom, were hung on either side, and the ties and rails were rolled along by manpower to the front of the device, where they were manhandled onto the grade.

The usual method of cut and fill was abandoned. Van Horne had decided at the outset to carry the line high, building timber trestles over the intervening gullies and filling them in later with materials brought in by rail. The cost of these trestles was about one-tenth the cost of the filling operation.

To Alan Brown, a pioneer in Ontario railway development, "the rock cuttings were wonderful." Brown, who travelled the line shortly after it was completed, said he felt weak in his powers of description: "It is impossible to imagine any grander construction. . . . Everything is synonymous with strength. . . . The bridges, the tunnels, the rock cuttings almost make you aghast. . . ."

John Macoun, who visited the line in 1884, wrote that it was "indescribable, as we were tormented by flies, and our path was not strewn with roses." Yet there was a kind of perverse grandeur about the country through which the steel was being driven. Superintendent John Egan found himself waxing poetical about it to the press: "The scenery is sublime in its very wildness; it is magnificently grand; God's own handiwork stands out boldly every furlong you proceed. The ravines and streams are numerous and all is picturesqueness itself. As to the character of the work, it will remain an everlasting monument to the builders."

To the men on the job – throats choked with the dust of shattered rocks, ears ringing with dynamite blasts, arms aching from swinging sledges or toting rails, skin smarting and itching from a hundred insect bites, nostrils assailed by a dozen stenches from horse manure to human sweat – the scenery was only a nuisance to be moved when it got in the way. The summers were bad enough but the winters were especially hard; in the flat light of December, the whole world took on a dun colour and the chill wind blowing off the great frozen inland sea sliced through the thickest garments.

Because of the isolation, conditions in the camps north of Lake Superior were undoubtedly the worst of any along the line of the railway. The navvies lived like men on another planet in gloomy and airless bunkhouses, which were little better than log dungeons. Into these hastily constructed temporary structures, often badly situated and inadequately drained, between sixty and eighty men were crammed. They slept in verminous blankets on beds of hay in double-decker bunks that extended around three sides of the building. The atmosphere was oppressive and the ventilation meagre. The faint light that entered from two small windows at either gable was rarely sufficient for reading or writing. The nights were fetid with steam from the wet clothes that habitually hung over the central stove. In the summer, the air was rancid with smoke from burning straw and rags set afire to drive off the maddening hordes of mosquitoes and blackflies. The board floor was generally filthy and the roof often leaked. Baths and plumbing were unknown; men washed and laundered or not as they wished; medical attention was minimal.

The conditions north of Superior, especially in the winter, made for a monotonous and unhealthy menu. The only real delicacy was freshly baked bread; otherwise the staples were salt pork, corned beef, molasses, beans, potatoes, oatmeal, and tea, varied by the occasional carcass of frozen beef. These was little if any fresh or green food to lighten this excessively coarse and heavy diet which, when it did not lead to actual scurvy, produced in most men a feeling of sluggishness and lassitude.

In spite of these circumstances it was usually not difficult to get cheap labour. Economic conditions were such that, in the summer of 1883, ordinary shovel men were being paid $1.50 for a ten-hour day along Lake Superior and in some instances as little as $1.00 a day, which was the going rate in the eastern cities. In the rare instances when strikes did occur, they were quickly broken.

Yet the conditions of the wage earners were far superior to those of the men who worked for themselves on small subcontracts, grading short strips of right of way with shovel and wheelbarrow, or clearing the line of brush and stumps for fixed prices, arrived at by hard bargaining. These subcontracts had one apparent advantage: the men were their own bosses. The advantage, however, was generally illusory; most of the self-employed men worked much longer hours under worse conditions than the wage earners, yet made no more money.

Living arrangements for those employed on small subcontracts were especially squalid. Harry Armstrong came upon one such camp of French Canadians that he thought the worst he had ever seen. It was a windowless cabin with nothing in the way of a floor except black mud, kept thawed by the heat of the stove. To bridge the mud there were several scattered poles across which the men were supposed to pick their way. Armstrong recalled

This rock cut near Winston's helps explain why Alexander Mackenzie thought of the ridges of the Canadian Shield as "impassable barriers." Van Horne's dynamite factories made them passable but at a cost in human lives. When one man tried to tamp a cartridge with a crowbar, he was blown to bits.

These rock men on Lake Superior had their wages raised to $2 a day when winter isolation made conditions unattractive. But when Van Horne boosted the price of board, the rise in wages appeared greater than it actually was. Men were paid only for the days they worked. Rain, illness, and construction delays kept them in the bunkhouse and reduced their take-home pay.

These log bunkhouses, sprinkled haphazardly through Superior's shattered forests, were uniquely Canadian.

that "all the refuse from table had been scraped off after each meal, which didn't improve the mud."

The camps of the Italian immigrants were even worse. One group, which took a contract clearing the line, lived during the winter in a kind of root cellar, dome-shaped and without windows. To enter, they crawled through an opening in the bottom, and there they lay most of the time, playing cards, but going out into the snow when the sun shone to do a little work. Once a week they bought a sack

of flour and a little tea on credit. By spring they had managed to clear half an acre.

Under such conditions the navvies turned inevitably to alcohol. By special act, the government had banned the sale of liquor along the line of the railway as far as the Manitoba border. Here, as everywhere else in Canada, government agents fought a running battle with whiskey peddlers. In May, 1881, the Thunder Bay *Sentinel* estimated that no fewer than eight hundred gallons of spirits were

The heavy, unvarying diet contributed to the listlessness evident in these bunkhouse men. The year is 1884.

sold every month to the twenty-five hundred people living between Whitemouth River and Lake Wabigoon. The price was fifteen dollars a gallon.

A regular count made by the CPR revealed that there were five thousand revolvers and three hundred shotguns and rifles, together with the same number of dirks and bowie knives, in the possession of railroad workers on the Lake Superior line. The North West Mounted Police did not patrol the Ontario section of the road; that job was left to the

local constabulary, some of whom were plainly corrupt.

Both Peninsula Harbour and Michipicoten were for several months under the control of gangs of desperadoes euphemistically called "vigilantes," who terrorized the citizens and held a tight rein on the whiskey trade, keeping out all competition and running the community for their own personal profit.

Such communities were isolated in winter because there was no continuous line of track between

Thunder Bay and Lake Nipissing. The contractors, supplied by boat, were strung out in sections of varying length, depending on the terrain; indeed, some contracts covered country so difficult that only a mile was let at a time. For administrative purposes, the Lake Superior line had to be divided into two sections: the difficult section led east from Fort William to meet the easier section, which ran west from Lake Nipissing, the point at which the Canada Central, out of Ottawa, joined the CPR proper.

In the summer of 1882, a young Scot of eighteen named John McIntyre Ferguson arrived on Nipissing's shore. Ferguson was the nephew of Duncan McIntyre, an uncle who knew exactly where the future railway was going to be located. The prescient nephew purchased 288 acres of land at a dollar an acre and laid out a townsite in the unbroken forest. He also built the first house in the region and, in ordering nails, asked the supplier to ship them to "the north bay of Lake Nipissing." Thus did the settlement unwittingly acquire a name. By 1884, when the CPR established its "company row," North Bay had become a thriving community. Ferguson went on to become the wealthiest man in town and, after North Bay was incorporated, its mayor for four successive terms.

By the end of 1882 the Canada Central had reached Lake Nipissing. By the end of 1883 the first hundred miles of the connecting CPR were completed. Early that year the crudest of tote roads, all stumps and mud, had reached the spot where Sudbury stands today. Here, as much by accident as by design, a temporary construction camp was established. It was entirely a company town: every boarding house, home, and store was built, owned, and operated by the CPR in order to keep the whiskey peddlers at bay.

The first men to examine the strange yellow-bronze rocks in the hills around the community made little or nothing from their discoveries. The earliest was probably Tom Flanagan, a CPR blacksmith, who picked up a piece of ore along the right of way and thought that he had found gold. He did not realize that he was standing not only on a copper mine but also on the largest nickel deposit in the world. Flanagan did not pursue his interest, but John Loughrin, who had a contract for cutting railroad ties, was intrigued by the formations. In February, 1884, he and three friends staked the land on what became the future Murray Mine of the International Nickel Company. It subsequently produced ore worth millions, but not for the original discoverers.

Other company employees became millionaires. One was a gaunt Hertfordshire man named Charles Francis Crean, who arrived on the first work train into Sudbury in November, 1883. On entering the company store, Crean noticed a huge yellow nugget being used as a paperweight. The clerk said the ore was probably fool's gold, but he let Crean have a piece of it. Crean sent it to a chemist friend in Toronto who told him it was an excellent sample of copper. In May, 1884, Crean applied for a mining claim and staked what was to become famous as the Elsie Mine.

A month later, Crean spotted some copper ore in the ballast along the tracks of the Sault Ste Marie

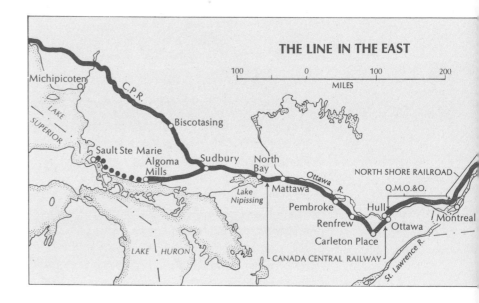

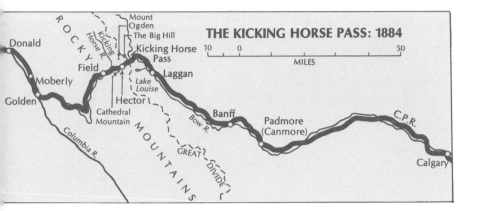

THE KICKING HORSE PASS: 1884

The Big Hill

branch of the railroad. He checked back carefully to find where the material had come from and was able to stake the property on which another rich mine – the Worthington – was established. Later he discovered three other valuable properties. Another prospective millionaire that year was a railway construction timekeeper named Thomas Frood, who acted on a trapper's hunch and discovered the property that became the Frood Mine, perhaps the most famous of all.

But for every fortune made in Sudbury there were a dozen lost: the story of northern Ontario mining is the story of happenstance, accident, and sheer blind luck. Sudbury itself was an accident, located by error on the wrong side of a lake and named by the contractor, James Worthington, after his wife's birthplace in England. Worthington had not intended to use such an unimportant spot on the map to honour his spouse, but the station up the line that was expected to be the real centre of the area had already been named, and he had to settle for the lesser community. He was not the only man to underestimate the resources of the Canadian Shield. Right up until the moment of Sudbury's founding, some members of Macdonald's cabinet, not to mention a couple of the CPR's own directors, were opposed to running a line of steel across those ebony scarps. It was only when the land began to yield up its treasure that the fuss about the all-Canadian line was stilled.

IN THE ROCKIES, that summer of 1884, the weather was miserable. The numbing rain turned the Kicking Horse into a torrent that spread itself across the Columbia flats, cutting the tote road so badly that it was almost impossible for the teams to struggle through. The speed of track-laying had slowed down once the pass was entered. The rails crept to within a few miles of the summit in the fall of 1883 and came to a halt for the winter. For all of the summer of 1884, the construction headquarters of the Mountain Division of the CPR remained near the summit at Holt City, later known as Laggan (the site of Lake Louise station today).

James Ross had announced that he would need twelve thousand men in the mountains that summer. By June they were pouring in. Every train brought several carloads of navvies who had come across the plains from Winnipeg. They tumbled off the cars and trudged up the right of way to the construction camps, in a land hitherto seen by only a handful of men.

The British novelist Morley Roberts, who arrived that summer, watched the tenderfeet from the cities heading off up the line to the various camps – a miscellaneous throng of about a hundred, loaded down with blankets and valises – and noted that many had never worked in the open air at all. Some indeed had not done a hard day's work in their lives:

"It was quite pitiful to see some little fellow, hardly more than a boy, who had hitherto had his lines cast in pleasant places, bearing the burden of two valises or portmanteaus, doubtless filled with good store of clothes made by his mother and sisters, while the sweat rolled off him as he tramped along bent nearly double. Perhaps next to him there would be some huge, raw-boned labourer whose

In the Rockies, long trains of horse-drawn sleighs were used to supply grade workers, tunnellers, and bridge teams.

belongings were tied up in a red handkerchief and suspended from a stick."

Behind the labourers came the first tourists, some of them travelling all the way from Winnipeg to gaze upon the wonders of the mountain scenery. Much of it was fast disappearing under the human onslaught. "Round me," wrote Morley Roberts, "I saw the primaeval forest torn down, cut and hewed and hacked, pine and cedar and hemlock. Here and there lay piles of ties, and near them, closely stacked, thousands of rails. The brute power of man's organised civilisation had fought with Nature and had for the time vanquished her. Here lay the trophies of the battle." The mountainsides that year were ablaze with forest fires started by the construction workers. At times the entire pass,

Tourists began to arrive as early as 1884. This picnic took place after the rails had reached the Columbia.

from the summit to the Columbia, and westward seemed to be aflame.

Avalanches were also frequent in the Rockies that season, many of them set in motion by the continual blasting that went on along the line. Everyone who witnessed one was awestruck. "They resembled exactly a large mow taken down with a scythe in the fields," Alexander Mackenzie wrote

to his daughter. (The former Liberal prime minister was on a tour of the North West as a guest of the railway and, as a result, was to change his mind about the barrenness of prairie land.) Sam Steele saw one avalanche descend five thousand feet from a summit with such velocity that it tore directly across a valley and up the opposite side for another eight hundred feet.

253

Under such conditions the work went on at a killing pace from dawn to dusk. On one contract the workmen averaged more than ten hours of labour a day every day for a month. Some of them had thirteen or fourteen hours a day to their credit. If rain made work impossible, they caught up in sunny weather. Some even worked by moonlight.

The railway workers lived in every kind of accommodation along the line – in tents of all shapes and sizes, in boxcars rolled onto sidings, in log huts and in mud huts, in shanties fashioned out of rough planks, and in vast marquees with handhewn log floors, log walls, and a box stove in the centre. Over the whole hung the familiar pungency of the bunk-house, an incense almost indescribable but compounded of unwashed bodies, strong tobacco, steaming wool, cedar logs, and mattress straw.

The work was often as dangerous as it was back-breaking. Near one of several tunnels along the Kicking Horse the cut in the hill was so deep that the men worked in three tiers. At the very top, the route was being cut through gravel; in the centre the gravel gave way to blue clay; below the clay was hard rock. The men on the lowest tier, working just above the layer of rock (which would have to be dynamited), attacked the clay from beneath. Twenty to thirty feet above them a second gang worked, chopping out the gravel and wheeling it

The mountain workers shown at the left are as tattered as the tents they live in. Note the presence of the dog and the open bottle, both of them necessary concomitants to the harsh existence of a railroad navvy in the Rockies.

Tunnel gangs (below) worked in tiers. The gang on the lowest level was never free of the warning cry "Look out below!" or "Stand from under!" as boulders, hurtling from above, threatened their lives.

Corey's Bro Tunnel No 14

This photograph of the great cut leading into the Corey Brothers' tunnel in the Rockies in 1884 illustrates the conditions described (overleaf) by Morley Roberts, the English novelist and adventurer who served his time as a rock worker for the CPR. The three tiers that he wrote about can easily be seen. At the top of the picture, the high gang clears away the stumps and underlying rocks beneath the forest floor. The men in the middle are chopping out the intermediate layer of gravel. Below the gravel was blue clay and below that hard rock, which had to be blasted. It was scary work for those at the lower levels.

257

away in barrows. The high gang removed the top layer of sand and stumps. Those at the very top worked in comparative safety; the middle gang was in some peril because they had to watch out for rocks that might topple down on them; but the lowest gang was in constant danger – from both benches above them came a continual shower of rocks. Morley Roberts, who worked on the lowest tier, reported that he never felt safe for a single moment. Every sixty seconds or so, all day long, a warning cry would be heard and a heavy stone or boulder would come thundering down the slope, scattering the men on both sides. On his third day on the job an eighty-pound rock put him out of action for five days. The literate vagabond whiled away his convalescence with a copy of Thomas Carlyle's *Sartor Resartus.*

Since it was impossible to take heavy drills down the dizzy inclines of the Kicking Horse, all blasting holes had to be punched out by hand. The men hammered the broken rocks into smaller pieces and shovelled them into carts and barrows. In spite of such primitive techniques, James Ross's work force managed to move a million and a half cubic yards of earth and rock and, in addition, drill half a mile of tunnels during the 1884 season.

Van Horne had decreed that all bridges be made of timber in order to save money. Even without the cost factor, the necessity of pushing the line through on time would have dictated this swifter method of construction. There was no way in which iron girders or quarried stone could be transported down the gorge of the Kicking Horse until the rails were laid.

In order to get around the face of some of the bluffs without drilling tunnels or making expensive cuts, the railway resorted to "grasshopper trestles," so called because the outer posts extended far down into the gorges, standing in steps cut in the rock, while the inner posts, like a grasshopper's forelegs, were very short and sometimes non-existent. Later on these trestles were replaced by walls of masonry built by Scottish stonemasons.

On its queasy descent from the Great Divide, the road switched back and forth across the Kicking Horse by truss and trestle eight times. Before the right of way could be cleared, a tote road had to be constructed to replace the dangerous surveyors' trail cut into the cliffside. This road ran a few feet above the bed of the railway and in one place was notched right into the cliff. On their first journey down the hazardous thoroughfare, men involuntarily hugged the upper side and uttered a sigh of relief when the journey was over.

The choice of the Kicking Horse Pass had presented the CPR with a considerable dilemma. The river drops eleven hundred feet in the first three and a half miles of its headlong race down the western slopes of the Rockies. Under the terms of its contract with the government, the CPR was pledged to a maximum gradient of 2.2 per cent, or about 116 feet to a mile; but to build the road as Rogers had located it, the line would have been forced to cross several unstable boulder slides and to pass under an immense glacier. In addition, it would have been necessary to drill a fourteen-hundred-foot tunnel – and that would have delayed the railway for almost another year. Sandford Fleming suggested to Van Horne that the company build a temporary line dropping quickly down from the summit into the comparative level of the valley of the Kicking Horse by means of a grade of 232 feet per mile – twice as steep as that allowed by the contract and four times as steep as the ideal maximum. Fleming's suggestion was accepted, and thus was born the "Big Hill" between the stations of Hector and Field. It was an eight-mile horror. The grades would be the steepest ever regularly operated for any considerable period of time by a standard-gauge railroad and the so-called temporary line – an eight-mile diversion from the original location – would last for a quarter of a century.

Even a 2.2 gradient can cause runaways. The first train that tried to descend the Big Hill ran away and plunged to the river below, killing three men. Safety switches were installed every two

Along the Kicking Horse canyon, Donald Mann's supply train wends its slow way over the perilous tote road cut into the cliffs just above the railroad's grade. Another contractor, Herbert Holt, was almost killed here when his horse slipped over the edge. Both Mann and Holt became wealthy entrepreneurs in twentieth-century Canada.

miles and manned twenty-four hours a day but these did not always work. A second train lost control after passing over a safety switch and headed straight into a tunnel where sixty men were working. The engineer slammed the engine into reverse, set the whistle, and jumped. When the tender derailed, the train came to a stop.

At the top of the Big Hill, every passenger train was required to stop to have its air brakes tested. Brakemen jumped off at intervals and trotted beside the cars to make sure the wheels were not sliding or heating unduly. Boxcars and flatcars were restricted to a speed of six miles an hour. All trains were required to stop at the safety switches and start up again after the switchman re-aligned the track onto the main line. The bigger engines were limited to seventeen loaded cars in daylight and twelve at night; smaller engines could not even pull these loads. Powerful water brakes were brought into service when the steeper inclines were reached and the trains began to slide downhill like toboggans. In spite of these precautions runaways continued to occur. One train lost a forty-ton wing plough, which plunged three hundred feet into the river. And there were several cases of locomotives roaring down the slope so fast that the men tending the safety switches could not operate them in time to save train or crew.

The upward journey was a slow and difficult operation. At least four big engines were required to pull a train of 710 tons to the summit. Under such conditions it took an hour to move eight miles. Such a train could not be long – fourteen to twenty freight cars or eleven passenger coaches. When the Prince of Wales visited Canada, it took five engines to pull his entourage back over the summit.

All of this was expensive and time consuming; the use of four locomotives meant that there were four times as many chances for delay through engine failure. And in the winter, when the winds shrieked off the Yoho ice-fields in forty-below weather, smothering the mountain slopes in immense

260

drifts of cement-hard snow, the difficulties were compounded. But it was not until 1909 that the CPR decided to drill the remarkable spiral tunnels, which make a figure eight deep within the bowels of Cathedral Mountain and Mount Ogden. It took ten thousand men two years to do the job, but there was not an employee in the operating division of the CPR who did not believe that it was worth it.

Nonetheless, the steeper line allowed Van Horne to push the railroad down the Kicking Horse to its junction with the Columbia by September. By January it had moved on down the Columbia for seventeen miles to the point where the line would cross over to the mouth of the Beaver at the foot of the Selkirks.

Here, at a spot known simply as First Crossing (it would later be named Donald, after Donald A. Smith), the work came to an end for the season and another garish little community sprang into being on the frozen river bank. On November 15, Jack Little, the telegraph operator, set down on paper the events of one single moonlit night:

". . . the Italian saloon . . . [is] a little hut, 12 x 16, and it dispenses beer, cigars, and something more fiery, in unlimited quantities. The barkeeper is a woman . . . there is an accordion squeaking in the corner, and it and the loud coarse laugh of the barmaid make an angelic harmony. . . . On all sides we hear the music of the dice box and the chips . . . the merry music of the frequent and iniquitous drunks; the music of the dance and the *staccato* accompaniment of pistol shots; and the eternal music, from the myriad saloons and bars along the street, of the scraping fiddle. In the French Quarter a dance is going on. The women present are Kootenai Squaw, 'the first white lady that ever struck Cypress' and two or three of the usual type of fallen angels. A gang of men and boys line the walls and a couple of the lads dance with the damsels in the centre. There is a lamentable want of a sense of shame at Columbia Crossing. . . .

In the "gambling, drinking, fighting little mountain town" of Donald, police and prostitutes occupied identical log cabins. Indian packers galloped through the narrow streets and railroad navvies squandered their pay in the saloons, until James Ross moved his entire work force to a new campsite on the far side of the Columbia.

"During our walk we met plenty of 'drunks.' The contractor is as drunk as his employees, and the deadbeats are as drunk as usual. There is a good deal of card-playing . . . all through the night. . . .

"Below the high bank, on the dry land left by the receding river, several teamsters have camped for the night preparatory to crossing in the morning. The ferry boat with its one light is making its last trip for the night across the narrow space of water, becoming narrower day by day as the ice encroaches from the banks. On the opposite side of the river lights shine out from rafts and shacks, while above them the dark pine forest stretches its gloomy line. The scene behind is growing livelier as the hours grow shorter. There is a row at one of the card tables. A pistol shot follows. A man is seen standing back a rough crowd with drawn revolver while another man is lying in a pool of his own blood. Well, it is all very interesting, no doubt, and has the great charm of being 'western' which makes up for a multitude of sins. . . ."

Van Horne's Pacific terminus

ALL DURING THE SPRING of 1884, Van Horne, who had moved his headquarters to Montreal, was trying his best to get out to British Columbia to settle on the Pacific terminus of the railroad. A variety of problems kept forcing him to postpone the journey. He was faced daily with a mixed bag of executive decisions, many of them niggling but all, apparently, requiring his personal intervention. No detail was too small for Van Horne to handle. Even the bill of fare on the newly acquired lake boats was subjected to his trencherman's scrutiny. ". . . altogether too many dishes offered," he told Henry Beatty. "Fewer varieties, but plenty of each, I have always found to be better appreciated than a host of small, made-up dishes. . . . Plenty of fresh fish . . . is what people expect to find on the lakes and it is, as a rule, the scarcest article in the steamers'

"The table was very fair," Van Horne wrote after a trip on one of the CPR's lake steamers, *"except that the coffee was bad, being too weak . . . and poor in quality as well, containing a considerable percentage of burnt peas."* He was equally solicitous of the needs of rail passengers. *"We cannot consent,"* he wrote to one executive, *"to the use of inferior cars in this line."*

larders. . . ." From that moment, Lake Superior trout and whitefish became standard Canadian Pacific fare.

Many of his actions in 1884 were designed to further the interests of the railway in the years to come. He worried about grain buyers swindling prairie farmers and told John Egan that if the buyers would not pay a fair price the market must be stimulated by dropping in outside buyers with private assistance to shake it up. He was distressed by the erection of flat warehouses. His experience in Minnesota had convinced him that much more modern elevators would be needed. Van Horne also did his best to persuade the farmers to forget soft wheat and concentrate on harder varieties. The best of these was Red Fife and, as an inducement, Van Horne offered to carry the seed free to any farmer who ordered it.

In spite of the need to cut costs he had no intention of pinching pennies where the railway's public image was concerned. He was determined, for instance, that the woodwork of the passenger cars be hand carved. As he told the board of directors: "Every foot of imitation carving will affect the opinion and attitude towards us of the Company's employees. We want them to have confidence in us – we want every clerk, conductor and brakeman to regard this Company as above all mean pretence. So everything must be of the best material, and be exactly what it pretends to be. Otherwise, their attitude and their service to us will not be what it ought to be."

Van Horne took special delight in personally designing sleeping cars and parlour cars. To this end he engaged noted artists to handle the interior decoration. As for comfort, he once, as an object lesson to his own people, made a comic illustration showing a tall, fat man attempting to squeeze into one of the short berths provided by United States railroads. He made sure that CPR cars were constructed of larger dimensions with longer and wider berths. Van Horne himself thought in terms of bigness. He liked big houses, "fat and bulgy like myself," with big doors, big roofs, big windows, big desks, and vast spaces.

His whole philosophy was based on permanence. The railway, as he saw it, was to become a kind of religion among the men who worked on it, and also among the people who travelled on it. "You are not to consider your own personal feelings," he told a trainman who had engaged in a dispute with an irritable passenger. "You are the road's while you are on duty; your reply is the road's; and the road's first law is courtesy."

His power, by 1884, was enormous. Lord Dunmore said that "no other man commands the same army of servants or guides the destiny of a railway over such an extent of country." Van Horne, "the ablest railroad general in the world," as Jason Easton, his American contemporary called him, was in charge of the equivalent of several army divisions. Yet at the same time he continued to indulge his various exotic tastes. His collection of Japanese porcelain was rapidly becoming the finest in the world. He recognized French Impressionists long before they were popular or valuable. When he discovered, to his chagrin, that his architects had designed the Banff Springs Hotel so that it faced away from the mountains, he personally sketched in a rotunda that could redress the oversight. The log station houses and chalets in the Rockies and Selkirks were also his idea. He scribbled a sketch on a piece of brown paper and turned it over to a designer with a brief order: "Lots of good logs there. Cut them, peel them, and build your station." In various ways, the general manager was helping to transform the face of his adopted land.

He finally saw the Pacific Coast in late summer. The expedition to British Columbia was arranged in July, and on August 4 a distinguished party arrived at Victoria and moved swiftly across to Port Moody, then designated as the terminus of the transcontinental line. The settlement, perched on a narrow bank at the head of Burrard Inlet, was basking in the belief that it was to become the greatest metropolis on the coast.

"Port Moody . . . has no rival," exclaimed the *Gazette*, the locality's pioneer newspaper. "There is no place upon the whole coast of British Columbia that can enter into competition with it . . . these declarations are sweeping but incontrovertible."

The paper could hardly wait for Van Horne to arrive in order that the new metropolis could be laid out. Its editor wrote lyrically of gigantic markets, theatres, churches, paved streets, hotels, shops, and warehouses rising "like magic." But it was all tragically premature. Van Horne was disturbingly non-committal. He wanted first to examine the mouth of Burrard Inlet and its two settlements – the tiny community of Hastings, surrounding the mill of that name, and another properly called Granville but dubbed "Gastown" after a former saloon-keeper, John "Gassy Jack" Deighton.

In fact, Port Moody would not do. There was no room on that crowded ledge for a substantial city. The railway alone would require four hundred acres of level ground, and even that much space did not exist. To reclaim it from the tidal flats would cost between two and four million dollars. But there *was* plenty of level ground in the vicinity of Coal Harbour and English Bay at the inlet's mouth. If Van Horne could persuade the provincial government to subsidize the continuation of the line from Port Moody, then it was his intention to build the terminus at that point.

This decision ensured the swift decline of Port Moody. In vain, the merchants sent off petitions of protest. The general manager was already planning to name the new terminus Vancouver. The proximity of Vancouver Island would help to identify its position in the minds of world travellers.

Van Horne had his first view of the Fraser Canyon on August 9. Yale was all but finished as a community. Kamloops was the new mecca. The town, which had suffered a decline after the gold rush, perked up with Van Horne's announcement that it would be a divisional point. Here were repeated all the spectacles attendant on the construction period – the hotels jammed with men, some

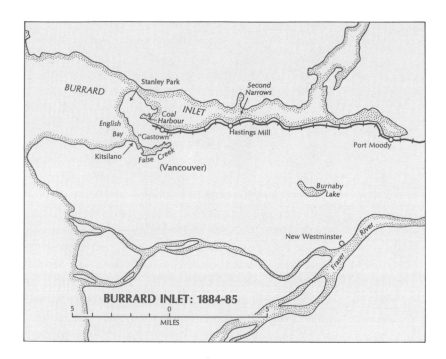

BURRARD INLET: 1884-85

sleeping in the bar room and some on billiard tables, some gambling their savings away and some drinking them up. The courts were crowded with liquor cases, presided over by the former premier, George Walkem, himself no mean toper. "Judge Walkem carried away dead drunk at 7 a.m. when everybody was looking on," Cambie scribbled in his diary one day, noting, however, that Walkem recovered sufficiently to open court at 10.30 a.m. and, presumably, to levy the usual fines for intoxication.

It was Andrew Onderdonk's job to continue the railroad for the CPR from the end of the government section at Savona's Ferry to meet the railway builders coming from the east. On August 11, Van Horne, together with Major Rogers and S. B. Reed, set off along the route of the line that would take them directly through Eagle Pass and then on across the mountains to the Columbia.

It was a truly fearful trip. The members of the party were forced to leave most of their spare clothing at End of Track and push on by freight team, scow, and, finally, pony train. An early fall of snow had deposited three feet of slush on the mountain

The beginnings of Port Moody. When Van Horne arrived, the local paper reported that a city of 100,000 would rise on the spot within a few years. Van Horne took one look at this narrow strip of shoreline and dismissed the idea. When the rival New Westminster paper reported his decision, the Port Moody editor refused to believe it, calling the statement a "choice assortment of cast iron lies."

Kamloops in 1884. The railway ran right down the centre of the main (and only) street. The settlement was little more than a shack-town. "For water," one resident wrote, "you went to the river and dipped in a bucket." But Van Horne was diplomatic enough, when he arrived on the scene, to refer to the community's "thriving and progressive look."

This is the wagon road through Eagle Pass, as Van Horne experienced it in 1884. Through this scarred land, made wretched by pelting rain, his party made *its hungry way towards the Selkirks, following a route almost identical with that travelled a generation before by Walter Moberly, the first surveyor.*

trails, already littered with the cast-offs of other travellers. While crossing Summit Lake, Van Horne tumbled into water that was only a degree or so above freezing. The entire trip was one that few people had ever made. In another fifteen months it would no longer be necessary.

The party was without food for two days, probably as a result of Rogers's eccentric provisioning. When they finally arrived at the most forward of the camps on Rogers Pass, the general manager's sensitive nostrils detected the aroma of ham cooking. "It was then," he later recalled, "that I learned that a man can smell ham ten miles away."

On this journey several new Van Horne legends were forged. When the general manager reached the Mountain Creek trestle he was told that a few days before several men had crashed to their deaths in the ravine below. The floor of the trestle, one hundred and sixty feet above the torrent, consisted of two loose planks and nothing more. One of the general manager's companions was barely able to negotiate the bridge by crawling inch by inch on his hands and knees, but Van Horne stepped confidently out on the shaky planks, strode across the trestle, and returned just as imperturbably.

He liked to take curves on the newly constructed road at the highest possible speed. Once, with a dangerous trestle looming up ahead, the engineer balked.

"Here," Van Horne said, "get down and I'll take her over myself."

"Well," said the engineer, "if you ain't afraid, guess I ain't neither."

When the general manager left the mountains and rolled across the prairies in the comfort of his private car, he was able to witness the by-products of his handiwork: Calgary, Medicine Hat, Moose Jaw, and Regina slowly changing from tent and shack towns to permanent communities; crops being harvested; sod houses going up; and a veneer of civilization spreading out over the raw prairie. As he sped towards Winnipeg, Van Horne could note at every siding the bleak symbols of a vanished past – great stacks of buffalo bones being loaded into boxcars. The general manager had made his gardening expertise pay off: the bones were shipped to Minneapolis and sold as fertilizer for seven dollars a ton. Back in Montreal, no matter was too small to occupy him. At one point he personally dictated changes in some drawings of the mountains: he wanted to see steam and not black smoke issuing from the locomotives pictured in the foreground of Mount Stephen; that would give more emphasis to the presence of the railway.

More and more, however, he was concerned about costs. Over and over, in his wide ranging correspondence, he used the phrase "we have not a dollar to spare." Staffs were reduced to the bone, and repairs to locomotives were cut back to the minimum. To John Ross, on the Lake Superior line, he wrote: "By cutting every corner and cheapening the work in every practicable way, we may be able to build the line for the money available. . . . If we cannot do that, we must stop the work."

As the months went by Van Horne's communications with his deputies in the field became more and more insistent. ". . . we are again very near our *danger line*," he informed John Ross in October. All pretence at building a first-class line had been abandoned. Even the ballasting of the rails had to be discontinued except where it was necessary to preserve them from damage. After November 1, not even a fence could be built or a nail driven without Van Horne's permission. That was how tight money had become.

Outwardly, the general manager maintained his air of bluff confidence. When a Scottish friend of W. B. Scarth's asked if the CPR was a good investment, Van Horne replied: "I have no hesitation in expressing my opinion in the strongest possible terms that it will pay handsomely" – and he went on to say why: its entire debt was only one third that of the Northern Pacific on a mileage basis, and even less in comparison with other United States transcontinental railways. The CPR's advantage as a through line was greater, and the road itself was far better built.

But Van Horne's real expression of confidence in the railroad went much further than words. He himself had sunk almost every dollar he had in Canadian Pacific stock. If the road failed, he was prepared to go down with it.

The edge of the precipice

ONCE AGAIN, the railway was in a critical financial position. "I *feel* like a man walking on the edge of a precipice with less 'nerve' than is comfortable or even *safe* in such a case," George Stephen wrote to the Prime Minister at the end of 1884. ". . . the ordeal I am going through is not easy to stand."

The ordeal had begun that summer – only a few months after Parliament had reluctantly passed the loan of $22,500,000. By September the credit of the company at home and abroad was gone. Stephen and Donald A. Smith had been dipping lavishly into their private fortunes in an attempt to sustain it. They were close to the bottom of the barrel.

Almost all of the spring loan had been gobbled up by the railway builders on the Shield and in the mountains; what was left was being paid out only as the work was done; often these payments were very late. The grain elevator at the lakehead had cost three hundred thousand dollars. Then there were the terminals, shops, and equipment, spread over more than two thousand miles. In the first ten months of 1884 the company found it had spent eight million dollars on essential work that had not been contracted for.

The railway was working on a margin that was terrifyingly narrow. A few days' delay in the subsidy could mean that thousands of men would not be paid. Yet for a variety of reasons the payments were often slow or slender.

There were other problems. Expensive tote roads had to be constructed out of Lake Nipissing

and Michipicoten and across the Selkirk Mountains. Vast quantities of construction equipment and supplies had to be brought in, especially before the onset of winter. For all of this the company was forced to lay out funds months in advance; but in Schreiber's strict interpretation of the contract terms, the subsidy did not apply to these preliminary steps of construction.

The real fear was that the government would stop payment altogether. This it was empowered to do if its engineers estimated that there were not enough funds left to complete the line. By October, 1884, it was becoming increasingly clear that if the company had to find funds to repay its loan of the previous November, together with interest and dividends, the coffers would be empty and construction must cease.

Wages were suspiciously slow. Thousands of men on the Lake Superior section were facing long delays in pay. The company was using every possible excuse to stave off creditors and employees. At the end of October the CPR announced that the men in the eastern division would henceforth be paid by cheques drawn on the Bank of Montreal; the reason given was that it was too dangerous to carry around more than a million dollars in cash. The real reason was that Van Horne had decided on a daring though barbarous gambit. He intended to keep nine thousand men at work all winter in the remotest areas with plenty of good food. They would be paid by cheque, which they would be unable to cash. If any man wanted to get away he would find it almost impossible to do so; the isolated conditions would make it difficult to leave before spring, at which time the general manager believed funds must be forthcoming.

In those desperate months, Van Horne and Stephen leaned heavily on Thomas Shaughnessy, a man apparently able to make one dollar do the work of a hundred. Shaughnessy was rising rapidly in the ranks; one day he would be president. He never showed the slightest tremor of panic as he kited cheques, kept creditors at bay, denied funds,

On the Little Pic River, R. G. Reid built huge towers
of masonry to carry the span, but in the fall of 1884,
when the CPR began to feel the pinch, Van Horne
was forced to ban all further use of stone and steel.

*The Red Sucker trestle was built entirely of timber. To save money, Van Horne
carried the line high. Later on he planned to fill in trestled gorges like this one.*

made partial payments, and generally held the company together. In Toronto, the heads of the big wholesale houses, under Van Horne's and Shaughnessy's persuasion, extended millions of dollars in credit so that supplies could go forward.

While Shaughnessy was using extraordinary measures to keep the company solvent, Stephen was slowly committing his entire personal fortune and those of his closest colleagues to its further support. The previous winter, he, Donald Smith, Angus, and McIntyre had put up a total of $2.3 million in their own bonds and securities as collateral against CPR bank loans. But in May, McIntyre dropped right out of the Canadian Pacific, refusing to stay even as a director or to have anything to do with the management of a company he clearly believed would go to the wall. Baron Reinach went with him, and Stephen was forced to use more of his fortune to buy out both men's stock.

In the face of these defections, the steadfastness of Donald A. Smith was refreshing. Smith was prepared, like Stephen, to invest all of his own money in the Canadian Pacific. Stephen, who went to London in July, was able that month to "*melt*," as he put it, a number of land grant bonds into cash by giving the personal guarantee of Smith, Angus, and himself to a British bank for a four-month loan.

The continued attacks on the Canadian Pacific affected Canada's own credit position on the other side of the Atlantic. Leonard Tilley, the finance minister, arriving in London in June and hoping to float a loan of five million pounds, was alarmed at the propaganda campaign that had been organized. Tilley got his money only with difficulty and not at the rate he expected. A week later CPR stock dropped to a record low of 39 on the New York board.

In mortgaging the railroad, Stephen had made it impossible to raise any further funds except through the sale of outstanding stock. But the government lien, together with the bitter campaign being waged against the CPR in New York and London, had frightened off potential buyers. Unless he could make an arrangement to get rid of that lien he faced an impossible situation. It was a maddening dilemma: as soon as the CPR became a through line the profits would roll in, for it held a mileage advantage over other transcontinental railroads. But could the CPR be completed? By October, Stephen realized that there was not enough money to do the job.

He set off for England for the third time that year to raise more funds. The loan he had negotiated in July would shortly be due. Worse, the five-million-dollar loan he had raised in New York the previous year by pledging ten million dollars' worth of CPR stock was also due in November – and the stock was too low to be of any use. There were other worries. Looking beyond the financial watershed of November, Stephen could see the dark month of February looming up. Then the railway would be forced to pay its guaranteed dividend of five per cent. The government was responsible for three per cent, but the CPR would somehow have to find the cash for the remainder – an amount in excess of one million dollars.

Nevertheless, Stephen began to see some tiny pinpoints of light at the end of the tunnel down which he had set his course. The New York loan he solved by the now familiar device of using his own funds and those of some of his friends. He simply bought up the stock held as collateral and paid off the debt. Then in London, Charles Tupper came to his aid and drafted a plan for relief of the railway which he shot off to Tilley in Ottawa. It was all very tentative; nobody knew whether any further plan to aid the CPR could be forced down the throats of the Cabinet. Still, it was a straw at which Stephen could grasp. And, finally, by pledging $385,000 worth of Toronto, Grey and Bruce bonds, which he, Donald Smith, and R. B. Angus held among them, he was able to raise a loan of a quarter of a million from a Scottish financial institution. It was this small bit of Highland good cheer that prompted the president to send off to Smith one of the most memorable cablegrams in

Canadian history . . . and certainly the shortest.

Both Stephen and Smith had come from small Scottish towns in the countryside drained by the River Spey, in a land once dominated by the Clan Grant. Stephen remembered, and knew that Smith would remember also, a great rock which dominated the valley no more than three miles from Dufftown, in Banffshire, where he had been born. Everyone knew the meaning of that rock: it was a symbol of defiance. In the brave old days, when clan battled clan, a sentinel had kept watch on its stark promontory, and when the enemy was sighted and a fiery cross borne through Speyside, this rock had become a rallying place for the Clan Grant. The rock was known as Craigellachie, and it was this defiant slogan that Stephen dispatched to his cousin. Into one brief, cryptic sentence, the CPR president managed to convey all the fierce passions, bold defiance, dark hatreds, and bright loyalties inherited from his Scottish forbears. "Stand fast, Craigellachie!" the cable advised, and Donald Smith, when he read it in Montreal, must himself have heard, as in the distance, the clash of warring claymores and the wild skirl of battle.

As the CPR's financial crisis worsened, construction became cruder and standards dropped. This log trestle over the Nepigon is a far cry from the one on page 271.

The critical year

EIGHTEEN EIGHTY-FIVE was perhaps the most significant year of the first Canadian century. After that year nothing could ever be the same again, because for the first time Canadians would be able to travel the length of their nation without setting foot in a foreign land. A series of devices came into being that year that would also help to bind the country together. The single-pole electric trolley had just been invented and was demonstrated for the first time at the Toronto Agricultural Fair of 1885. That same year Gottlieb Daimler took out his historic patent for an internal combustion engine and Karl Benz built the first automobile – a three-wheeled one. The presence of radio waves was confirmed and the long-distance telephone put into use. Like the railway, these new aids to communication would help stitch the awkward archipelago of population islands into a workable transcontinental reality.

The concept of a transcontinental railway was also responsible for changing the casual attitude towards time. Heretofore every city and village had operated on its own time system. When it was noon in Toronto, it was 11.58 in Hamilton, 12.08 in Belleville, 12.12½ in Kingston, 12.16½ in Brockville, and 12.25 in Montreal. As the railways lengthened across the continent, the constant changing of watches became more and more inconvenient. Schedules were in a state of total confusion. Every railroad had its own version of the correct time, based on the standard of its home city. There were, in the United States, one hundred different time standards used by the various railroads.

On New Year's Day, 1885, the Universal Time System was adopted at Greenwich. About a year earlier the major American railways and the Canadian Pacific had brought order out of chaos as far as their own schedules were concerned by adopting "railway time." The change was a fundamental one, for it affected in a subtle fashion people's attitudes and behaviour. Such concepts as promptness and tardiness took on a new meaning. The country began to live by the clock in a way it had not previously been able to do.

Much of the credit for this went to Sandford Fleming, who had realized very early that a transcontinental railway would immediately raise difficulties in the computation of time. In 1876 he prepared a memorandum on the subject, which was widely circulated, and in 1885 the Canadian Institute recognized him as "unquestionably the initiator and principal agent in the movement for the reform in Time-Reckoning and in the establishment of the Universal Day."

Eighteen eighty-five was as dramatic a year as it was significant. As the nation became vertebrate, events seemed to accelerate on a collision course. In Montreal, George Stephen was trying to stave off personal and corporate ruin. In Ottawa, John A. Macdonald faced a cabinet revolt over the railway's newest financial proposals. In Toronto, Thomas Shaughnessy was juggling bills like an accomplished sideshow artist in order to give Van Horne the cash he needed to complete the line. On Lake Superior, Van Horne was trying to link up the gaps between the isolated stretches of steel – they totalled 254 miles – so that the CPR might begin its operation. In Manitoba, the political agitation against both government and railway was increasing. In St. Laurent on the Saskatchewan, Louis Riel was back from his long exile and rousing the Métis again. On the far plains, the Cree chieftains, Big Bear and Poundmaker, were petitioning for new concessions. And in the mountains, the railway builders faced their last great barrier – the snow-shrouded Selkirks.

Van Horne had thought long and hard about using the Rogers Pass in preference to the longer but easier Columbia Valley. On the one hand there would be steep gradients for some forty miles. That would mean heavy assisting engines and costly wear

on the track. Against that there was the saving of nearly seventy-seven miles, which meant a reduction of two hours in passenger time and four hours for freight trains. This latter consideration was of great importance when competing for through traffic. Van Horne, who disdained circumlocution, opted for the Rogers Pass.

There were problems in the Selkirks, however, on which no one had reckoned. By 1885 the right of way had been cleared directly across the mountains. More that a thousand men were toiling away in the teeth of shrieking winds that drove snow particles like needles into their faces. Seen from the summit, the location line resembled a wriggling serpent, coiling around the hanging valleys, squeezing through the narrow ravines, and sometimes

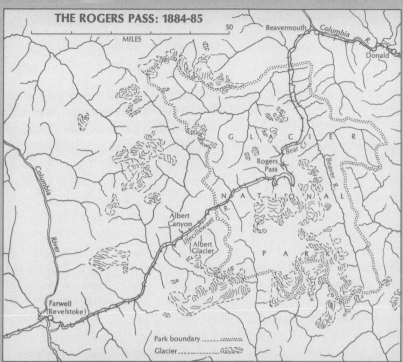

THE ROGERS PASS: 1884-85

Park boundary ....
Glacier ....

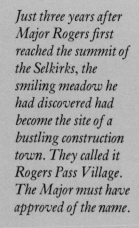

Just three years after Major Rogers first reached the summit of the Selkirks, the smiling meadow he had discovered had become the site of a bustling construction town. They called it Rogers Pass Village. The Major must have approved of the name.

vanishing into the dark maw of a half-completed tunnel. High above, millions of tons of ice hung poised on the lip of the mountains, the birthplace of the avalanches and snowslides that constantly swept the area.

An average of fifty feet of snow fell each winter on the Rogers Pass. This natural phenomenon posed a threat to the entire operation of the railway. In midwinter, the pass was almost impossible to breach. The snowslides – solid packs of ice – were sometimes fifty feet thick. Through this frozen jungle the railroad builders intended to force the line.

A Selkirk snowslide was a terrifying spectacle. A quarter of a million cubic yards of snow could be detached from a mountain peak and come tearing down the slopes for thousands of feet, ripping out cedars, seizing boulders in its grip, and causing an accompanying cyclone more fearful than the avalanche itself. A few seconds before the body of the avalanche struck, the pressure of this gale force wind, known as the flurry, snapped off huge trees several feet in diameter fifty feet above the base. One such flurry was known to have picked up a man and whirled and twisted him so rapidly that when he dropped he was a limp mass without a bruise or a break in skin or clothing yet with every bone in his body either broken or dislocated. Another knocked eight loaded freight cars off the rails.

Apart from the slides, there were the prodigious falls of snow. In one six-day period, eight and a half feet of snow fell. Sometimes three weeks could pass without the blizzard ceasing. In the winter, the scene from the Rogers Pass was eerie. The traveller, gazing westward, looked down into a two-thousand-foot gorge, muffled in a white blanket twenty feet deep. Above and around him the glaciers dangled, shimmering in the sunlight. At one spot, forty-two glaciers were visible, the largest being the vast Illecillewaet, which would for more than half a century be one of the great Canadian tourist attractions until the changing climate caused it to recede.

This scenery, an uncalculated asset in the summer, was an uncalculated liability in the winter. The problems of the Selkirks delayed the opening of through passenger service to the Pacific by at least six months. In the winter of 1885-86 entire sections of completed track were swept away by snowslides and the line had to be closed. In the end, the company was forced to construct almost six miles of snow sheds at a cost of forty dollars a foot.

For the next quarter-century, this westward descent, like that of the Big Hill in the Rockies, was an operating nightmare. In March, 1910, a snowslide which caused the loss of fifty-eight lives finally convinced the CPR that it must abandon the Rogers Pass. This resulted in a second engineering feat, equal to the drilling of the spiral tunnels – the boring of the longest double-track tunnel on the continent, the five-mile-long Connaught. (Today the Trans-Canada highway runs through the Rogers Pass, but it is passable only in summer.)

Snow or no snow, the line had to be driven to completion somehow by the end of 1885. As winter gave way to spring, every mile of the right of way was throbbing with activity.

The mountain streams tumbling down from the glaciers above had cut deep gouges in the naked rock, and it was over these gulches that the longest and the highest bridges were required. Built entirely of timber, they had few counterparts in the world. The Mountain Creek bridge, which rose more than 175 feet above the torrent, was one of the largest wooden structures ever built, being twelve hundred feet long. The bridge over Stoney Creek was the highest in North America, supported on wooden towers two hundred feet high, set in concrete.

On the far side of the pass, where the Prussian blue waters of the Illecillewaet raced downhill between thick jungle walls, the line made a double loop, curving first to the left, then swinging back across the valley to the very tip of the great glacier and then, a mile farther on, twisting back again in the shape of an inverted S. This was three more miles of railway than Van Horne had counted on; it took nine and a half miles to reach the level of the stream four miles from the summit. But it was necessary to avoid the snowslides, and for future tourists, swaying down this dramatic slope from the vantage point of an observation car, the experience would be electrifying. This was the same trail, bestrewn with devil's club and skunk cabbage, that Major Rogers and his nephew Albert had toiled up on their voyage of discovery in 1881, and that a hungry Van Horne had struggled over in 1884. Nobody except an enthusiastic mountaineer would ever have to make that journey again; and only a few, gazing up at the shattered rock of the clefts and tunnels and the pilings of the matchstick bridges, would let their thoughts rest upon the thousands of sweating workmen who had made it possible.

The famous "loop" on the Illecillewaet, rendered obsolete by the Connaught Tunnel. From here, where the railway crossed Loop Creek at Cambie station, the traveller could see three other sections of track: directly ahead, to the right, and on the far left (where roofs of shacks peek through the trees). This was the centre point of a giant inverted S.

Big Bear (centre), photographed at Fort Pitt at the time he was forming the Cree council. Of all Indians, he took the most active part in the rebellion.

The return of Louis Riel

To THOSE who had known the North West before the time of the steel, the railway was a symbol of the passing of the Good Old Days. To the Indians it was a new kind of boundary, as solid in its own way as a wall. To the white settlers of northern Saskatchewan, its change of route had meant disappointment. To the farmers of Manitoba it spelled monopoly and grinding freight rates. To the halfbreeds, it stood for revolutionary social change.

From Winnipeg to Edmonton, the North West was in a ferment. Whites, Indians, and half-breeds were all organizing. At the end of July, 1884, the Crees of the North Saskatchewan, who had come to the point of rebellion earlier in the year, were

welded into an Indian council by Big Bear, the most independent of the chiefs. The Indians felt that the government had deceived them, and the Indians were right. Ottawa had promised to save them from starvation, yet already their meagre rations had been cut back as part of an official policy of retrenchment. It was plain that the eastern politicians had little understanding of the North West; the new minister of the interior, Senator David Macpherson, had not even ventured as far as Winnipeg.

The white settlers were equally disaffected. In addition to the burgeoning Manitoba Farmers' Union, other organized groups were petitioning Ottawa for redress. Their demands were similar: local autonomy, land reform, control of their own railways, reduction of protective tariffs, and an end to the CPR monopoly.

Gabriel Dumont, "the Prince of the Prairies." He knew the plains "as well as a housewife knows her own kitchen." A brilliant tactician, famed for his generosity to unlucky members of the buffalo hunt, his only weakness was gambling. He could play cards for three days and three nights without stopping to eat.

The English and Scots half-breeds and the French-speaking Roman Catholic Métis had another grievance. They wanted what the government had granted in Manitoba after the first collision with Louis Riel – a share in the aboriginal title to the land. Time after time they had been put off.

By the spring of 1884, protest meetings were becoming common at St. Laurent near Duck Lake on the South Saskatchewan – the strongest and best established of the Métis communities. At this point the united half-breed community decided that Louis Riel was the only man who could lead them to force the government's hand. He was a long distance away and many years out of touch, living in poverty and teaching school at a Jesuit mission at Sun River, Montana. Distance held no terrors for the Métis. Four of them saddled up their horses that May and set out on a seven-hundred-mile ride to meet their Messiah.

The most interesting member of the delegation was Gabriel Dumont, the most popular and respected man along the Saskatchewan – a natural leader, though totally unlettered and almost apolitical. Dumont had been for years chief of the buffalo hunt – a legendary rider, sharpshooter, drinker, gambler, and even swimmer. He was forty-seven and had been chief of his people since the age of twenty-five, much beloved by all who knew him. "One might travel the plains from one end to the other and talk to the Métis hunters and never hear an unkind word said of Dumont," Sam Steele was to recall. "When in trouble the cry of all was for Gabriel."

In 1884 the cry was for Gabriel again. But Dumont knew that he could not lead his people in a battle with the government of Canada: he had no English and no gift for oratory. He was a man of action, a prairie general who would shortly become the tactician of the last stand of the Métis empire against the onrush of civilization. Riel would be that empire's king.

The four delegates arrived at Riel's home on

Edgar Dewdney (front, centre), photographed in Regina in 1885 with the members of his North West Council.

June 4, 1884. Riel was under doctor's orders to avoid excitement, a counsel he only occasionally remembered to follow. He was clearly aroused by the message the delegation brought to him. The sense of power, which he had enjoyed in his brief time as master of Fort Garry, was still within him; so was the mystic conviction that he had a divine mission to perform. Undoubtedly he felt keenly the plight of his people, as he had fifteen years before. Added to that was his own sense of injury at the hands of the Canadian government. Canada, he believed, owed him both land and money. After some consideration he told the delegation that he would return to Canada temporarily to fight not only for his personal rights and those of his people but also for the white settlers and the Indians.

On the surface, Riel did not appear to sanction trouble. His meetings were enthusiastic but outwardly peaceful. The Métis demands were codified and sent to Ottawa; they included requests for land

scrip, better treatment for the Indians, responsible government with vote by ballot, parliamentary representation, reduction of the tariff, and the building of another railway to Hudson Bay. In spite of the clamour, the government remained curiously inattentive.

The resident priest at St. Laurent, Father André, wrote three letters to Dewdney in January and February, 1885, stating clearly that unless the government took some action to redress grievances there would be an uprising under Riel in which the Indians would join. By this time Riel was acting very strangely indeed. There is no doubt that he believed himself to be God's envoy. He prayed daily, told of revelations he had experienced in the night, recounted the visitations of saints, and repeated conversations he said he had had with the Holy Ghost.

Father André's repeated warnings were supplemented by others from Joseph Howe, the

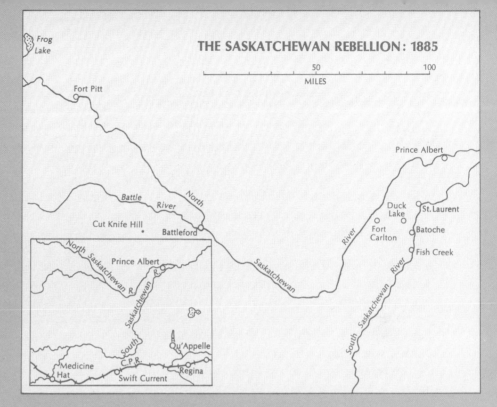

The adversaries at Duck Lake, Louis Riel (left) and Major L.N.F. Crozier sketched by a contemporary artist.

Mounted Police inspector at Prince Albert, from Major L. N. F. Crozier, his superior at Battleford, and from D. H. McDowell, the representative of the district on the Territorial Council. All urged that Ottawa take some action; but the government's only response was a vague set of promises for the future and the establishment in January of that favourite Canadian device for procrastination, a commission to examine the question of land scrip for the Métis. This served only to infuriate Riel and his followers.

In the face of these vacillations Major Crozier's misgivings increased. He wired Dewdney in February urging that some accommodation be made with the Métis; delay would be dangerous. But the Prime Minister's mood that spring seemed to be delay, as George Stephen was finding to his own frustration.

Riel's memory went back to those intoxicating moments in December, 1869, when he had been

able to deal with Canada on equal diplomatic terms and secure concessions for his people as the result of a bold *fait accompli*. Something along the same lines was in his mind in the early months of 1885. He would not need to resort to bloodshed; the threat of it would bring the Canadian government to its senses. But conditions had changed since 1869 and Riel ignored one vital factor – the presence of the railway.

By March 13, Crozier was expecting a rebellion. The NWMP commissioner, A. G. Irvine, dispatched a hundred reinforcements to Prince Albert. Events began to accelerate. On March 18, Riel took prisoners, seized arms in the St. Laurent-Batoche area, and cut the telegraph line between Batoche and Prince Albert. The following day, he set up a provisional Métis government, as he had done in 1869.

In the week that followed he and his followers, in Crozier's words, "robbed, plundered, pillaged and terrorized the settlers and the country." Dewdney wired Macdonald on March 22 that it was imperative that an able military man be in the North West in case the militia had to be called out. The next day Macdonald dispatched Major-General Frederick Dobson Middleton to the Red River with orders that the militia should move.

It was Riel's intention to seize Fort Carlton and establish it as the capital of his new government. Crozier decided to hold the Fort with his policemen and a detachment of volunteers from Prince Albert. But on March 25 he sent a sergeant and seventeen constables to get provisions and ammunition from the trader's store at Duck Lake. The detachment was halted by a large party led by Dumont, who actually went so far as to prod the ribs of the NWMP interpreter with a cocked and loaded rifle while the Indians jeered at the police: "If you are men, now come in." The party retreated.

This was too much for the impatient Crozier. Without waiting for Irvine and his reinforcements, the superintendent set out with his fifty-five Mounted Policemen, forty-three Prince Albert volunteers, and a seven-pound cannon in tow.

Dumont, on horseback, watched them come. His Métis dismounted and began to creep forward through a curtain of falling snow, partially encircling the police.

Crozier drew his twenty sleighs up in line across the road and ordered his men to take cover behind them. A parley took place under a rebel white flag with Dumont's brother Isidore and an Indian on one side and Crozier and a half-breed interpreter, John McKay, on the other. When Crozier extended his hand to the Indian, the unarmed native made a grab for McKay's rifle. Crozier, seeing the struggle, gave the order to fire. Isidore Dumont toppled from his horse, dead. The rebels were already on the move, circling around the police left flank. Crozier put spurs to his horse and galloped back to the police lines through a hail of bullets. The Indian was already dead.

At this moment, with the Métis pouring a fierce fire on the police from two houses concealed on the right of the trail and outflanking them on the left, Louis Riel appeared on horseback through the swirling snow at the head of one hundred and fifty armed Métis. He was grasping an enormous crucifix in his free hand and, when the police fired at him, he roared out in a voice that all could hear: "In the name of God the Father who created us, reply to that!"

Within thirty minutes Crozier had lost a quarter of his force killed and wounded. The Métis had suffered only five casualties. The North West Mounted Police were in retreat. The Saskatchewan Rebellion had begun.

Impending crisis

SUNDAY, JANUARY 11, 1885, was the Prime Minister's seventieth birthday, and on Monday all of Montreal celebrated this anniversary, which also marked his fortieth year in politics. As he drove through two miles of flaming torches on that "dark soft night," under a sky spangled by exploding rockets, to a banquet in his honour, he was in the mellowest of moods. In his speech he could not help adding to the eulogies that he heard on all sides about the great national project, which was nearing completion. "In the whole annals of railway construction there has been nothing to equal it," he said. Only a few of those in attendance – George Stephen was one – could appreciate the irony of that statement. The Prime Minister might just as easily have been referring to the immensity of the financial crisis that the railway faced.

Just the previous Friday, Stephen had dispatched one of his frantic wires to the Prime Minister: "Imminent danger of sudden crisis unless we can find means to meet pressing demands." That week, rumours of the company's financial straits began to leak out. Within a fortnight the stock was down below 38; not long after it hit a new low of $33\frac{1}{8}$.

Financially, it was an ingenious scheme. Politically it was disastrous. The previous year, Blake had taunted the Government about the CPR loan: "Don't call it a loan. You know we shall never see a penny of this money again." Macdonald could foresee the hazards of allowing Blake to cry: "We told you so!"

The horrifying prospect of the April dividend hung like a spectre over the CPR executive committee. The company's books were about to close. If it did not advertise the dividend, the world would assume that the Canadian Pacific was bankrupt. Again, the only hope was the government. Surely it would come to the assistance of the company on a temporary basis, making an advance on supplies before the end of January: those funds could be paid back out of the monthly estimates. Stephen wired Macdonald on January 20: "The dividend must be cabled to night. . . . Can I trust to this? Please answer. I cannot delay advertizing dividend any longer."

Now the Prime Minister was forced into a corner. He must break the news to Stephen that there was no hope of further assistance. He faced a revolt in his cabinet; three ministers were opposed to further relief and one of these, Archibald McLelan, the Nova Scotian who was Minister of Fisheries, was pledged to resign if any further public monies were advanced to the CPR. The Prime Minister wired Stephen that there was little chance of legislation that session. He would, however, be able to carry an advance of enough money to pay the dividend if it would enable Stephen to postpone matters until 1886.

This was worse than no answer at all. As Macdonald himself knew, the railway could not stay afloat until 1886. Stephen realized what he must do.

In one of his directors' meetings, Stephen, in a speech that Van Horne later characterized as the finest he had ever heard, turned to Smith and said, simply: "If we fail, you and I, Donald, must not be left with a dollar of personal fortune." Smith had silently agreed. Now the two Scotsmen pledged

Stephen had worked out with Tupper and Macdonald a scheme whereby the unissued stock of the CPR would be cancelled by government legislation, the lien on the railway removed, and a more or less equivalent amount of cash raised by mortgage bonds applied to the entire main line of the railway, with principal and interest on them guaranteed by the government. About half the cash from these bonds would be used to help pay off the loan of 1884. The rest would go to the company as a loan to pay for expenditures not included in the original contract. The remainder of the 1884 loan would be paid off in land grant bonds.

In 1884, William Notman photographed George Stephen's new home on Drummond Street, Montreal, in all its Victorian opulence. The picture was taken a few months before the CPR president pledged it – contents and all – to raise enough cash to keep the company solvent. Treasury officers inventoried all his possessions: art collection, furniture, marble statuary, linen, china, and silverware. Then Stephen "without a flicker of an eyelid signed it all away." That act, he told Macdonald, was "simply absurd on any kind of business grounds." But it helped save the railway. The famous mansion is now the Mount Stephen Club.

the remainder of their joint fortunes and all their personal assets – everything they possessed – to raise the six hundred and fifty thousand dollars necessary to pay the dividend and an additional one million dollars on a five-month note to provide the short-term funds the company would need to carry it over the coming weeks. If the CPR crashed, Stephen and Smith would crash with it.

The two financiers could not, unaided, save the railway with a million dollars. The demands of the contractors would consume that sum in a few weeks. Already the three-month notes given to satisfy clamorous creditors were coming due and Macdonald was still vacillating. Even the normally ebullient Van Horne was in a private state of gloom. Outwardly he remained supremely confident. "Go sell your boots, and buy c.p.r. stock," he told one worried creditor. Inwardly he must have had his doubts. The absence of the pay car was threatening to close down the railway. At Beavermouth on the Columbia, there was strike talk. On Lake Superior, men were threatening to lynch a contractor whom they blamed for holding back their wages.

On March 18, Stephen made an official application to the Privy Council for a loan of five million dollars. When it was rejected, Stephen vowed he would leave Ottawa, never to return. The company was finished. Its directors were ruined men.

Van Horne this time made no attempt to hide his feelings. Collingwood Schreiber recalled a scene in his office – "the only time I believe his iron nerve was ever shaken" – when the general manager very slowly and very softly revealed the depth of his despair: "Say, if the Government doesn't give it [the loan] we are finished."

And then, as if the railroad itself had given the cue, succour came from the North West in the most perverse and unexpected form. The Métis under Louis Riel had raised the flag of insurrection.

Earlier that year, Van Horne had held a significant conversation with John Henry Pope, who had talked about a possible prairie revolt.

Van Horne remarked that he could get troops from Kingston or Quebec to Qu'Appelle in ten days.

In late March, Van Horne was reflecting on that promise: *How could the government refuse to aid a railway that sped troops out to the prairies, took the Métis unawares, and crushed a rebellion?* He immediately offered to the Privy Council the services of the railway to move troops, if needed, from Ottawa to Qu'Appelle. He made only one stipulation: he and not the army was to be in complete control of food and transport.

It sounded like a foolhardy pledge. There were four gaps, totalling eighty-six miles, in the unfinished line north of Lake Superior. Between the unconnected strips of hastily laid track was a frozen waste. Could men, horses, guns, and supplies be shuttled over the primitive tote roads which crossed that meeting place of blizzards? The members of the Council refused to believe it.

"Has anyone got a better plan?" Macdonald asked. There was no answer. Van Horne was told to prepare for a massive movement of men, animals, arms, and equipment.

The first intimations of the impending Saskatchewan rebellion appeared in fragmentary reports in Ontario newspapers on March 23. By the following day, Van Horne's plan was in operation, although Joseph-Philippe-René-Adolphe Caron, the Minister of Militia and Defence, was still unsure it would work. The engagement at Duck Lake took place on March 26; when the news burst upon the capital, the country was immediately mobilized.

In Ottawa on the very morning of the Duck Lake tragedy, George Stephen had just finished scribbling a note to Macdonald confessing failure and asking that the Privy Council decision rejecting his proposal be put into writing. There was nothing more that the CPR president could do. The fate of the CPR now lay with the railway itself. If Van Horne's gamble worked, then the politicians and the public would have the best possible proof that the presence of a transcontinental line could hold the nation together in time of trouble.

Toronto, Saturday, March 28, 1885. The Queen's Own and the 10th Royals leave the drill shed to receive clothing and equipment. A "war artist" was on hand.

Marching as to war

ON MARCH 27, all of settled Canada learned from its newspapers that a bloody rebellion had broken out in the North West. Ten members of Crozier's mixed force of police and volunteers lay dead at Duck Lake. Dumont's victory was beyond dispute. The Indians were about to rise. Prince Albert, Fort Carlton, Batoche, Fort Pitt, and perhaps Fort Qu'Appelle, Calgary, Edmonton, Moose Jaw, and Regina were all threatened. A wave of apprehension, anger, patriotism, and excitement washed over eastern Canada.

The government had already called out the permanent force – A and B batteries from Quebec and Kingston. On March 27, several militia regiments were ordered to be ready to move immediately to the North West. This aroused a flurry of speculation: How on earth were they to get there? There would be 3,324 men in all.

When the news was confirmed that the entire force was to be shipped west on the new railroad, a kind of frenzy seized the country. To a considerable extent the social life of the towns revolved around the militia. Now these men were parading through the streets for the first time in earnest. Never before had Canadians witnessed the kind of

spectacular scenes that took place during late March and early April – the cheers for Queen and Country, the blare of martial music, the oceans of flapping banners, the young men in scarlet and green marching behind the colours, the main streets jammed with waving thousands, the roll of drums, the troop trains puffing through the small towns and off into the Unknown – the singing, the cheering, the weeping and the kissing and the bitter-sweet good-byes. All this sound and spectacle, pumped up by a fanfaronade of military oratory – together with the terrible news on April 2 of a massacre of priests and civilians by Big Bear's Indians at Frog Lake – kept the country on an emotional binge for the better part of a fortnight.

The first units called out were the Queen's Own Rifles, the Royal Grenadiers, and the Infantry School, all of Toronto. The scenes on Monday morning, March 30, were chaotic and extravagant. It seemed as if every single citizen who could walk or crawl had come from miles around to line the route of march from the drill shed to Union Station.

Down the streets the young men came, as the crowd around them and above them, before them and behind them shouted itself hoarse. Bouquets of flowers drifted down from the windows above.

Handkerchiefs fluttered. A thousand flags snapped in the breeze. Those who could not move along beside the troops began to cry "Good-bye, Good-bye!" as the musicians struck up the song that became a kind of theme all over Canada that month, "The Girl I Left Behind Me."

To the foot of York Street, by the station, the people had been pouring in an unending stream. The immense crowd filled the Esplanade from one end of the station to the other, swarming over the roofs of freight cars and perching in every window.

Jammed into the cars, the men leaned out and waved. The train began to crawl forward. Above the continual roaring, individual good-byes could be heard. Then the band of the Queen's Own struck up "Auld Lang Syne" and, as the engine bell began to ring, the men joined in. Slowly the train drew away through the yards, where the top of every freight and passenger car was black with waving well-wishers, and then through the driving sleet and the whirling snow towards the dark forests and the unballasted track of the new Canada.

These scenes were repeated over and over again during the days that followed. In Kingston, hundreds crammed the town square to greet the incoming troops. In Montreal, the crush of onlookers

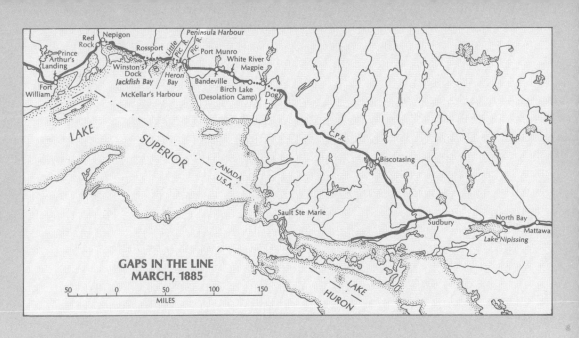

GAPS IN THE LINE
MARCH, 1885

50   0   50   100   150
MILES

was so great that a vast double window burst out from a three-storey building, injuring twelve persons. In Ottawa, the station platform was "a dense mass of enthusiastic, patriotic, jostling, laughing, shouting and war-fever-stricken individuals of all ages, sizes, sexes and complexions." In Quebec, "the scene presented beggars description."

Only the Governor-General's Body Guard, the oldest cavalry regiment in Canada, departed in comparative quiet and secrecy, the authorities fearing for the safety of the horses. The Guard was kept on the *qui vive* for several days while final arrangements were made to get the horses over the gaps in the line. When the regiment left, their colonel, George T. Denison, and his officers had not slept for three nights, having remained booted and spurred and ready to move for all of that time.

The trains sped off at staggered intervals towards Dog Lake, where the real ordeal would begin. The officers, at Van Horne's insistence, were given first-class accommodation even though he doubted he could collect for it. But for the sake of the railway's long-term image it was "important that the report of the officers as to the treatment of the troops on our line should be most favourable." As for the men themselves, Van Horne ensured that

there would, whenever possible, be mountains of food and gallons of hot coffee. Better than anybody else he knew what the troops were about to face. He could not protect them from the chill rides in open flatcars and sleighs, or from the numbing treks across the glare ice, but he could make sure that his army marched on a full stomach.

At Dog Lake, the men left the shelter of the cars and were packed into sleighs which set off behind teams of horses down the uncompleted right of way or along tote roads that circumvented the unbridged ravines and unfilled cuts. In some places the sleighs encountered boulders seven or eight feet high; in others they pitched into holes as deep as graves – the occupants flung over the dashboards and into the steaming haunches of the terrified horses. "No description," wrote one man, "could give an idea of the terrible roads through the woods." One sleigh overturned no fewer than thirteen times. Men were submerged in six feet of powdery snow, often with all their equipment. One member of the London Fusiliers was completely buried under an avalanche of baggage; a comrade was almost smothered when a horse toppled onto him.

The men crouched in the bottoms of the sleighs, wrapped in their greatcoats, but nothing could keep

291

The 10th Royal Grenadiers arriving at Desolation Camp. Sleep was impossible When they tried to light fires, the embers vanished in three feet of snow. One observer said that there was more heroism displayed here than later in the heat of battle.

AN OCCASIONAL SPILL.

F. W. Curzon, the artist who accompanied the 10th Royals, portrays the trip in open flatcars between Desolation Camp and Port Munro. The inset drawing shows the ordeal in the sleighs across the Dog Lake gap.

out the cold. For some units, it was so intense that any man who left any part exposed even for a few minutes suffered frostbite. "What they passed through that night all hope will never require to be repeated," a reporter travelling with the Grenadiers wrote back.

The entire gap between Dog Lake and Birch Lake took some nine hours to negotiate, and at the end stood a lonely huddle of shacks, which was swiftly and accurately named "Desolation Camp." It deserved its title. A fire had swept through the scrub timber leaving the trees a spectral white, and a cutting wind, rattling through the skeletal branches, added to the general feeling of despair. The only real shelter was a tattered tent, not large enough to accommodate the scores who sought refuge in it. Yet some men had to remain there for hours, their drenched clothing freezing to their skins in temperatures that dropped as low as thirty-five below. The 10th Royal Grenadiers arrived at five one morning and waited seventeen hours for a train without even the warmth of a fire to greet them.

Some members of the Queen's Own were rendered hysterical by the cold; when the trains finally arrived they had to be led on board, uncomprehending and uncaring. Although most troops had had very little sleep since leaving civilization, they were denied it at Desolation Camp because sleep could mean certain death when the thermometer dropped. The Halifax Battalion, the last to arrive, had to endure a freezing rain, which soaked their garments and turned their greatcoats into boards. When men in this condition dropped in their tracks, the guards were ordered to rouse them by any means, pull them to their feet, and bring them over to the fires to dry. There they stood, shivering and half-conscious, until the flatcars arrived.

In these cars, sleep again was all but impossible. There was no roof, and the wind and snow blew in through the crevices between the planks. Rough benches ran lengthwise and here the men sat, each enveloped in his two issue blankets, packed tightly together, or huddled on the floor.

For the Governor-General's Body Guard, the journey was complicated by the presence of the animals. The men were obliged to gather railway ties and construct flimsy ramps up which the horses could be led to the cars. The boards were sheathed in ice and had to be covered with blankets so that the animals would not lose their footing. All had to be watered and fed before the men could rest. Nor could they be moved by sleigh; the cavalrymen rode or led their animals the entire distance. When the cavalry moved by train, the horses were placed in exactly the same kind of flatcars as the men. Unloading them occupied hours, for it was necessary to remove all the hind shoes to prevent injuries to men and steeds.

The track that led from Desolation Camp to the next gap at Port Munro was of the most perfunctory construction. The ties had been laid directly onto the snow and in some sections where a thaw had set in, four or five ties in succession, spiked to the rails, would be held clear off the ground for several inches. Trains were thrown off this section of track daily and the rails were slowly being bent by the heavy passage. It was rarely possible to exceed five miles an hour. "It was," a member of the Queen's Own Rifles wrote home, "about the longest night any of us ever put in."

At Bandeville, the half-way point, the men were fed sandwiches and hot tea. Some were so stiff with cold they had to be lifted out of the cars. Others were so bone weary that when they reached the warmth of the eating house they dropped off into a sleep so deep it was almost impossible to awaken them to eat. After Bandeville, the troops faced another chilling seven hours before End of Track at Port Munro was reached. Here, in a deep, natural harbour, lay the schooner *Breck*, "open at both ends and leaky into the bargain." It was capable of accommodating some two hundred men who slumbered in comparative comfort, huddled together in the hold on mattresses composed of equal parts of hay and dirt, and later of water.

There followed a forced march across the glare ice of Lake Superior to the next piece of track at McKellar's Harbour, a journey of some eight hours Here, for many, the sun proved to be the enemy. For those who had been issued with snow glasses the glare on the ice was searing enough; they arrived at their destination with their faces scorched and blistered sometimes almost beyond recognition. Others managed to make eye-coverings, Indian-fashion, out of strips of birchbark with thin slits cut into them. But there were some who were rendered painfully blind.

The troops, buffeted by piercing winds on one side and blistered by the sun's glare on the other, were eventually strung out for seven miles across the lake. Marching was almost impossible on the glassy surface. Then, after ten miles, the texture changed and deep cuts, broken blocks of ice, and rocks frozen into the surface began to lacerate the feet of the men and officers, especially those who had left home in light shoes. Some threw their kits away, bit by bit; some collapsed in their tracks; others became temporarily deranged; one man was ruptured. The baggage sleighs picked up the casualties.

"I can tell you I'll never forget that march," a member of the Queen's Own Rifles wrote home. "We dared not stop an instant as we were in great danger of being frozen, although the sun was taking the skin off our faces. One man of our company went mad and one of the regulars went blind from snow glare."

Those units that travelled the same gap by night endured equally fearful conditions. Any man who drifted away from the column knew that he faced almost certain death. To prevent this, guards were assigned to ride around the column to head off drifters and stragglers. At that, the night was so dark and the way so difficult that the guide appointed to lead the troops across lost his way and the ordeal was lengthened by several hours.

The travail of the cavalry was again far more strenuous. The infantry was marched across the ice as far as McKellar's Harbour, where a short piece of line had been laid to Jackfish Bay. But because of the nuisance of loading and unloading horses, the Governor-General's Body Guard decided to ride or walk their steeds the full distance. For the last twenty miles they faced "a vast prairie or desert of ice," with no track of any kind. The surface was obscured by a crust under which two or three inches of water lay concealed. Above the crust there was a blanket of light snow. This treacherous surface was broken by patches of glare ice. Through this chill morass the horses, all of them lacking hind shoes, slipped, floundered, and struggled for mile after mile.

Out of Jackfish Bay, where the next gap began, the bone-weary troops, gazing from the rims of the cutters, began to gain some understanding of Van Horne's feat of railway construction. There they could see the gaping mouth of one of the longest tunnels on the road, piercing a solid wall of rock, one hundred and fifty feet high, for five hundred feet. For miles on end the roadbed had been blasted from the billion-year-old schists and granites – chipped into the sheer surface of the dark cliffs or hacked right through the spiny ridges by means of deep cuts. In some places it seemed as if the whole side of a mountain had been ripped asunder by dynamite and flung into the deep, still waters of the lake.

The voyage between Winston's Dock and Nepigon was again made on rails laid directly over the snow. The scenery grew grander as the cars crawled along and the soldiers began to stand up in their seats to see "sights which we will never forget" – the road torn out of the solid rock for mile after mile, skirting the very lip of the lake, from whose shores the mountains rose up directly for hundreds of feet above the track.

There was one final gap yet to come, and for many it would be the most terrible of all. This was the short march over the ice of the lake between Nepigon and Red Rock. It was no more than ten miles but it took some troops six hours.

"*The Midnight Tramp of the Royal Grenadiers,*" *as rendered by*
W. D. Blatchly for the Illustrated War News. *The troops blundered*
out "into the solemn darkness of the pines and hemlocks"
along a narrow, snow-choked trail where any false step spelled
disaster. But worse was to come on the melting ice of Nepigon Bay.

"The worst ice that mortal man ever encountered" faced the troops who floundered across Nepigon Bay. This was the final gap in the Lake Superior line.

Although officers enjoyed the dubious comfort of the caboose, some preferred to sit up with the men in open flatcars. Only when Red Rock was reached were the troops accommodated in real passenger cars (below). By then most were too weary to care.

The 10th Grenadiers started out in the evening along a trail so narrow that any attempt to move in a column of fours had to be abandoned. It was almost impossible to stay on the track, and yet a single misstep caused a man to be buried to his neck in deep snow. When the troops emerged from the woods and onto the lake they were met by a pitiless rain that seemed to drive through the thickest clothing. Every step a man took brought him into six inches of icy porridge. To move through this slush the men were forced to raise their knees almost to their waists, as if marking time; in effect, they waded the entire distance. Now and then a man would tumble exhausted into the slush and lie immovable and unnoticed until somebody stumbled over him. Captain A. Hamlyn Todd, of the Governor-General's Foot Guards, counted some forty men lying in the snow, many of them face down, completely played out. Some of these could not even speak. A member of the York Rangers described one such case: "On the way across one of the boys of the 35th was so fagged out that he laid down on the sleigh and could not move an inch. Captain Thomson asked him to move to one side but not one inch would he stir, so he caught hold of him like a bag and baggage, and tossed him to one side to let him pass."

When Red Rock was finally reached, the men were like zombies. They stood, uncomprehending, in ice-water ankle-deep, waiting for the trains; and when these arrived they tumbled into the cars and dropped in their tracks, lying on the floor, twisted on the seats all of a heap, sleeping where they fell. There was tea ready for them all but, cold and wet as they were, many did not have the strength to drink it. The ordeal was at an end; the track, as they well knew, lay unbroken all the way to their destination at Qu'Appelle. There would be no more marching until the coulees of Saskatchewan were reached – time enough then to reckon with Dumont's sharpshooters. For the moment, at least, they had no worries; and so, like men already dead, they slept.

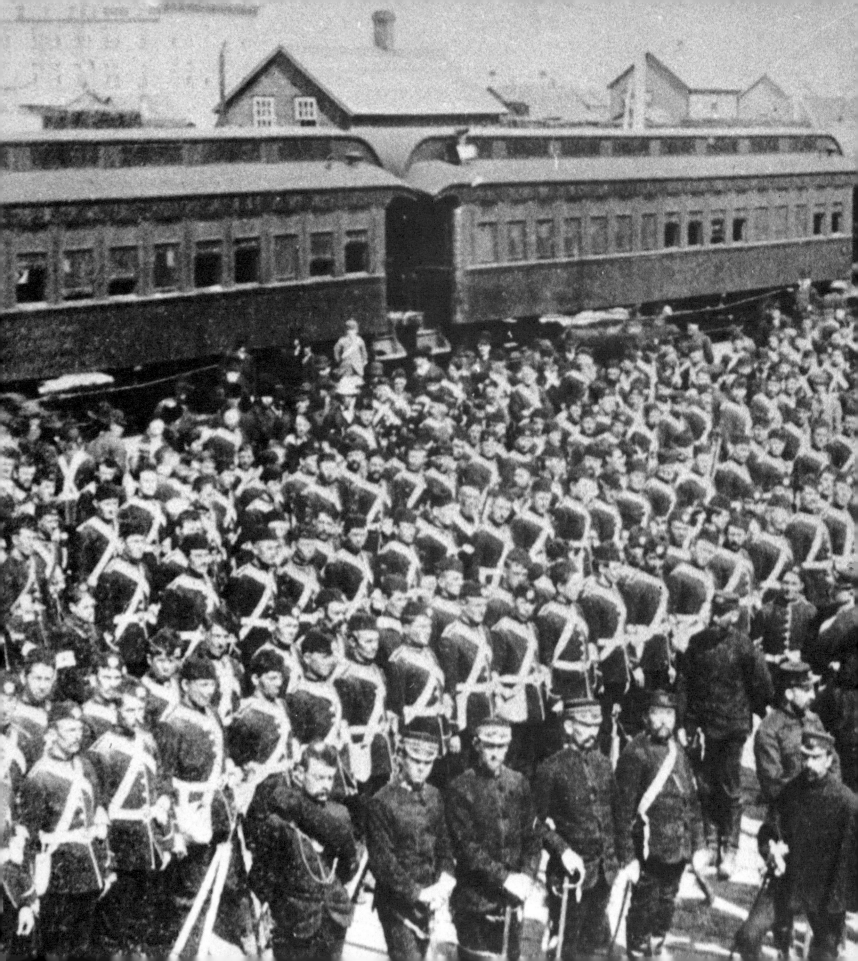

7

❧❧❧❧❧❧❀❧❧❧❧❧

A Land No Longer Lonely

❧❧❧❧❧❧❀❧❧❧❧❧

The CPR station, Winnipeg, 1885. The troops arrived in remarkably good spirits and with a new awareness of the land and the railway's relation to it. Amazed by the engineering marvels they had seen, they would soon gaze on the wonders of the plains and gain a fresh conception of the vastness of the new Canada.

The cross-fertilization process begins as troops from Quebec arrive at Port Arthur. With the Shield finally breached, Canada at last had an accessible frontier from which to draw new blood, new strength, and new ideas. It was no longer necessary to travel on foreign soil to reach the North West. As the Quarterly Review *put it, "there is no longer any reason why Canada's sons should 'go to the States' to make a new start in life."*

Stephen throws in the towel

WILLIAM VAN HORNE was not a man given to rash or boastful promises. When he said that he could move troops from eastern Canada to Qu'Appelle in ten days, he was actually giving himself a cushion of twenty-four hours. The first troops to leave Ottawa on March 28 arrived in Winnipeg exactly one week later. Within two days they were on the drill ground at Qu'Appelle. Two hundred and thirty miles to the north at Batoche, Riel was in control. Battleford was under siege by Poundmaker's Indians. Big Bear's Crees, following the massacre at Frog Lake, were roaming the country around Fort Pitt, killing, looting, and taking prisoners. But by mid-April, not much more than a fortnight after Duck Lake, the entire Field Force, save for the Halifax Battalion, was in Saskatchewan and ready to march.

The rebellion wrenched the gaze of settled Canada out to the prairie country and focused it on the railway. Every major newspaper sent a war correspondent with the troops. For week after week in the columns of the daily press, as the journalists digressed on the grandeur of the scenery, the impressive size of the newly created cities, and the wonders of the plains, Canadians were treated to a continuing geography lesson about a land that some had scarcely considered part of the nation. Until 1885, it had been as a foreign country; now their boys were fighting in it and for it, and soon anyone who wanted to see it could do so for the price of a railway ticket.

The Halifax Battalion was especially delighted to discover so many fellow Nova Scotians working along the line and living in the western towns. "I was surprised at the size of the city of Winnipeg," a Nova Scotian wrote home, "and the magnificent character of the buildings and the splendid wide streets, three times as wide as in Halifax. The stone and brick stores on every hand indicate a surprising degree of enterprise in this city. . . . There are a great many Nova Scotians in both the police and fire departments." No longer would these Maritimers think of the North West as the exclusive property of Ontario.

If Riel's rebellion helped change eastern attitudes to the prairies, it also helped change them towards the CPR. Van Horne was later to remark that the railway should have erected a statue to the Métis leader. As early as April 6 he was able to tell a friend in Scotland that "there is no more talk about the construction of the Lake Superior line having been a useless expenditure of money, nor about the road having been built too quickly. Most people are inclined to think it would have been better had it been built three or four weeks quicker."

Yet – and Van Horne must have felt the irony of the situation – the CPR was in worse financial shape than ever. It had cost almost a million dollars to ship the troops west, and that bill was not immediately collectable. It was a strange situation: at the moment of its greatest triumph, while the troops were speeding west on the new steel to the applause of the nation, the CPR's financial scaffolding was collapsing, and scarcely anybody in Ottawa appeared to be concerned.

The president himself wanted out; Ottawa had become painful to him. George Stephen was determined to shake the slush of the capital from his boots, never to return.

On March 26, the day of the bloody engagement at Duck Lake, he went to his room in the Russell House and packed his bags. He had already written to the Prime Minister explaining that, as a result of a conversation that morning, he was satisfied the government could not aid the railway.

Brandon in 1885: the wheat market. In just four years the first of the CPR towns had grown out of all recognition. "Here," one soldier wrote home, "the grandest reception of all was received. Half the population seemed to be assembled at the station, and as many as could do so entered the cars to welcome the volunteers. . . . The young ladies . . . overcame their native shyness and conversed quite freely. One having announced her determination not to leave the Ottawa car until she had shaken hands with everyone in it, stayed so long that two young gallants had to lift her off the train before it started. The kind action of the Brandon folk . . . will not soon be forgotten. . . ." Thus were the young Canadians from the East introduced to traditional western hospitality.

303

"I need not repeat how sorry I am that this should be the result of all our efforts to give Canada a railway to the Pacific ocean. But I am supported by the conviction that I have done all that could be done to obtain it." That was it. The great adventure was over. Stephen prepared to return to Montreal to personal ruin and public disgrace.

Among the crowd in the lobby that evening was Senator Frank Smith, Minister without Portfolio. A Toronto wholesale grocer and supplier to the CPR, he was personally involved in railways as well as in allied forms of transportation. When he spotted the downcast Stephen walking towards the office to pay his bill, he hurried towards him, urging him not to leave. "No," said Stephen, "I am leaving at once; there is no use – I have just come from Earnscliffe and Sir John has given a final refusal – nothing more can be done. What will happen tomorrow I do not know – the proposition is hopeless."

But Smith, whose powers of persuasion were considerable, managed to induce Stephen to stay, promising that he would make a final effort that evening to change the Prime Minister's mind. He drove to Earnscliffe for a midnight interview, leaving a friend, George Campbell, with orders to remain with Stephen and not to allow any other person access to him.

When Smith returned at 2 a.m. he was able to convince Stephen that he should not give up the ghost. Guarded by the vigilant Campbell, the CPR president agreed to revise his proposal for relief while Smith worked on Macdonald and the Cabinet. It was said that for Campbell the three days that followed were the most anxious of his life. He was the constant companion of "a man torn with anguish and remorse whose heart seemed to be breaking with compassion for friends whose downfall he felt himself responsible for."

Stephen had his revised proposition ready for the Privy Council the following day. That it was not rejected out of hand must be seen as a victory for Frank Smith, a powerful politician with a vast following among the Roman Catholics of Ontario. McLelan might resign if the loan went through, but Smith made it clear that he would resign if it did not; and Smith controlled more votes.

Over the next fortnight, as the troops from eastern Canada were shuttled off to the plains, a series of protracted negotiations took place regarding the exact terms of the proposed loan. With every passing day, Stephen grew more distraught. Reports were coming in of a serious strike at Beavermouth, where an angry mob of navvies was on the march. Stephen warned Tilley of the "utter impossibility of averting an immediate & disastrous collapse" unless some way could be found to give the company temporary aid to tide it over while the matter was being discussed at painful length in the Cabinet and in Parliament. Tilley was not helpful; he believed the government would have to take over the railway.

Once again the CPR president was at the end of his tether. Once again he told Macdonald: ". . . it is impossible for me to carry on." The delay had rendered him "utterly unfit for further work." He was sick at heart, fed up with politicians, betrayed by the very man in whom he had placed his confidence. Yet he could not quite bring himself to leave. He waited four more days. Silence. Finally, on April 15, Stephen gave up. That evening he took the train back to Montreal, to the great mansion on Drummond Street in which he must have felt a trespasser since it was, in effect, no longer his. And there the following morning the dimensions of the disaster the railway faced were summed up for him in a curt wire from Van Horne:

"Have no means paying wages, pay car can't be sent out, and unless we get immediate relief we must stop. Please inform Premier and Finance Minister. Do not be surprised, or blame me if an immediate and most serious catastrophe happens."

Riot at Beavermouth

Crowfoot and his family, photographed just before the rebellion. The Blackfoot chief did not attack, not because he loved the whites, but because he saw the ultimate futility of revolt.

OF ALL the mercurial construction camps along the CPR's mountain line, the one at the mouth of the Beaver River was the most volatile. It was dominated by saloons – forty of them – all selling illegal whiskey at fifty cents a glass, and it was awake most of the night to the sound of dancing, singing, and revelry.

By late March, the complaints over lack of pay began to gather into a discontented rumble. The men had been content to go without wages in the winter, but by early spring funds were needed for homesteads in Manitoba, Minnesota, and Dakota. Inspector Sam Steele counselled patience. He feared that a strike, if it came, would swiftly develop into a riot, sparked by a large number of "ruffians, gamblers and murderers from the Northern Pacific who had left it on the completion of that road." He wired the Prime Minister that a strike was imminent but got no action. Macdonald had more serious troubles in Saskatchewan on his mind. At this critical point Steele was felled by a massive attack of Rocky Mountain fever; he was so ill he could scarcely lift his head from the pillow. With the strongest force for law and order thus incapacitated, the men struck and began marching by the thousands up the line towards Beavermouth.

The news of the work stoppage had barely reached the Mountie when a frantic wire arrived from the Mayor of Calgary: the entire North West seemed to be up in arms; Riel had struck; the Crees were on the verge of joining the rebellion; Crowfoot and his braves were camped on the very edge of Calgary. "For God's sake, come; there is danger of an attack by the Blackfeet!" Everything seemed to be crowding in on Steele at once. He could only reply that the situation at Beavermouth was so dangerous that he could not spare a man. He had only eight as it was.

The construction camp at
Beavermouth, in the winter
of 1884-85. James Ross had
moved his navvies across
the river from Donald
in order to isolate them
from the gamblers and
whiskey peddlers, but the
plan did not work. The
coarser elements soon moved
across the Columbia bridge
and began to build saloons,
dance halls, and brothels
out of cedar logs. When Ross
refused to allow CPR trains
to provide the underworld
with food or supplies, an
upsurge of petty thievery
and discontent followed,
which helped to spark the
riot over lack of wages.

307

The indomitable Sam Steele, seated in front of his mountain headquarters. "We were rarely to bed before two or three a.m. and were up in the morning between six and seven," he recalled in his memoirs.

The strikers moved resolutely towards Beavermouth, gathering strength as they went. The ailing Steele received a deputation and warned them that "if they committed any act of violence, and were not orderly, in the strictest sense of the word, I would inflict upon the offenders the severest punishment the law would allow me."

Three hundred armed strikers began to police the line, bringing all work to a halt. A trainload of men sent to End of Track was driven back. James Ross himself mounted the engine, told the engineer to put on all steam, and ran it through the armed mob as bullets whistled past his cab. The train entered the narrow canyon of the Beaver, an easy place to defend with a few men. Here the track-laying began again.

On came the strikers, firing as they advanced, while the tracklayers worked in the canyon. Steele's second in command, a thickset sergeant with the appropriate name of Fury, drew his party across the mouth of the canyon to meet the advance. When they arrived, Fury announced that he would shoot the first man to cross the line. An uproar followed, but the strikers were cowed and returned to Beavermouth, allowing the tracklayers to finish their day's labour.

Sergeant Fury returned to his bedridden superior to find that one of the constables, attempting to arrest a contractor named Behan for being drunk and disorderly, had been driven off by the mob. "We must take the man at any cost," Steele told him. "It will never do to let the remainder of the gang know they can play with us." Fury accordingly set off with two constables to arrest the offending contractor, whom they found in a saloon "in the midst of a gang of drunken companions." The constables seized their quarry and dragged him out, but an angry mob of two hundred armed men retrieved Behan and the police were forced to retreat.

Fury, badly mauled, returned to ask Steele for orders. "Take your revolvers," Steele said, "and shoot anyone who interferes with the arrest!"

Events were now building to a climax. Steele was too weak to watch what happened, but the local stipendiary magistrate, George Hope Johnston, gave him a running account from the barracks window. He watched Fury and three policemen start off for the bridge across the Beaver, enter the log town, and disappear between the cabins. A few moments later the sharp crack of gun-fire echoed through the valley.

"There is one gone to hell, Steele," Johnston said.

Sick or not, Steele had to see for himself. He crawled to the window in time to see two of his men dragging a prisoner across the bridge. The prisoner was "fighting like a fiend, while a woman in scarlet followed . . . with wild shrieks and curses."

It was time for Steele to take over. He called on Johnston to get the Riot Act and, seizing a Winchester from the constable on guard at the jail, ran to the bridge, levelled his rifle at the crowd, and told the strikers to halt.

"Look at the——," someone cried; "his own death bed makes no difference to him!" Nonetheless, everybody stopped. One of the constables knocked the struggling prisoner insensible and pulled him by the collar the rest of the way. The woman in red started to scream: "You red-coated ——!" Steele turned to his men: "Take her in, too!" Then he started forward onto the bridge to face the sullen mob.

Johnston had been forced to kick the orderly-room door in, the constable with the key having been too busy with the riot. He arrived at last with the Riot Act. Said Steele: "Listen to this and keep your hands off your guns, or I will shoot the first man of you who makes a hostile movement." There was silence. Sergeant Fury had already put a bullet into the shoulder of a man who tried to keep him from taking his prisoner.

After the Riot Act was read, Steele spoke again:

"You have taken advantage of the fact that a rebellion has broken out in the North West and that I have only a handful of men, but, as desperate diseases require desperate remedies, and both disease and remedy are here, I warn you that if I find more than twelve of you standing together or any large crowd assembled, I will open fire upon you and mow you down! Now disperse at once and behave yourselves!''

Steele's full force of eight Mounted Police now stood in line behind them, rifles cocked. Steele stood his ground with Johnston and watched the grumbling mob slowly break up. The following morning the town and all the line were "as quiet as a country village on Sunday." Steele arrested all the ringleaders in the riot, brought them to court, and fined them each one hundred dollars or six months in jail.

There was no further violence. Steele, still convalescent, donned his uniform and headed for Calgary where he was given a unique command. His task was to organize a cavalry detachment and strike off in pursuit of the rebel Cree chieftain, Big Bear. It was, perhaps, the most remarkable case on record of instant recovery from Rocky Mountain fever.

The eleventh hour

WHEN STEPHEN LEARNED from Van Horne on April 16 that the CPR pay car could not be sent out, he immediately wired the news in cipher to John Henry Pope in Ottawa. Van Horne had hinted at the imminence of a "serious catastrophe." Another riot was likely if wages were again held up. The Minister of Railways was Stephen's last hope.

Pope went straight to the Prime Minister and again pointed out the obvious: if the CPR went bankrupt, the Government could not survive. At last the vacillating party leader was forced into a decision. With very little heart he decided that, once again, he must help to bail out the CPR.

Fortunately, the mood of the country was beginning to change. Because of the railway, the government had a good chance of localizing the Saskatchewan Rebellion. First, however, there was a nasty wrangle in the caucus. McLelan resigned and Macdonald had to use all his political muscle to bring the party into line; he bluntly promised to resign himself if his followers failed to back his proposal for another loan.

In one crowded week, events took on momentum of their own. The railway still had no money to pay its men. The relief bill could not be passed before a long debate in Parliament. Macdonald privately asked the Bank of Montreal to advance five million dollars to the CPR, explaining that he intended to bring some resolutions before Parliament regarding financial aid "at an early date." That was not good enough for the bank; it refused to advance a nickel to the faltering company. The same day – April 24 – at Fish Creek, a coulee not far from Batoche, a handful of Métis under Gabriel Dumont fought General Middleton's superior force to a standstill, immobilizing him for a fortnight. There was better news from Battleford, where the siege was finally lifted by Colonel William Dillon Otter's division. In London three days later, Sir Henry Tyler told a Grand Trunk meeting that the CPR was finished.

On May 1, the reluctant Prime Minister acted. He gave notice to the House of the resolutions he proposed to submit. The following day, there was more bad news from Saskatchewan: Colonel Otter had suffered a defeat at the hands of Poundmaker and his Crees. And still there was to be a delay. Macdonald was determined to postpone the debate on the railway resolutions until he had forced his pet franchise bill through the House. This was a measure that would remove control of the terms of the federal franchise from provincial legislatures. To Stephen, it seemed as if the Prime Minister was putting a petty squabble with the provinces ahead of what he was prone to call "this great national undertaking."

Col. W. D. Otter, who led the Toronto contingent to the North West, was rendered snow-blind en route. He relieved Battleford from siege but was later beaten by Poundmaker at Cut Knife Hill.

He was beside himself at this politicking. J. J. C. Abbott had "fairly scared" him with the news that it might be five or six weeks before the CPR resolutions became law. The railway could not hold out for anything like that time. It was essential that the government guarantee a loan at the bank. Even a million dollars would help. That sum in Thomas Shaughnessy's hands could give the company perhaps three weeks' breathing space. On May 5, at the government's request, the Bank of Montreal advanced three-quarters of a million dollars. It was not much, but it was something.

The real problem was pay. Both the March and the April wages were due and all along the line the grumblings began to be heard, mingled with reports of real privation. It was clear that the CPR would have to have a government advance or another bank guarantee if it was to stay alive. Somehow the railway had to find money, not just for wages, but also for the interest payments on the bonds of the Ontario and Quebec Railway, due on the first of June. "If we default," Stephen reminded the Prime Minister on May 12, ". . . then goodbye to the C.P.R. . . ."

The resolution of the CPR's various financial crises was always theatrical, fraught with the same kind of tension that audiences had come to expect from the stage melodramas of the era, in which the heroine was saved at the last instant from the Fate Worse than Death. Such a moment came less than a week before the interest on the O and Q bonds was due. The directors of the company waited breathlessly outside the Privy Council door while the Cabinet argued about guaranteeing another bank loan. Finally the word came that it had been done.

Van Horne raced immediately to the company's office to telegraph the news to Shaughnessy. The operator seemed too slow and so the general manager pushed him aside and began ticking off the message himself. It had been a near thing. "The advance we are now making is quite illegal and we are incurring the gravest responsibility in doing so," Macdonald wrote to Stephen.

John Henry Pope was not able to present the railway resolutions until June 16. By that time the rebellion in Saskatchewan had been crushed. Riel and Poundmaker were both prisoners. Dumont had vanished over the border. Sam Steele was in hot pursuit of Big Bear. Schreiber had already informed Tupper (in England) that "the House and country are both in favour of the CPR and that should now be doubly the case when the fact is patent to the world [that] but for the rapid construction . . . Canada would have been involved in a frightful waste of blood and treasure quelling the rising in the North West."

Edward Blake had no intention of giving in without a fight. He was prepared to oppose the relief bill as he had opposed the whole concept of a privately owned transcontinental railway from the very beginning. But this time Macdonald was in a strong position, for the railway had proved itself; no matter what Blake and his colleagues said, it had saved the country. He made that point when he rose to speak:

"Late events have shown us that we are made one people by that road, that that iron link has bound us together in such a way that we stand superior to most of the shafts of ill-fortune, that we can now assemble together, at every point which may be assailed, or may be in danger, the whole physical force of Canada by means of that great artery, against any foreign foe or any internal insurrection or outbreak."

The debate that followed, as Joseph Pope recalled it, was "acrimonious and unpleasant." It was a foregone conclusion that the measure would pass; what was less certain was the company's ability to survive during the time it would take to turn the bill into law. If the Opposition kept on talking the CPR could collapse.

The loan from the bank ran out; the chances of another were slim. The melodrama continued until the very last hour. By July, the CPR's credit had reached the snapping point. One creditor would wait no longer. The company owed him four hun-

dred thousand dollars and could not meet its obligations. On July 10, it is said, the debt was due. If it was not paid, the CPR was faced with total collapse.

The debate had occupied the best part of a month. The morning of July 10 came and the bill still had not passed the House, which did not sit until 1.30 that afternoon. According to O. D. Skelton, Van Horne's sometime confidant, the four-hundred-thousand-dollar debt was due at three o'clock. At two that afternoon a majority of the Commons voted in favour of railway relief. With the Lake Superior line complete and only a few dozen miles remaining in the gap between the Selkirks and the Gold Range, the railway was saved. It is doubtful whether history records another instance of a national enterprise coming so close to ruin and surviving.

In England, Tupper was working on the great financial house of Baring Brothers to market the new CPR bonds when they were issued. By the time Stephen reached London, he found they had taken the entire issue. In Canada, the CPR got the money it needed to finish the line; and it never had to ask for a government loan again.

A land no longer lonely

THE FRONTIER was melting away. The old, free days of whiskey peddlers and gamblers, of log towns and unfenced prairie were vanishing. On the heels of the railway came Timothy Eaton's new catalogue: for as little as two dollars the ladies of Moose Jaw or Swift Current could order one of several models of the new Grand Rapids Carpet Sweeper or for twenty-five cents a patented Hartshorn window shade with spring rollers. The violent days were over – gone with the buffalo and the antelope, gone with the whooping crane and the passenger pigeon, gone with the Red River carts

and the nomads who used to roam so freely across that tawny sea of grass.

The native peoples had made their final, futile gesture in the deep coulees of the North Saskatchewan country in May and June. Gabriel Dumont met the militia at Fish Creek on April 23, luring them into a kind of buffalo pound and vowing to treat them exactly as he had the thundering herds in the brave days before the railway. Here his force of one hundred and thirty Métis, armed with obsolete weapons, held back some eight hundred men under General Middleton, the bumbling and overcautious British Army regular. On May 2, at Cut Knife Hill, Chief Poundmaker and 325 Cree followers emerged victorious against cannon, Gatling gun, and some 540 troops under Colonel Otter.

These were the last contortions of a dying culture. The Canadian government had eight thousand men in the field, transported and supplied by rail. The natives had fewer than one thousand, and these were neither organized nor in all cases enthusiastic. Riel planned his campaign according to the spiritual visitations he believed he was receiving almost daily. The more practical Dumont used his knowledge of the ground, his skill at swift manoeuvre, and his experience in the organization of the great hunts to fend off superior forces. In mid-May Dumont fought his last battle at Batoche. It lasted for four days until the Métis ammunition ran out. Riel surrendered and Dumont fled to the United States, where he subsequently re-enacted the incidents of 1885 in Buffalo Bill's Wild West Show. In the weeks that followed, the Indian leaders surrendered too, or fled over the border.

In the great trench between the Selkirk Mountains and the Gold Range through which the Columbia flowed, the old frontier life still existed. The last rail was laid on the Lake Superior section on May 16, but in British Columbia construction continued for most of 1885. On the Onderdonk side, the rails were ascending the western slope of the Gold Range from Eagle Pass Landing on Shuswap Lake. On James Ross's side, the rails were moving up the

By 1885, Calgary was no longer a tent town but a thriving community stretched across the prairie along the line of the railway. The I. G. Baker store, left foreground, provided a link with the settlement's past.

Van Horne, an avid gardener, saw the value of buffalo bones as fertilizer and had them gathered and stacked along the sidings. This was all that remained of the great herds that once roamed the plains.

These Canadian militiamen, marching towards Battleford
under that pukka British officer, Major-General
Frederick D. Middleton, stopped at Qu'Appelle Lake to
fish, bathe their feet, and have their picture taken.

With the Onderdonk section of the line completed, the contractor prepared to make as much profit as possible before turning it over to the CPR. The first excursion to the Fraser Canyon, shown here, bore a more than casual resemblance to a roller-coaster ride. The CPR was not happy with the government section, and an acrimonious dispute followed. Compare the photograph on the right with an earlier view of the same scene on page 194.

eastern slopes of the same mountains from Farwell, on the Columbia, soon to be renamed Revelstoke.

Again in Farwell the CPR brooked no opposition from local merchants or speculators in the matter of real estate profits. A. S. Farwell, the surveyor, had secured one hundred and seventy-five acres for himself on the banks of the Columbia; as he had anticipated, the railway location went right through his property. However, he refused the terms offered by the CPR, and a long and expensive lawsuit followed, which he eventually won. For practical purposes, he lost. The company followed its practice of moving the location of the station and laid out another townsite which became the heart of the business section.

What the CPR wanted in British Columbia was a gift of land in return for establishing a town or divisional point. The general manager had no in-

This is how the most expensive section of Vancouver's modern waterfront looked in October, 1885, when it was known officially as "Granville" and unofficially as "Gastown" after "Gassy Jack" Deighton, the ship's captain and saloon-keeper who was for some time its leading citizen. Almost all of this shoreline was appropriated for the CPR by Van Horne on the spurious excuse that the company would require it for dockage. He claimed that the depth of the water made piers impossible. This, as it turned out, was pure nonsense.

tention of locating the smallest station where "it will benefit anybody who has imposed upon us in the matter of the right of way." In his dealings with William Smithe, the Premier of British Columbia, he struck a hard bargain. He knew that the provincial government was anxious to see the CPR extend its line to a new terminus at Granville on Burrard Inlet because it would help the sale of public land in the area. In return, Van Horne asked for almost half the peninsula on which the present metropolitan area of Vancouver is situated. He settled for an outright gift of six thousand acres from the government. In addition, the Hastings Mill had to give up immediately four thousand acres of land and an additional one thousand acres annually in return for an extension of its lease to 1890.

Van Horne let the private speculators know that if they did not deal liberally with the company, the CPR shops and works would be moved away from their property. In the end, the landholders had to yield a third of the lots in each block they held. The railway, in short, would dominate the new city. No street could be continued to tidewater without its permission.

"Keep your eyes open," Van Horne is said to have told a colleague after an all-night poker session in which he himself had been badly taken. "These damned Vancouver fellows will steal the pants off you." But Van Horne was engaged in a larger game for higher stakes. Besides the huge land grant he had managed to secure almost all of the foreshore of the future city, which he had insisted upon because, he said, the depth of the water made piers impossible; the railway would need all that land for dock facilities. Future events were to prove that this was not necessary, and, as later generations slowly realized, the railway would have had to come to the mouth of the inlet anyway, whether or not it was given as much as an acre of free real estate. Van Horne may have been skinned at poker in the last of the frontier railway towns, but he was the real winner in a much more important game of skill and bluff.

The last spike

EDWARD MALLANDAINE, aged seventeen, wanted to fight the Indians. When the news of the rebellion reached Victoria, where he lived and went to school, there was no holding him, and his father, a pioneer architect and engineer, did not try to hold him. He booked passage to New Westminster, took the CPR as far as Eagle Pass Landing, and then trudged along the partly finished railway until he reached the foot of the Kicking Horse, where he learned that the rebellion was over.

Disappointed and disgusted, he headed west again, through the Rogers Pass and into Farwell, with its single street lined with log and frame shacks. There was a feeling of excitement in Farwell that summer of 1885. The town was the half-way point between the two ends of track: freight outfits bustled in from the Rogers and the Eagle passes; boats puffed into the new docks from the mines at the Big Bend of the Columbia; a new post office was opening. Young Mallandaine decided to stay for a while and go into business for himself. He opened a freighting service between the town and Eagle Pass Landing, taking a pony through the Gold Range twice each week along the tote road carved out by the railway contractors and soliciting orders for newspapers and supplies from the navvies along the way. It was hard going but it made a profit.

Each time Mallandaine made his way through Eagle Pass, the gap was shorter. By October it became clear that the road would be finished by first snow. Now, as the boy moved through the mountains, he noticed the wayside houses shut up and deserted, contractors' equipment being shifted and carted away, and hundreds of men travelling on foot with all their belongings to the east or to the west.

An oppressive silence settled on the pass — a silence broken only by the hideous shrieking of the construction locomotives echoing through the hills, as they rattled by with flatcars loaded with steel

The wagon road through Eagle Pass as Edward Mallandaine
saw it in the late summer of 1885. As the gap between
the two lines narrowed, activity slowed down and it
seemed as if "some scourge had swept this mountain pass."

320

rails. Mallandaine felt a kind of chill creeping into his bones – not just the chill of the late October winds, sweeping down through the empty bunk-houses, but the chill of loneliness that comes to a man walking through a graveyard in the gloom. There was something eerie about the sight of boarded-up buildings, dump cars left by the way-side, and portions of contractors' outfits cast aside along the line of the tote road. And the silence! Not since the days of the survey parties had the moun-tains seemed so still. Mallandaine decided to return to Victoria. There was, however, one final piece of business which he did not want to miss: he was determined to be on hand when the last spike on the Canadian Pacific Railway was driven.

On the afternoon of November 6, the last con-struction train to load rails left Farwell for Eagle Pass. Mallandaine was one of several who climbed aboard and endured the "cold, cheerless, rough ride" that followed. Far into the darkness of the night the little train puffed, its passengers shiver-ing with cold. Mallandaine, lying directly upon the piled-up rails and unable to sleep, was almost shaken to pieces as the train rattled over the unballasted roadbed. Finally it came to a stop. The youth tum-bled off the flatcar in the pitch dark, found an abandoned boxcar, and managed a short sleep. At six that morning the track crews were on the job. By the time Mallandaine awoke, the rails had almost come together.

At nine o'clock, the last two rails were brought forward and measured for cutting, with wagers being laid on the exact length that would be needed: it came to twenty-five feet, five inches. A peppery little man with long white whiskers cut the final rail with a series of hard blows. This was the leg-endary Major Rogers. One of the short rails was then laid in place and spiked; the second was left loose for the ceremony. The crowd, which included Al Rogers, Tom Wilson, Sam Steele, and Henry Cambie, waited for the official party to appear.

It is perhaps natural that the tale of the driving of the last spike on the CPR should have become a legend in which fancy often outweighs fact; it was, after all, the great symbolic act of Canada's first century. Two days before the spike was driven, George Stephen had cabled from England: "Rail-way now out of danger." Nine days after the spike was driven, Louis Riel kept his rendezvous with the hangman at Regina. In more ways than one the completion of the railway signalled the end of the small, confined, comfortable nation that had been pieced together in 1867.

It is not surprising, then, that some who were present that day in the mountains should have re-called half a century later that the spike was made of gold. But there was no golden spike. "The last spike," said Van Horne in his blunt way, "will be just as good an iron one as there is between Mont-real and Vancouver, and anyone who wants to see it driven will have to pay full fare."

The very simplicity of the scene at Eagle Pass – the lack of pomp, the absence of oratory, the plainness of the crowd, the presence of the work-men in the foreground of the picture – made the spectacle an oddly memorable one. Van Horne and a distinguished party had come out from Ottawa, Montreal, and Winnipeg for the occasion. The big names included Donald A. Smith, Sandford Flem-ing, John Egan, John McTavish, the land commis-sioner, and George Harris, a Boston financier who was a company director. Meanwhile, on the far side of the mountains, Andrew Onderdonk's pri-vate car "Eva" came up from Port Moody with Michael Haney aboard, pulling the final load of rails to the damp crevice in the mountains which the general manager, with a fine sense of drama, had decided years before to name Craigellachie.

It was a dull, murky November morning, the mountains sheathed in clouds, the evergreens drip-ping in a coverlet of wet snow. Up puffed the quaint engine with its polished brass boiler, its cordwood tender, its diamond-shaped smokestack, and the great square box in front containing the acetylene headlight on whose glass was painted the number 148. The ceremonial party descended and walked

1. *Major A. B. Rogers*
2. *Michael Haney*
3. *William Cornelius Van Horne*
4. *Sandford Fleming*
5. *Donald A. Smith*
6. *Edward Mallandaine*
7. *Henry Cambie*
8. *John McTavish, CPR land commissioner*
9. *John Egan, western superintendent*
10. *James Ross*

There were two photographs taken of the famous ceremony at Craigellachie.
The one above is the more familiar, though it hides the presence of
Major Rogers. Tom Wilson can just be seen, wearing a wide-brimmed
western hat and craning his neck, above the crowd at the very rear.
Sam Steele was also present but is not shown. The bearded man in the
left foreground, facing the camera, is Frank Brothers, roadmaster,
who retrieved the last spike to prevent it from being stolen. It was stolen
anyway, years later, from the desk of CPR president Edward Beatty.
The spike that Smith bent on his first try is at the Strathcona home
in Scotland, though parts of it were split off to make jewellery for the wives
of those who were present that day. Other covetous wives were given
spurious relics.

After the trainload of dignitaries rolled off towards the Pacific, the workmen left behind posed for their own versions of a last spike ceremony. Most of them are not identifiable, but in the picture above Tom Wilson can be seen, third from the left. The second man from the right in the front rank is Charles A. Stoess, the engineer in charge of building the snowsheds in the Selkirk Mountains. The end piece of the final sawn rail and the last tie were also chipped away for souvenirs.

through the clearing of stumps and debris to the spot where Major Rogers was standing, holding the tie bar under the final rail. By common consent the honour of driving the connecting spike was assigned to the eldest of the four directors present – to Donald A. Smith, whose hair in five years of railway construction had turned a frosty white.

Now that moment had arrived which so many Canadians had believed would never come – a moment that Sandford Fleming had been waiting for since 1862, when he placed before the government the first practical outline for a highway to the Pacific. The workmen and the officials crowded around Smith. Young Edward Mallandaine squeezed in behind him, right next to Harris, the Boston financier, and directly in front of Cambie, McTavish, and Egan. As the photographer raised his camera, Mallandaine craned forward. Fifty-nine years later, when all the rest of that great company were in their graves, Colonel Edward Mallandaine, stipendiary magistrate and reeve of the Kootenay town of Creston, would be on hand when the citizens of Revelstoke, in false beards and borrowed frockcoats, re-enacted the famous photograph on that very spot.

Smith's first blow bent the spike badly. Frank Brothers, the roadmaster, pulled it out and replaced it with another. Smith posed with the uplifted hammer. The assembly froze. The shutter clicked. Smith lowered the hammer onto the spike. The shutter clicked again. Smith began to drive the spike home. Save for the blows of the hammer and the sound of a small mountain stream there was absolute silence. Even after the spike was driven home, the stillness persisted. "It seemed," Sandford Fleming recalled, "as if the act now performed had worked a spell on all present. Each one appeared absorbed in his own reflections." The spell was broken by a cheer, "and it was no ordinary cheer. The subdued enthusiasm, the pent-up feelings of men familiar with hard work, now found vent." More cheers followed, enhanced by the shrill whistle of the locomotive.

All this time, Van Horne had stood impassively beside Fleming, his hands thrust into the side pockets of his overcoat. In less than four years, he had managed to complete a new North West Passage. Did any memories surface in that retentive mind as the echoes of Smith's hammer blows rang down the corridor of Eagle Pass? Did he think back on the previous year when, half-starved and soaking wet, he had come this way with Reed and Rogers? Did he reflect, with passing triumph, on those early days in Winnipeg when the unfriendly press had attacked him as an idle boaster and discussed his rumoured dismissal? Did he recall those desperate moments in Ottawa and Montreal when the CPR seemed about to collapse like a house of cards? Probably not, for Van Horne was not a man to brood or to gloat over the past. It is likelier that his mind was fixed on more immediate problems: the Vancouver terminus, the Pacific postal subsidy, and the Atlantic steamship service. He could not predict the future but he would help to control it, and some of the new symbols of his adopted country would be of his making: the fleet of white Empresses flying the familiar chequered flag, the turreted hotels with their green château roofs, boldly perched on promontory and lakefront; and the international slogan that would proclaim in Arabic, Hindi, Chinese, and a dozen other languages that the CPR spanned the world.

As the cheering died the crowd turned to Van Horne. "Speech! Speech!" they cried. Van Horne was not much of a speechmaker; he was, in fact, a little shy in crowds. What he said was characteristically terse, but it went into the history books: "All I can say is that the work has been done well in every way."

Major Rogers was more emotional. This was his moment of triumph too, and he was savouring it. In spite of all the taunts of his Canadian colleagues, in spite of the scepticism of the newspapers, in spite of his own gloomy forebodings and the second thoughts of his superiors, his pass had been chosen and the rails ran directly through it to Craigellachie. For once, the stoic major did not trouble to conceal his feelings. He was "so gleeful," Edward Mallandaine observed, "that he upended a huge tie and tried to mark the spot by the side of the track by sticking it in the ground."

There were more cheers, some mutual congratulations, and a rush for souvenirs – chips from the tie and pieces hacked off the sawn rail. Then the locomotive whistle sounded again and a voice was heard to cry: "All aboard for the Pacific!" It was the first time that phrase had been used by a conductor from the East, but Fleming noted that it was uttered "in the most prosaic tones, as of constant daily occurrence." The official party obediently boarded the cars and a few moments later the little train was in motion again, clattering over the newly laid rail and over the last spike and down the long incline of the mountains, off towards the gloomy canyon of the Fraser, off to the soft meadows beyond, off to the blue Pacific and into history.

This photograph of the first labourer, an Indian, to work on the CPR in British Columbia was taken immediately after the railway was completed and was found recently in an album of pictures donated to the British Columbia archives by Gladys Weeks, Andrew Onderdonk's youngest daughter. It is entitled simply: "His Occupation Gone."

With the ceremony at Craigellachie finished and the last rail securely spiked and ballasted, a handcar loaded with Andrew Onderdonk's workmen rolls back towards Kamloops.

ACKNOWLEDGEMENTS

The picture research for this book was done in public archives and libraries across Canada from Montreal to Victoria (in addition to several in the United States), and I should like to thank all the people who so kindly assisted me in my searches. Additional pictures come from four private collections, those of Ed McKnight of Acton, Ontario, Walter Coucill of Toronto, Ida Schneider of Toronto, and Taylor Stoess, also of Toronto, whose grandfather built the great snowsheds in the Selkirks. I should like, in addition, to acknowledge the special assistance of Omar Lavallée, CPR historian, Stanley Triggs of the Notman Photographic Archives, and Bill Brooks of McClelland and Stewart.

PICTURE CREDITS

Order of appearance in the text of pictures listed here is left to right, top to bottom. After the first recording, principal sources are credited under these abbreviations:

BCA	Provincial Archives, Victoria, British Columbia	MHS	Minnesota Historical Society
CB	Courtney C. J. Bond	MM	McCord Museum, McGill University
CP	Canadian Pacific	MTLB	Metropolitan Toronto Library Board
GAI	Glenbow-Alberta Institute	NPA	Notman Photographic Archives
MA	Manitoba Archives	OA	Ontario Archives
		PAC	Public Archives of Canada

Front cover	Glenbow-Alberta Institute		Library Board (John Ross Robertson Collection)	26/27	PAC	46	MTLB
Back cover	Canadian Pacific			28	BCA; Culver Pictures	47	MTLB; MTLB; NPA
		15	Manitoba Archives	29	Notman Photographic Archives (2)	48	MTLB
1	Public Archives of Canada	16	PAC	30	NPA	49	MTLB
		17	PAC	32	PAC	50/51	Jerry Kozoriz
2/3	Stoess Collection	18	MTLB (2)	34/35	PAC	52	GAI
4/5	GAI	19	MTLB (3)	36	PAC	54	PAC
6/7	Vancouver City Archives	20	Alberta Provincial Library	37	Schneider Collection (4)	55	BCA
10/11	PAC	21	Courtney C. J. Bond	39	PAC (2)	56/57	PAC
12	PAC	22	MTLB; PAC	40	PAC (2)	59	BCA
13	Provincial Archives, Victoria, B.C.	23	GAI	41	MTLB (2)	60	CB
		24	PAC	43	PAC	62	BCA
14	Metropolitan Toronto	25	PAC	44	MTLB	63	PAC
				45	PAC	64	BCA
						65	Coucill Collection

Every reasonable effort has been made to ascertain ownership of the illustrations used.
Information would be welcomed which would enable the publisher to rectify any error.

66 BCA	125 MTLB (2)	199 Vancouver Public Library	263 GAI (2)
67 MTLB	127 MTLB (3)	200/201 BCA	264 NPA (2)
68/69 PAC	129 MTLB (2)	202 MTLB	266 CB
70 MTLB	130 MTLB	203 PAC	267 BCA; PAC
71 PAC; MTLB	131 MTLB	204 PAC	268 BCA
72 MTLB	133 MTLB	205 PAC	270 McKnight Collection
73 PAC	134 MTLB	206 PAC	272 NPA
74/75 BCA	135 MTLB	207 PAC	274 CP
76 PAC; BCA	137 MTLB	209 PAC	276/277 CP
77 BCA	138/139 PAC	210/211 MM	277 CB; BCA
78 MTLB	140/141 CB	212/213 MM	279 Coucill Collection
80 MA	142 CB	215 CP	280 GAI
82 MA	143 MTLB	216/217 BCA	281 Montana Historical Society
83 PAC	144/145 MA	218 MA	282 NPA; MA
84 MA	147 PAC	219 PAC	283 PAC; CB
85 MA	148 PAC (3)	220 PAC	285 PAC
86 MA	149 PAC (2)	221 NPA	286/287 NPA
87 PAC; MTLB	150/151 Canadian Pacific	222/223 NPA	289 PAC; MTLB
88 PAC	153 NPA	225 PAC	290 MTLB (3)
91 MTLB	154/155 PAC (2)	226 GAI	291 MTLB; CB; MTLB
92/93 MTLB	156/157 PAC	228 MTLB	292 PAC (2)
94/95 MTLB	159 PAC	229 MTLB; PAC	295 PAC
96 MTLB	160/161 GAI	230 GAI	296 PAC
97 PAC (2)	162/163 GAI	231 GAI	297 GAI; MTLB
98 PAC	164/165 GAI	232 GAI (2)	298/299 PAC
99 BCA	166 CP	233 NPA; GAI	300 OA
100/101 PAC	168/169 GAI	235 MM	302/303 MA
103 PAC	170 PAC	237 PAC	305 GAI
104 BCA	172 Saskatchewan Archives	239 NPA	306/307 GAI
105 BCA	172/173 PAC	240/241 McKnight Collection	308 GAI
107 MA	173 CB	242 McKnight Collection	310 MTLB (John Ross Robertson Collection)
108 McCord Museum of McGill University	174/175 NPA	245 PAC	312 GAI; PAC
109 MTLB	176/177 PAC	246/247 Ontario Archives	314/315 Kalamazoo Public Museum (through GAI)
110 CB	179 GAI	248 MA	316 BCA
111 Minnesota Historical Society	180 CB	249 OA	317 BCA
112 MHS	181 Coucill Collection	250 CB	318 BCA
113 MHS	182/183 Stoess Collection	251 CB	320 BCA
114 MHS	184 CB	252 GAI	322 GAI
115 NPA	185 GAI	253 MM	323 CP
116 MHS	186 CB	254 GAI	324 PAC
119 NPA	188/189 Robert N. Smith	255 MM	325 CP
121 MTLB; PAC; MTLB	191 Valerie J. May	256/257 MM	327 BCA
122 MTLB	192 PAC	258/259 MM	328 BCA
123 PAC	193 BCA	260 MM	336 PAC
124 MTLB (2)	194 CB; MM	261 NPA	
	195 NPA	262 GAI (2)	
	196/197 PAC		

INDEX

(Numerals in italics refer to illustrations)

ON THE MAKING OF THIS BOOK

Type was set by Mono Lino Typesetting Co. Ltd.,
the book was prepared for lithography by Herzig Somerville Ltd.,
printed by Ashton-Potter Ltd.,
and bound by Hunter Rose Company.

THE NEW NORTH-WEST PASSAGE.